D0015818

Same Knight,
Different Channel

Other Sports Titles From Brassey's

Pro Basketball Prospectus 2003 Edition by John Hollinger

Blue Ribbon College Basketball Forecast 2003–04 Edition edited by Chris Dortch

String Music: Inside the Rise of SEC Basketball by Chris Dortch

Pro Football Prospectus 2003 Edition by Sean Lahman and Todd Greanier

Blue Ribbon College Football Forecast 2003 Edition edited by Chris Dortch

Dominance: The Best Seasons of Pro Football's Greatest Teams by Eddie Epstein

Paths to Glory: How Baseball's Championship Teams Were Built by Mark Armour and Daniel Levitt

Throwbacks: Old School Baseball Players in Today's Game by George Castle

Same Knight, Different Channel

Basketball Legend Bob Knight at West Point and Today

Jack Isenhour (signature)

Jack Isenhour

Brassey's, Inc.

WASHINGTON, D.C.

Copyright © 2003 by Brassey's, Inc.

Published in the United States by Brassey's, Inc. All rights reserved. No part of this book may be reproduced in any manner whatsoever without written permission from the publisher, except in the case of brief quotations embodied in critical articles and reviews.

Library of Congress Cataloging-in-Publication Data

Isenhour, Jack.
    Same knight, different channel : basketball legend Bob Knight at West Point and today / Jack Isenhour.— 1st ed.
        p. cm.
    ISBN 1-57488-556-1 (hardcover : alk. paper)
    1. Knight, Bobby. 2. Basketball coaches—United States—Biography. I. Title: Basketball legend Bob Knight at West Point and today. II. Title.

GV884.K58I74 2003
796.323'092—dc21

                        2002156004

Softcover ISBN 1-57488-634-7

Printed in the United States of America on acid-free paper that meets the American National Standards Institute Z39-48 Standard.

Brassey's, Inc.
22841 Quicksilver Drive
Dulles, Virginia 20166

Text design by Pen & Palette Unlimited

First Edition

10 9 8 7 6 5 4 3 2 1

For Mike Silliman

The wilderness had patted him on the head ...
had taken him, loved him, embraced him, got
into his veins, consumed his flesh, and sealed
his soul to its own by the inconceivable
ceremonies of some devilish initiation. He was
its spoiled and pampered favorite. Ivory? I
should think so. Heaps of it. Stacks of it.

— Joseph Conrad, *Heart of Darkness*

Contents

Acknowledgments ix

Part I. INDIANA CLASSIC 1

Chapter 1. I'm No Friend 3

Chapter 2. Appropriate Decorum and Civility 10

Chapter 3. Heroes and Cowards 17

Chapter 4. The Bob Knight Clinic for
            Anger Management 23

Chapter 5. Bigger Than Elvis? 31

Part II. SCARY GUYS 41

Chapter 6. Come to Papa 43

Chapter 7. Beast Barracks 54

Chapter 8. Scary Guys 65

Chapter 9. Second-Class College 75

Chapter 10. Prize Recruits 81

Chapter 11. The Summer of 1963 89

Chapter 12. Showing Signs 98

Chapter 13. Single-Minded Roughnecks 108

Chapter 14. Too Much of What He Was 115

Part III. BOBBY BALL 123

Chapter 15. Jug of Booze 125

Chapter 16. Bobby Ball 128

Chapter 17. Wrong on Both Counts 136

Chapter 18. Firsts 141

Chapter 19. Frightful Shoulders 151

Chapter 20. Scramble Them Brains! 160

Chapter 21. Long-Ball Hitter 166

Chapter 22. Who's Silliman? 172

Chapter 23. Roasted, Salted Pecans 178

Chapter 24. Bisons, Peacocks, Redmen 184

Chapter 25. I'll Take Manhattan 192

Chapter 26. The National Implausible Tournament 198

Chapter 27. An Evening with Bob 203

Chapter 28. What West Point Is All About 214

Part IV. FIRED! 219

Chapter 29. An Absolute Moron 221

Chapter 30. A Five-Fish Riot 231

Chapter 31. Looking Forward to Going Forward 237

Chapter 32. Uh Huh. Right. 249

Chapter 33. Talking Points 263

Chapter 34. It's Only Sports 271

Chapter 35. Dunn Deal 279

Part V. MEDIA WARS 287

Chapter 36. Midnight Madness 289

Chapter 37. Riding in Cars with Bob 296

Chapter 38. Grandpa 302

Chapter 39. The Bob Knight Practice 309

Conclusion An American Institution 315

Index 322

About the Author 330

Acknowledgments

There is no book without Dana Moore, Bob Knight, and Frank Weimann of The Literary Group International. I'd like to thank all my teammates and others associated with the 1965–66 West Point basketball team; the family and friends of Mike Silliman; Eleanor Dale Davis, who has always been there; and editor Kevin Cuddihy.

I also owe a debt to those who came before: John Feinstein for *A Season on the Brink;* Rick Atkinson for *The Long Gray Line: The American Journey of West Point's Class of 1966;* Joan Mellen for *Bob Knight: His Own Man;* Stephen E. Ambrose for *Duty, Honor, Country: A History of West Point;* Phil Berger for *Knight Fall;* Rich Wolfe for *Knightmares/ Oh What a Knight;* Bob Hammel, the co-author of *My Story;* Tates Locke and Bob Ibach for *Caught in the Net;* Peter C. Bjarkman for *Hoopla: A Century of College Basketball;* and, finally, the scores of sportswriters who learned to write well enough in second grade to provide a running history of Bob Knight over the past thirty-seven years.

Part I

INDIANA CLASSIC

Chapter 1

I'm No Friend

Bloomington, Indiana, June 23, 2000. The eleventh annual Indiana University Golf Classic starts in a half-hour, and the golf carts are lined up five deep outside the on-campus clubhouse. The greeters, college kids wearing white polo shirts with an Indiana-red Golf Classic logo on the breast, scurry about hauling clubs from cars, directing players to the buffet inside. Clear and sunny, not too hot, it's a perfect day for golf and sunscreen.

The clubhouse, modest as these things go, sits on a gentle slope just above the parking lot. Built in 1979, the low-slung stone affair has a Frank-Lloyd-Wright-on-Prozac feel about it. Just below the clubhouse, a silky green par-three course snakes its way down the hill and out of sight. To the right is a driving range, where a handful of people are getting in a few last-minute practice swings.

I walk up the sidewalk past the golf carts. There's a white tent set up just outside the clubhouse, people sitting at a half dozen or so round tables eating lunch. Coach Bob Knight is hunched over one table surrounded by ex-players. Since former NBA superstar Isiah Thomas isn't here this year, Knight is the only name above the title. I try to make eye contact to nod hello, but he doesn't see me.

I'm right on time despite having been pulled over by a Kentucky State Trooper during my Nashville-to-Bloomington run. I took a chance, told him who I was going to see—nobody's neutral on Bob Knight—and he smiled, letting me off with a warning. Not bad for seventy in a fifty-five zone. Coach Knight would have been proud. On a cross-country recruiting trip during his West Point days, he's said to have come home with a glove compartment stuffed full of speeding tickets, one from every state he'd crossed.

I check in at the registration desk on the far side of the tent, get my complimentary Indiana Classic polo shirt and baseball cap, both emblazoned with the event logo. The Indiana Classic is a golf tourney that raises money for basketball scholarships, about fifty thousand dollars a year, and the logo, designed by the wife of a Knight crony, reflects the schizophrenic nature of the event: it's a guy in a basketball uniform whacking a basketball with a golf club. I double-check the shirt to make sure it's the right size and notice it's a Tommy Hilfiger. That surprises me. I figured Knight for more of a bare-basics, Champion kind of guy.

Inside, I grab a chicken sandwich, chips, and bottled water and join the seven or eight other guys sitting at Knight's table. Still no eye contact. He seems wary, but then he always seems wary.

Back home in Nashville, I jokingly told friends I was going up to Bloomington to interview "my close personal friend Bob Knight." But I'm no friend. I'm a player. From his first team at West Point back in the mid-sixties. And the interview will be the first real conversation I've had with the man in more than thirty years.

"What kind of relationship do you have with Knight?" friends ask.

I'm at a loss. "Relationship" implies some kind of two-way, back-and-forth thing. There's none of that. He's the coach. I'm the player. I was never one to offer feedback, at least not within earshot, and he never asked for any. Like during that heated Boston College scrimmage in 1965. Knight threw an arm around my shoulder, pointed out a cheap-shot artist on the BC squad, and told me to get in there and hammer the guy. I went. I hammered. Got under the kid on a rebound, leveled him off, and he crashed to the hardwood, all elbows and knees. No questions asked. No explanation needed. He's the coach. I'm the player. Now I worry I'm still susceptible. Worry he might shout, "Hey Ike"—that's what Knight always called me—"how about giving me twenty after you drive that golf cart into the side of the clubhouse?" I worry that as I drop to do the push-ups alongside the crumpled cart, he'll be needling me about my form. "For Christ's sake, keep your back straight!" Being around Knight is like going to your parents' house for Christmas. You revert to child-player status, and I'd no sooner call him "Bob" to his face than call my mother "Louise." He's "Coach." And although I'm in my mid-fifties now, I'm still scared to death of the son of a bitch.

Relationship? Think general and private, fly swatter and fly.

The ex-players now surrounding Knight are middle-aged, graying, and most, like him, are wearing the uniform of the day: baggy, knee-length shorts and tucked-in polo shirts, belts curving beneath ample paunches. Many have donned hats, but not Knight. So his face is sun-reddened, setting off the silver hair, chopped off in a crew cut. His features are still sharp: that beak of a nose, those small, intense eyes set so deep they often appear to be black, onyx. He's better looking than he appears on television, charismatic, but there's an off-putting fierceness about him that keeps you at arm's length.

I munch on my sandwich, every now and then casting a glance in Knight's direction. After a while, I look down at my shirt to make sure I'm not invisible. Back in February, I had written Knight about doing a book chronicling his first year as a head coach, his first basketball team, the one at West Point in 1965–66. I'd spice it up with little asides on cadet life, prehistoric basketball, and the cultural stirrings that would come to full flower in the sixties. That year, 1965, was the year of the Voting Rights Act, the year passive resistance began giving way to Black Power, the year Lyndon Johnson sent the first "American boys ten thousand miles away from home to do what Asian boys ought to be doing," and the year Muhammad Ali knocked out Sonny Liston with a mystery punch in the first round in that noted fight mecca, Lewiston, Maine.

I received Knight's reply in early March. "I will be glad to do whatever I can to help," he wrote. But that was before Neil Reed and zero tolerance. So I'm not sure Knight will actually go through with it. I mean, what advice would I have given him if he told me this walk-on turned career journalist had resurfaced after thirty years—gotta be a liberal—asking to poke around in his past?

"Run like a deer!" I'd have told him. Nothing to gain. Lots to lose. Look at what John Feinstein did to you in *A Season on the Brink*, CNN-SI with the Neil Reed "You call that choking? I'll show you choking!" story. Zero tolerance means zero journalists, I'd have told him. You don't have to apologize for what you don't say. Or as one former Big Ten supervisor of officials once put it, "You can't quote silence." Luckily Knight never asked for my advice.

I had tried unsuccessfully to nail down a time for the interview. His secretary, the forever-patient Mary Ann Davis, said he'd be glad to do it, said to "just remind him" during the golf tournament. And while I was a little concerned, I knew Knight was legendary for helping ex-players. So I'm hoping he's thinking, "Here's this guy who made it through the mill and I'm willing to help him out," even though the only time Knight called my name was when officials told him to shut me up or risk a technical.

Tee-off time. Knight is among the few stragglers remaining at the tables under the tent. Most of the six-man teams have marshaled golf carts, heading in all directions for the staggered, shotgun start. Knight is about to get up when he's approached by a squirrely little man carrying a basketball. He hands Knight the ball and a black Sharpie pen. "For charity," says the guy, smarmy smile. Maybe. Knight skewers him with an "Oh really?" glare. In the past several months, some people whose charities he's given time and money to over the years have turned on him, joined the thumbs-down hoard baying in the coliseum. Knight hands the ball back unsigned and rises, muttering something about charities under his breath. It's the only time I'll see Knight refuse an autograph.

People close to Knight tell me the last few months have been the worst ever. They say they've never seen him so down, and they're worried. He feels betrayed, one says, and not only by outsiders, but by people inside the university. He's angry, and there are rumors he's going to ask for some of the money back from the chair he helped endow in

Indiana University's history department; that he'll swear off public appearances; that he'll refuse to wear his trademark Indiana-red sweater at ball games, in favor of the team colors of friends who have been loyal, such as the green and gold of Baylor, where former assistant Dave Bliss is now coach. Friends are concerned that such mean-spirited acts of defiance will turn even more people against him.

I hang back, still hoping to make contact, but Knight heads down the slope to his golf cart. I wonder what the squirrelly guy did that turned him off. What can I learn from it? Maybe I can do the book without Knight, but I don't think so. He's critical. So I'd best not piss him off.

Earlier in the year, a magazine writer working on a profile was following Knight through a typical day when he made the mistake of sticking a tape recorder in Knight's face at the wrong moment. "This interview is over," snapped Knight and ran the guy off. The writer couldn't have been happier. He had his story: "Hothead Coach Berates Mild-Mannered Reporter." With Knight delivering that gimme, there was no need for the have-stereotype, will-travel reporter to look beyond the obvious. Now I'm wondering if Knight has a thing about tape recorders.

At least that reporter had actually met him. A lot of writers who have never been in the same county with Knight pretend to know the man. He's the guy who threw the chair: the foul-mouthed, foul-tempered, petty tyrant; the "classic bully" who steamrolls anybody who gets in his way—player, fan, ref, athletic director, secretary, even his own son. He's an out-of-touch, out-of-control, testosterone-infused beast, a speed-popping John Wayne with a saddle burr, stomping around as a quavering staff, family, and wife wait for him to explode at the first provocation. People who don't know Bob Knight are sure they have him all figured out, while people who have been friends for decades say they don't know him at all.

For years I've been telling friends that if you want to get a feel for what big-time basketball is really all about, just watch Knight raging on the sidelines. Maybe that works in reverse. Maybe the intensity of the game itself helps explain what Knight is really all about. That and his time at West Point. Anyway, that's what I'm thinking coming in.

I join my golf group and we convoy three carts out to the fourteenth tee, a 223-yard par three. There are four members of Knight's first basketball team in the group, but you couldn't tell it by looking at us. Aside from our combined age of 220 years, I'm the tallest at only 6′ 2″, and then there's the posture.

"They don't look like basketball players," a rival coach once remarked as he watched Army warm up before a game. "They stand up too straight. Basketball players slouch."

Two years before, Knight had invited a few of these guys with good posture up to Bloomington for the Indiana Golf Classic. Since then, the West Point contingent has grown, and this year John "Jocko" Mikula has rounded up a total of fourteen ex-players, eight from Knight's first team.

Jocko tees up his ball, takes a practice swing. A guard on Knight's first squad, Jocko looks nowhere near his fifty-five years. He is one of the few players recognizable on first meeting without a double take: same sandy brown hair, broad shoulders, open manner, easy laugh.

Jocko takes a swipe and hits a grass-cutter about fifty yards. His swing needs some work, but at least he keeps his head still, thanks to a mysterious fever he picked up in Vietnam that has left him with what looks like a permanent crick in his neck. Doctors think the high fever brought on something called "ankylosing spondylitis," a form of progressive arthritis. Now when you call his name, Jocko turns his whole body, leading with a shoulder. He has learned to live with the pain and is quick to say the ailment hasn't hurt his golf game. That's because he wasn't worth a damn to begin with.

Jocko hands me the baby blue driver—we're sharing my wife's clubs—and I dribble the ball off the tee. I'm relieved I even hit the damn thing.

Jocko is not the only West Pointer here with a medical memento from Vietnam. Midway through the course, we run across Bill Helkie. The word "lumbering" still comes to mind. A forward on Knight's first team, the 6′ 4½″ Helkie learned basketball playing against black kids on the playgrounds of South Bend. At Army, Helkie was an unapologetic gunner, a zone buster from what is now three-point range. "A man open underneath the basket," Helkie used to say, "is in a good position to rebound."

Several years out of Vietnam, mysterious lumps, some the size of golf balls, began to appear all over Helkie's body. First he had them removed, but he's long since given up on that. Nobody can figure out what causes them. Helkie thinks it might have something to do with his exposure to Agent Orange, but he can't prove it.

Jocko observed that in the jungles of Southeast Asia everybody was "getting bitten by all sorts of creatures" carrying who knows what kind of exotic tropical diseases. He may be on to something. There were so many unexplained fevers going around in Vietnam that the doctors finally assigned them their own acronym: FOUO, "fever of unknown origin." I know this because it was an FOUO that got me out of combat after six months as an infantry platoon leader. The highlight of my two-week stay in the hospital was a fainting spell that left me facedown in a half-dozen bowls of soup. No harm done. This being an Army mess hall, the soup wasn't hot.

We hack our way around the course. I get accolades for speed, if not skill. I've given up on the traditional practice swing and just step up and flail away. At the end of eighteen holes, we're only one over par, and I think our group has done pretty well. Then they tell me the winner in these "best ball" things will be fifteen or twenty under. No free golf balls for this bunch. Golf over, the schedule calls for us to reassemble later beneath the football stadium. I never even catch a glimpse of Knight. We started on opposite sides of the course and never crossed paths.

Chapter 2

Appropriate Decorum
and Civility

By Big Ten standards, Indiana's football arena is small. The less than imposing Memorial Stadium, "The House," as players call it, seats a little more than fifty-two thousand. While some schools are forever expanding their stadiums, Indiana hasn't added a seat since the place opened in 1960. No need. Over the years there have been about twenty thousand empty seats for an average game. That's not surprising for a football team that hasn't won a conference championship since Lyndon Johnson was president. In the Big Ten, only Northwestern draws fewer fans. All this helps explain the nickname for the Memorial Stadium banquet hall where the Indiana Classic golfers reconvene at 7 P.M.

During the football season, this banquet hall, officially known as the "Hoosier Room," is a traditional pre-game gathering place for the Hoosier Hundred, a group of fat-cat football fans who have contributed twenty-five hundred dollars or more to the athletic department. But the room's unofficial nickname suggests that years of losing football teams have created a bit of tension between the athletic department and the boosters. For to some Indiana insiders, this pleasant banquet hall is known not as the Hoosier Room, but as the DCSC—"Downtown Cock Suckers Club."

Tonight the DCSC is the site of the first of two Indiana Classic receptions and banquets where the 150 or so cleaned-up golfers share drinks, Italian food, and conversation. The group is mostly men—ex-players,

Indiana fans, the West Point contingent—many sporting sunburned faces and reeking of strong-smelling deodorant soap. There's a lot of milling around in the cocktail-party area in the back next to the bar while a few people browse at the souvenir table, shopping for Indiana merchandise. While the school's colors are officially "crimson and cream," that translates into simple red and white for the T-shirts, baseball caps, and the like. Down a couple of steps from the upper level is the main room, a buffet line on the right. Soon the tables on the main floor are full, folks digging into plates weighed down with spaghetti and meat sauce.

The West Point group sits at one of the long, rectangular tables on the upper level. Knight is sitting a couple of tables over. He's still ignoring me, which would be normal except for the interview request. I'm wondering when would be the right moment to approach him. I'm being cautious. Don't want to spook him. This is nothing special to Knight, bad temper or not. I'm treating him just like any other celebrity with an attitude.

The program is underway, and the towering Mike Noonan takes the podium, his "aw shucks" manner winning people over before he ever says a word. The $6\,^1/_2'$ Noonan was the tallest guy on Knight's first West Point team, a happy-go-lucky kid until Coach got hold of him.

They had asked me to speak. I assumed this was because of the newspaper column I wrote defending Knight that appeared in a couple of newspapers, including the Bloomington *Herald-Times.* In the column, I tried to make the case that discipline is neither outmoded nor unique to the Indiana basketball program.

"Behind closed doors," I wrote, "there is still a whole world out there where strict discipline, abuse, is creating not only great soldiers and athletes, but policemen, fighter pilots, astronauts—even doctors and lawyers. And wherever there is a difficult regimen, there is somebody there to drive people—usually the young—to do things they don't want to do."

I went on to say no matter how much I'd like to, I still didn't believe that a pat on the back and a kind word alone would get the job done.

"So just to be safe," the column concluded, "I'm going to pass on all the lawyers, airline pilots, and brain surgeons coming out of 'I'm Okay,

You're Okay University.' Just to be safe, I'll be sticking with the Bob Knight grads."

Notice I didn't say anything about Knight grabbing player Neil Reed by the throat.

Since I'm no speaker, I offered to read a shortened version of the column. Too serious, they said, need to keep it light. So I suggested Mike Noonan, a sophomore center on the 1965 team.

When Army Assistant Coach Bob Knight came to recruit him, Noonan was "livin' on stamps," by himself, in a trailer in tiny Elgin, Illinois. Noonan was not all that impressed with the twenty-four-year-old Knight, had hardly even heard of West Point. Still Knight talked Noonan into visiting the Academy. But it wasn't the visit to West Point that sold Noonan; it was the visits to the other schools. There everybody seemed rich by comparison.

"I owned two pairs of jeans and two flannel shirts," said Noonan, "and these guys had cars, and I said even if I got a full ride I wouldn't have two nickels to rub together."

Up at West Point, they wouldn't offer a car, but since Noonan, like all cadets, would be a soldier in the U.S. Army, just about everything else was taken care of: food, lodging, clothes. And then there was the modest salary of $111 a month and a first-class education.

But for this seventeen-year-old, there was one deciding factor. "I knew everybody got uniforms," said Noonan. For the first time in his life, he wouldn't have to worry about his wardrobe.

So Noonan strolls to the podium, the easygoing kid now an affable country lawyer in Frostburg, Maryland. *Keep it light.* Noonan bemoans the lack of crime in peaceful Frostburg, which is bad for business, and claims to be a founding member of an organization called "Lawyers Without Clients." He tells a couple of G-rated Knight stories, saying he is being extra careful since after his last talk he'd been exiled from the prime real estate behind the Indiana bench to the upper forty of the balcony in Assembly Hall, the IU basketball arena.

The speeches over, the golf tourney winners are announced, trophies and prizes awarded. Knight doesn't speak. This seems to be proof that he is indeed cutting back on public appearances in reaction to the zero-tolerance policy announced during a news conference a little over a month before.

On May 15, 2000, Indiana University President Myles Brand had called the media together to announce Knight's fate after a seven week, "wide-ranging investigation" brought on by allegations that Knight had choked player Neil Reed during a 1997 practice. During the investigation a tape surfaced showing Knight grabbing Reed by the throat with one hand. Reed's head snaps back, and it's all over in about the time it takes to read this sentence. Reed called it "choking." Not Knight.

"You're going to choke somebody, you better use two hands. That's how you choke somebody," Knight would say.

While IU investigators decided that neither the Reed altercation nor several other incidents they looked into rose to "the level of dismissal," they did identify "a protracted and often troubling pattern in which Coach Knight has a problem of controlling his anger and confronting individuals."

Knight was suspended for three games, fined thirty thousand dollars, and given one last chance to clean up his act under what Brand called a "zero-tolerance policy." That policy prohibited "inappropriate physical contact" with players, coaches, women, and small children; required Knight to comply with a TBA "code of conduct" for IU athletes and coaches; and, in paragraph three, contained an admonition to be, well, nice.

"Public presentations and other occasions during which Coach Knight is a representative of Indiana University," pronounced Brand, "will be conducted with appropriate decorum and civility."

Remember, Knight had to agree to this in order to hang on to his job. The goal, chimed in IU trustees' president John Walda, was to "protect and enhance the image of Indiana University."

The word "muzzled" comes to mind, followed closely by "lawsuit."

Any restrictions on what Knight could and could not say might have gotten a bit tricky for IU lawyers. Say Indiana was playing archrival Purdue, and Knight said something lacking the "appropriate decorum and civility," perhaps told an official, "That was the worst fucking call I've ever seen!" and said it loud enough for the TV cameras to pick it up, to the shock and dismay of schoolmarms all across America. If President Brand had decided that was another example of a "lengthy pattern of troubling behavior," Coach Knight would have been history. Or would he?

Indiana University is a government institution and, as such, is subject to the free-speech restrictions of the United States Constitution. While private employers can fire you for simply saying "fuck," the government cannot, thanks in part to a California teenager.

On April 26, 1968, a smart-ass kid named Paul Robert Cohen strolled down a corridor in the Los Angeles Courthouse (that's *courthouse*—one of those places full of judges, cops, and lawyers). Cohen was wearing a jacket with a pithy thought for the day scrawled across the back. "Fuck the Draft," it said. Cohen "was arrested, tried, convicted, and sentenced to thirty days," about that fast, for "maliciously and willfully disturbing the peace."

Supreme Court Justice John Harlan wore this one out.

"One man's vulgarity is another's lyric," rhapsodized Harlan in the 1971 *Cohen v. California* decision. The question, Harlan said, was whether states "acting as guardians of public morality, may properly remove this word [fuck] from the public vocabulary." They can't, said Harlan. So "fuck" was still in.

Harlan's reasoning? The phrase "Fuck the Draft" is a whole lot stronger than something like "Doggone the Draft!" or "Down with the Draft!" So to deprive Cohen of the use of the word "fuck" would have watered down his right to free speech. The First Amendment to the Constitution won't let government do that. "Freedom of speech" they call it, and everybody in America owns a piece of that franchise, even Bob Knight.

And Knight's employer, the state of Indiana, the government, according to a 1972 Supreme Court decision, "may not deny a benefit [such as a job] to a person on a basis that infringes on his constitutionally protected interests—especially his interest in freedom of speech."

In other words, Indiana University couldn't fire Bob Knight for what he said. Mostly. There are a few exceptions, things like libel and sexual harassment, but none apply here.

As New Jersey Judge Harvey Smith put it in a 1975 decision:

> Statutory attempts to regulate pure bluster
> Can't pass what is called constitutional muster.
> Use of vulgar words that may cause resentment
> Is protected by the First Amendment.

All this to say that it looks like Bob Knight has a constitutionally protected right to say, "That's the worst fucking call I've ever seen!" to an official, at a news conference, on ESPN, and in front of women, children, and blue-haired grannies. So before anybody at IU could fire Bob Knight, the lawyers were charged with making sure he was doing more than just saying something. If not, that image the trustees were so concerned about could have collected some major smudges as Indiana University became the laughingstock of academe when its name ended up on the yokel side of a high-profile free-speech case.

Of course, three months later, Knight would come through for the IU lawyers when he grabbed that kid. Grabbed him. Now he'd done more than just say something. But we're getting ahead of ourselves.

A month after the press conference announcing the zero-tolerance policy, the thirty-thousand-dollar fine, and the three-game suspension, President Myles Brand would step forward to defend the right of an Indiana University employee to speak his mind. Not Bob Knight, Murray Sperber, the English professor who has been a longtime critic of Knight.

"Professor Sperber," as the dean of the Indiana College of Arts and Sciences put it, "is free to say whatever he wants and wherever he wants."

Unlike Coach Knight. So what we're left with is a cadre of IU administrators—government representatives, a benevolent Big Brother—picking and choosing who is allowed to say what. All with the best intentions, of course.

———◆———

Back at the DCSC, it's well past nine, and the bull session with the West Point players is still going strong. Coach Knight notices the staff is hanging around, and volunteers to lock up so they can go home. One of the women who's been working with Knight for a couple of decades makes it clear that's not an option. I get the impression that Knight is not to be trusted with the keys. Someone suggests we adjourn to the lobby of the Hampton Inn, where most of the West Point crew are staying. A half-hour later, we reassemble for more lies and more beer, except for Knight, who doesn't drink.

I sit on the outside of the circle. I'm running out of time. I decide that if Coach doesn't say something about the interview, I'll confront him. Around ten-thirty Knight gets up to leave, and I'm right on his ass. When he stops to sign an autograph, I station myself between him and the door.

Is this a wasted trip? Is the book dead? Will he treat me with "appropriate decorum and civility"?

He turns.

"Coach," I say, "when do you think we can get together and talk?" I say nothing about an "interview." That sounds too much like a reporter.

He glances at me, completely benign, like we'd been chatting all night. "I'll pick you up here in the morning," he says.

Just that easy.

Chapter 3

Heroes and Cowards

Saturday, June 24. I'm up at 6:30, going over my notes, studying. I've seen Bob Knight humiliate reporters who ask "dumb questions."

Downstairs I splurge on a donut, gulp coffee, then retreat to my room. I have two pages of questions, a page more than I need. What do I absolutely have to get out of him? What do I need to avoid? During my research, I've pinpointed all the firsts—first win, first loss, first player to quit, first time he got thrown out of a game, first instance of chair abuse. But I expect this will be only one of several interviews, so I want to stay away from anything controversial.

I decide to concentrate on the early part of the book: chapter and verse of how he came to be named head coach. When did he get the offer? When did he tell the players? What were the circumstances? If there's time left, I'll move on to specific games.

I go over and over the first question. It will set the tone. The question needs to be something that lets him know what the book is about, but doesn't sound like something coming from a typical sports reporter. Ready, I head back down to the lobby at a quarter to eight. I get another cup of coffee, sit in a chair just inside the front door across from the registration desk. Can't miss him here. I act nonchalant. Although I'm dying to pull out my notes for a last once-over, I don't want him to catch me at it.

It starts to rain. Great, I think. That means less golf, more time to talk. I check my watch. We could spend the whole day together.

Eight-thirty. When my teammates come by, I tell them I'm waiting for Knight. Nine o'clock, no Coach. I begin wondering what he meant by "morning." Registration for today's golf tourney starts at eleven. I check to see if there have been any calls. Nope. The rain stops. Golf is back on. I give up on Knight at ten-thirty, go back upstairs to call my grown son and wish him a happy birthday. The rest of the day is scheduled. There's golf until 5 P.M., another reception and banquet beginning at seven, and the unofficial post-banquet cluster fuck that will last until all hours. I'm screwed. No interview today.

I head out to the golf course. Walking up to the clubhouse, I spot Knight down on the driving range. Looks like working on his swing is more important than talking to me. I'm not about to call him on it. See "Knight, celebrity." See "temper, bad." Maybe his alarm didn't go off, maybe his dog died, maybe he spent the morning guzzling Kaopectate. Celebrities don't have to make up excuses; others will do it for them.

I'll try for tomorrow, although officially I'm not here tomorrow. Officially, I'm heading home after two days of fun at the Indiana Classic. But I'll stay over. One day, two days. As long as Knight's in town, I'll be dogging his ass for the interview. Respectfully, of course. Persistent, but not pushy. Not like I'm entitled to anything.

Jocko Mikula and I corral a couple of golf carts and, with Knight pal Al Lo Balbo in tow, head out to the course. We're not playing today. We'll just follow people around, kibitzing. Rain is still threatening.

Alfred Anthony "Al" Lo Balbo, in his early eighties, is one of Knight's old cronies from the West Point days. Knight has flown him in from New Jersey for the tournament. Like any Knight-sponsored event, the Indiana Classic is a living history pageant. There'll be guys who coached him, played with him, or befriended him; guys from Orrville, Ohio, where he grew up; from Ohio State, where he played college ball; from Cuyahoga Falls, Ohio, where he first coached; and, of course, from West Point and Indiana.

Al Lo Balbo was born and raised in the Bronx, and he still has the accent and the swagger. He's a wiry little guy with huge hands, perfect for basketball. A year-and-a-half out of high school, Al was working in his parents' "sweet shop" when he was recruited—back when the idea of recruiting was in its infancy—to play at Iowa State in Cedar Rapids. This was in the early forties. He graduated *summa cum laude,* he'll tell you, majoring in education.

Lo Balbo is wearing a senior-citizen's special, a pastel polyester outfit with matching shirt and pants. He's lost most of his hair but has fashioned a comb-over that would be the envy of Purdue's Gene Keady. He's taken a long flap of white hair growing out of the base of his skull, swept it up over the top and sides, and sprayed it into place. The Lo Balbo swoop. I hear Knight needles him mercilessly about it, has gotten him to cut a lot of it, wants him to cut more.

Al Lo Balbo became Knight's assistant up at West Point after seventeen years as a high school coach at St. Mary's in Elizabeth, New Jersey. That's where he claims to have invented the pressure defense Knight is now famous for.

"As soon as that ball goes into the big man," said Lo Balbo, "we go diving down after it."

Sounds familiar.

In mid-afternoon, the rain returns, and the golf tourney is cut short. The reception and banquet at the Hoosier Room are a repeat of the night before: cocktails, dinner—spicy ribs and mild barbecued chicken this time—and speeches.

As the dessert is being served, chairs are scooted back and angled toward the podium. Tonight's West Point speaker will be Bobby Seigle. The shortest guy on Knight's first squad at 5'11", Bobby was the team's best ball handler and a "floor leader" who teetered on the fine line between leading and jumping to the head of the parade. Always yapping, he was famous for telling you to do something you were already going to do. "Go through!" he'd shout, after you were already two steps toward the baseline.

Seigle speaks first of the common bond between West Point and Indiana, Bob Knight, the "big, silver-haired guy" sitting in the back of the room.

I slip the tape recorder into my lap surreptitiously and turn it on, still not sure of Knight's stance on taping.

Seigle, a retired Army colonel, followed his brother to West Point and an Army career. He's one of the best preserved of the squad, not a contender in the potbelly sweepstakes, hair still dark with only a little gray at the temples. During the speech, he comes across like a commander speaking to his troops: authoritative, but approachable.

He tells the Indiana players they can thank the West Pointers for the Bob Knight that made his debut in Bloomington in 1971. The crowd laughs. They don't seem too thankful.

"You guys all owe us something," says Seigle. "Somebody had to train him to be who he is."

Knight did come of age during his years as head coach at West Point. It was an extraordinary run. In six seasons beginning in 1965, he had 102 wins versus fifty losses and four National Invitation Tournament (NIT) appearances at Madison Square Garden, back when that meant something. This by a coach at a military academy trying to recruit at the height of the Vietnam War.

In those days, West Point had trouble recruiting anybody, much less athletes. Here's how bad it got. Several years before the Vietnam War heated up, the Academy sifted through a pool of 3,012 nominees to come up with 1,582 physically, medically, and academically qualified applicants. A little over half of those, 847, ended up attending the school. Seven years later, in 1968, West Point admitted every single qualified applicant. In some years during the Vietnam War, the Academy wasn't getting enough applications to even fill the quota, then around a thousand.

Still Knight recruited successfully and won basketball games. You have to go back more than half a century to find a West Point coach anywhere near as successful. Only Leo Novak won more games (126), and it took him thirteen years (1927–39) versus Knight's six. Since Knight left, West Point basketball has languished except during a short period in the late seventies when one of Knight's former players led the team. A guy named Mike Krzyzewski posted a 73–59 record during five years at the Academy. No coach since has managed to bat even five hundred.

Knight brought the system that made good West Point teams sometimes play like great teams with him to Indiana, where he won three national championships. What was it about that first season at West Point that began the transformation of this hothead from Orrville, Ohio, into one of the most influential and controversial basketball coaches of all time? That's what I'm in Bloomington to find out.

"Now about heroes and cowards," says Seigle, getting to the heart of his speech. "We know that heroes set standards. We know that cowards abuse standards."

And in the wake of the Neil Reed flap, it was clear just who the heroes and cowards were.

"We know that heroes set higher standards for everybody to meet," continues Seigle, "because they know you can meet them."

During other speeches this bunch has been dutifully attentive. But now every eye is on Seigle, the room quiet, absent even the usual background murmur of a crowd this size: the tinkling silverware, shifting chairs, quiet asides.

"Heroes aren't quitters. Cowards are quitters," says Seigle, warming up. "Cowards die a thousand deaths and heroes die but one."

That last one didn't quite fit, but what the hell.

Then came the MacArthur quote. Douglas MacArthur, five-star General of the Army, hero of World War II and Korea, the soldier's soldier, enshrined in bronze at West Point, is the closest thing to a silver-tongued orator to ever come out of the Academy. No true West Pointer can make a speech without relying on ol' Doug. The man could pile it deep. Problem is, he was such a quote factory, it's hard to choose.

"Old soldiers never die, they just fade away"; "There is no substitute for victory"; "I shall return"—all good ones, but Seigle chooses a quote more in tune with the plight of the West Point athlete of the sixties. It dates from just after World War I when MacArthur, then the head man at the military academy, had the following chiseled in stone over the doorway to the gymnasium:

> Upon the fields of friendly strife are sown the seeds that, upon other fields, on other days, will bear the fruits of victory.

To a man, the West Pointers assembled in Bloomington were all too familiar with those "other fields." Every one of them had served in Vietnam, some twice, and several had been in the Gulf War. A helicopter pilot, Seigle himself had been in both hellholes plus Grenada.

"You're learning more than just how to move on a basketball court," says Seigle, not the first West Pointer to say playing for Knight was good preparation for combat.

"In some ways, I think combat was a little bit easier," said one.

And Knight himself is always talking about how he's trying to prepare players for life after basketball. When officers coming out of West Point are prepared, the troops serving under them are prepared. That saves lives.

"There are hundreds of thousands of soldiers walking free in the United States today because of the training principles we learned on that basketball court," says Seigle.

Later Knight, needling Mike Noonan, would sum up the difference between Noonan's speech and Seigle's.

"Noonan, you're a comedian," Knight said, "and Seigle is an orator."

"We know the difference between heroes and cowards," Seigle had said, gesturing in Knight's direction, "and that man back there is no coward."

"No coward." Put that first on the list of what Bob Knight ain't.

Chapter 4

The Bob Knight Clinic
for Anger Management

G o to the third light and turn left on College." Bob Knight is patiently repeating the directions to the location of tonight's post-Hoosier-Room *soiree*. "Go two more lights, turn left on Tenth." It's like he's on the sidelines telling players how to run an out-of-bounds play he just made up. He stops short of asking us to recite it back.

Thanks to great directions, we all wind up at Yogi's, a student hangout at the corner of Tenth and Indiana. The place is full, but Knight has reserved a private room for the insiders. Heads turn when Quinn Buckner and Knight walk by. A local celebrity, Buckner was the leader of Knight's undefeated 1976 national championship team at Indiana. A couple of gay guys give us the once over as we parade in, but the girls don't seem too interested. Buckner, Mike Noonan, and the other cigar smokers are soon exiled to tables on the tented patio out front, while the rest of the clan settle in with Knight in a back room.

There are three tables for two along the left-hand wall, the rest of the room filled with dark wooden booths. The Tenth Street sidewalk is visible through a glass door and picture window in the back wall. Knight sits in a booth by the window and is joined by Seigle and Mike Gyovai, a burly, senior forward on Knight's 1969–70 West Point team. Waitresses scramble around taking orders.

Wearing jeans and basketball shoes, Gyovai is about 6′ 4″, 220, still in great shape, still playing ball. I'm still playing too, but I wouldn't get near a court where this guy was playing. I can only imagine the damage he can do when up to speed.

Knight asks Seigle why he never made general. No mystery there, replies Seigle, and tells a long story about how he got crossways with some drunk he worked for at the Pentagon. Mike Gyovai punctuates Seigle's blow-by-blow account with an occasional "Why does that surprise you?" delivered like an "Amen!" coming from a front pew.

The talk turns to Ed Jordan, a guard on Knight's first team. In the early eighties, Jordan was about to get booted out of the Army after seventeen years, three short of retirement. This was just the latest slap in the face. He'd been passed over for promotion for well over a decade and was still a captain long after his peers had been promoted first to major and then lieutenant colonel. This because of some rhubarb about "supply accountability" when he was a twenty-four-year-old company commander. According to team scuttlebutt, Jordan had stayed in, suffering the humiliation, because he needed the medical insurance to cover a child with a rare growth disorder. Wrong, says Jordan.

"I stayed in because I liked it," he said.

Knight got wind of Jordan's predicament. "I'll see if I can help you out," Knight told him and called an old friend from West Point, a general who had just retired as head of Army personnel at the Pentagon.

"Next thing I know I was promoted to major," Jordan recalls. Not only that, Jordan would be promoted a second time before retiring as a lieutenant colonel after twenty-eight years in the service.

The retired general had a simple rationale for helping Jordan, said Knight: Jordan played basketball at West Point. Today Jordan knows Knight was somehow involved in his change of fate. Amazingly, Knight has never called him to take full credit for this life-altering favor.

And all I want is a simple interview. Not that it couldn't be life-altering. I figure Bob Knight is money in the bank.

Bob Seigle is entertaining Knight with tales from the modern Army. While more than half of the players on Knight's first team bailed as soon as their four-year commitment was up, Bob, like Ed Jordan, had made a career of it, retiring in 1993 after twenty-seven years.

Seigle tells Knight about some of the problems facing today's commanders. Problems unheard of when we graduated in 1966. In the old days, officers would seldom even share a beer with lower-ranking soldiers: "familiarity breeds contempt" and all that. So after taking over a unit, Seigle was surprised to discover the two lesbians, both married to men, who wanted their boss, a captain, to father their child. Seigle was even more surprised to discover the captain said "yes."

Knight, head bowed, listens closely, glancing up every now and then to show he's paying attention.

After tonight's "heroes and cowards" speech, I sense Seigle has risen to the top of Knight's list. Maybe that's how Knight views the world. Heroes and cowards. Us against them. Wrong against right. For a man as smart as Knight, he seems, on the surface at least, to acknowledge few gradations between right and wrong, at least in his public persona.

"I have always been too confrontational, especially when I know I'm right," said Knight in the "apology" he issued in the midst of the IU investigation. Maybe the problem is not so much the "confrontational" part as the "knowing you're right" part, this compounded by a conviction that "being right" is what matters most. That'll be a hundred dollars, please, see you same time next week.

I'm pretending to know Bob Knight, like every other La-Z-Boy psychologist in the country, when, truth is, I don't know him at all.

I had been reminded of this a couple of weeks earlier while agonizing over Knight's fate following the announcement of the zero-tolerance policy. In the days just prior to the coach's ESPN interview with Roy Firestone and Digger Phelps, I had come up with what I thought was a foolproof plan to hoist Knight's critics on their own petard.

We've all been privy to the Bob-Knight-is-a-maniac highlight reel: the tossed chair, the tirades, the Neil Reed grabbing, the speech in which he asked to be buried "upside down, so my critics can kiss my ass." We've all read the stories about the scuffle with the Puerto Rican cop, the forfeit of the game with the Soviet Union, the shouting match with the athletic director. Back in 1964, when Bob Knight first stomped into an officials' locker room in Portland, Oregon, he was said to have a "bad temper." Now these thirty-some years later he has "a problem with anger management." That's progress. A bad temper is a character flaw. A problem with anger management? That's a guilt-free affliction, like crossed eyes or prickly heat.

One of those geniuses who suddenly materializes to comment anytime a celebrity's flaws are made public stepped forward to explain that "anger management is about slowing people down so they don't react impulsively to their anger." Hmmm. Didn't they used to call that counting to ten?

Anyway, I'd come up with this foolproof plan Knight could use to outfox his critics. First he would admit to having an "anger management problem." That would gain him instant admission to the psychobabble theme park, a magical world of victimhood where you don't have character flaws, you have addictions and conditions and disorders, through no fault of your own, of course. Once you've admitted to a problem and sought "help," I figured, the touchy-feely folk are disarmed. Any future temper tantrum is just a little tangent on the path to "recovery."

I got so excited, I prepared a memo.

> May 30, 2000
>
> Coach,
>
> Here are four possible ways to seize the initiative on the anger issue and turn it to your advantage.
>
> (1) Establish a Bob Knight Clinic for anger management a la the Betty Ford Clinic.
>
> (2) Endow a chair in the IU psychology department to study anger.
>
> (3) Begin an annual "Conference on Anger Management."
>
> (4) Confess to being "addicted to anger." This takes the air out of any additional charges. Since the temper problem is already established, what's one more example?
>
> A variation on the theme is to narrow the subject to "Sports and Anger." Maybe get Latrell Sprewell and P. J. Carlesimo involved.
>
> I hope this helps.

It was a stroke of genius. Bob Knight would become the poster boy for anger management. He would be continually "struggling" with his "addiction," of course, and most days he would succeed in "conquering his demons," but, being human, sometimes he would fall off the wagon—

see that chair sailing over the scorers' table—and have to attend meetings again.

"Hi, my name is Bob, and I've been anger free for three nanoseconds."

I was loving this. I take some pride in being a cynic, but this was a new low.

Memo in hand, I breathlessly called Knight's secretary, Mary Ann Davis. I was desperate to share this "insight" with him before the ESPN interview with Roy Firestone and Digger Phelps that night. Was there a chance he could talk to me before the interview? If he didn't have time, I'd fax the memo up. Just give me the word. I'd be standing by. Mary Ann was polite—she's used to dealing with difficult people—but there was no phone call. No fax.

Thank God.

The big shock was not that Knight believed he could handle his anger without professional help. The big shock was that he would take that tack on national television. Going in, I thought the minimum he could do to quiet the howling jackals was to sign up for an anger-management class. After all, at least one Indiana trustee had suggested as much. Why not go along and get along? Didn't he learn anything at West Point? Spend a few hours chatting up a woman with a bad perm and funny glasses, pronounce yourself cured, and get on with your life.

No way.

"I think my wife is as good at anger management as anyone can imagine," Knight told Firestone and Phelps. "She's got magnets hung up all over the house that say, 'The horse is dead. Get off.'"

While Knight did admit his temper was a problem he'd recognized at least since he was a teenager, he didn't think it was all that big a deal.

"If you took the percentage of times I have really gone overboard," said Knight, "that's a pretty small percentage of all the circumstances I've been in."

All the taunting fans, bad calls, teenage players making dumb-ass mistakes.

"I have to be able to do all the time basically what I do most of the time now," said Knight.

My first thought was, "The man is in denial." And maybe he is. But based on what we do know about him, the response was in character. Here's a guy who has a reputation for honesty. And today, because of who he is, he can call an idiot an idiot and get away with it. That's what happens when adjectives like "legendary," "champion," and "hall-of-famer" get tacked on to your name. Who's going to challenge him? He's not diplomatic; he doesn't have to be. For most of his coaching life, insulated by success, Bob Knight has enjoyed the luxury of saying exactly what's on his mind. But what was he like back when he was Bobby Nobody?

Portland, Oregon. Christmas, 1964. Army was playing Washington State in the second round of the Far West Classic. They were led by second-year coach Tates Locke, a twenty-seven-year-old firebrand out of Ohio Wesleyan. Beside Locke on the bench sat a twenty-four-year-old assistant coach who was about to get thrown out of his first college game. His name was Bobby Knight.

Locke and Knight had been ragging the officials, as usual, and as the first half was winding down, the two already had three technicals between them: two on Locke, one on Knight. (Locke brags they led the nation in technicals that year. Knight denies it.) That's when the "charge" was called against Army.

The referee was about as easygoing as an official gets, remembered now for his ready, if incongruent, smile. He'd blow his whistle, smile, and nail you, so good-natured nobody could get pissed off at him. Well, almost nobody.

The charge is one of the trickiest calls in basketball. In the textbook charge, the man with the ball barrels straight into the chest of a defender. To get the call, the defensive player must be squared off, his chest perpendicular to the offensive player's direction of travel. He cannot be moving forward or to the side, and, on paper at least, he must give the offensive player an opportunity to get around him. As any coach will tell you, it's one of the most frequently botched calls in basketball.

So it's not surprising that Coach Knight, uh, took umbrage at "Smiley's" charge call. He leapt off the bench and threw a towel in the air.

The official, still smiling, looked at Knight and said, "If that towel hits the floor you got a technical."

Gravity being what it is, Knight got his second T. That really set him off, and he kept after the official right up until halftime.

Coach Locke made a few adjustments during the intermission, and when he was through briefing the players, he noticed Knight was missing. He looked outside.

"We've got about five minutes before tip-off," recalled Locke, "and here he comes down the hall with his head hanging to one side like it does when things aren't going too well."

Turns out Knight had spent most of halftime in the officials' locker room. They weren't swapping fish stories. Locke told Knight to shake it off. "We gotta get ready for the second half," he said.

"Well, don't worry about the tip," said Knight. "There won't be one. We just got another technical." Locke shook his head.

Knight had gotten a T during halftime.

"There's another thing," said Knight. "I won't be with you for the second half."

So Knight was thrown out of his first college game even before he became a head coach. There are two versions of what happened next. Locke's version is that Knight was allowed to sit in the stands with his new best friend, a Pinkerton agent. In the second version, Knight, banned from the arena, tried to sneak back in to watch the game. The smiling official spotted him and, still smiling, told Tates, "If that guy's not out of here in sixty seconds, this game is over." So out Knight went.

Army went on to win the game by five points.

So here's Bobby Knight, then little more than a boy, whose only stint as a head coach was one year with the high school junior-varsity team at that basketball powerhouse, Cuyahoga Falls, Ohio, taking on a major college official at the Far West Classic. The point is Knight was raising hell long before the adjectives started piling up behind his name. Bobby Knight, the nobody, was the same as Bob Knight, the legend.

And since Bob Knight, the legend, doesn't think he has an anger problem of any consequence, he's not going to say he does on ESPN or anywhere else. He doesn't think anger controls his life, and he doesn't think his perennial temper tantrums "define the person." And if he doesn't believe it, he's not going to say it. That would be hypocritical. That's another one of those adjectives you never see attached to Knight's name. So now we have a second thing we can add to the list of what Bob Knight ain't. He ain't a coward, and he ain't a hypocrite.

This brilliant insight dawns on me about two minutes into the ESPN interview. Not long after, I realize there's not going to be any Bob-Knight-endowed anger-management chair in the IU psychology department, there's not going to be any eat-your-heart-out-Jerry-Springer roundtable featuring Latrell Sprewell and P. J. Carlesimo, and there's not going to be any Bob Knight Clinic for Anger Management.

Pity.

———

Back at Yogi's, a pretty blonde in a tank top keeps prancing by outside the Tenth Street window, waving her arms, doing a little jig. It's the kind of antics people resort to when they are trying to get their face on TV. I expect this display is aimed at Knight, but he doesn't notice. I'm sitting in the booth across from Knight's, nursing my third iced tea. I figure if Coach ain't drinking, I ain't drinking. There might still be a chance for some manner of late-night, pre-dawn interview.

It's nearing midnight, and Knight has spent most of the time in a back booth with Seigle and Gyovai. Figuring he ought to spread it around, he decides to move up front to another group of players. Before he gets up, he nudges me with his foot.

"Let's get together tomorrow morning," he said. "I'll pick you up."

He does.

Like I said: Just that easy.

Chapter 5

Bigger Than Elvis?

C oach Knight strolls through the door of the Bob Knight School for Basketball around 10:30 on Sunday morning, and the intensity of play picks up as he walks the length of the field house. The school is held annually on the campus of Indiana University, and about five hundred boys ages nine to eighteen have signed up this year. For their $275 the boys get four days of total basketball immersion and two lectures a day from Coach Knight. The brochure emphasizes that "Coach Knight personally greets and signs autographs for all campers and their families." It's a chance to meet the most famous man in Indiana. That alone is worth the price of admission.

The boys are running drills to a cacophony of shouts, bouncing rubber balls. On a near court, one kid sets a low pick as a second rubs off a defender before taking a pass from outside and shooting a jumper. On the other end, a rebounder throws a baseball pass to a kid at half court, who passes to the wing man, who feeds the ball inside for a lay-up.

Knight huddles with Assistant Coach John Treloar, and the boys sneak glances at the winningest active coach in college basketball. Knight's wearing the *de rigueur* baggy shorts, tucked-in polo shirt, and basketball shoes, a belt all but disappearing beneath his potbelly. Face it, the man's fat. But this is not over-the-hill fat. This is power fat, like one of those nineteenth-century robber barons.

The scrimmaging begins.

A skinny, shirtless white kid—no chest, all ribs, maybe nine—wearing baggy, navy-blue polyester shorts that swish around his calves, brings the ball up the court, dribbling back and forth between his legs as naturally as breathing. He's so tiny, I'm surprised the ball will fit between his knobby knees. It's a beautiful thing. Graceful. Back in 1962, there was a kid on the West Point plebe team who demonstrated that move—once. In those days dribbling between your legs or behind your back, dunking, or even palming the ball were considered showboating, and few coaches would tolerate it.

On the other team, a black kid, a foot taller, wearing a shirt and baggy pants in a light, North Carolina blue, brings the ball up the court. He's also a good ball handler, but sloppy. He throws all his passes with one hand from over his head, arm uncoiling like a striking cobra. Problem is, with just the one hand, he can't pull the pass back if the passing lane closes. Knight 101.

Whistles blow, echoing throughout the field house, and the kids congregate in a horseshoe at Knight's feet. A couple of Indiana players, Dane Fife and Jeffrey Newton, part of the school staff, hover on the periphery.

You have to work hard to develop skills, Knight tells the group, but it takes more than skill to play basketball. The game is "four parts mental to one part physical," he says, repeating a familiar Knight mantra.

He points out Dane Fife, the 6′4″ Indiana guard. He says Fife is a good player, but he's not great, because he doesn't think. He'll be great, says Knight, if he can learn to do the little things.

Suddenly Knight is pointing toward the back of the group. It takes a minute, but the staff finally pinpoints the three boys, maybe nine, who were goofing off. They are pulled out, moved to the back, and made to face the wall. Discipline starts early at the Bob Knight School.

Knight pulls an older kid up out of the front row to demonstrate how to shoot a jump shot. Feet together. Head back. Follow through like your hand is going through the basket. I cringe when I notice Knight is moving the kid around with a hand clasped to the back of his neck.

The session over, the kids scatter, and, hands in pockets, Knight quietly talks to the three exiles serving time on the back wall. When he's done, he pats each on the top of the head with the flat of his hand. Go and sin no more. They have something to tell mama.

On the way back across the field house Knight is stopped several times: somebody's grandma wants a picture, a kid wants an autograph, a man wants to shake his hand.

Outside, after Knight chats with Assistant Coach Mike Davis for a few minutes, we climb into Knight's car, a roomy, nondescript American make. Given his reputation, you'd think he'd drive some kind of bully-mobile: a pickup truck, one of those muscle-bound SUVs, a Humvee. He doesn't fasten his seat belt.

I ask him if he still gets joy out of working with these kids. He ignores the question and tells me how the camp works, how some coaches don't really participate in their camps, how he makes three appearances a day, talking to them twice. I ask him if he ever recruited a kid out of the basketball school. Just one, he says.

Back in the late seventies, he approached a promising fourteen-year-old. "Do you want to play at Indiana?" Knight asked.

"Yes," the quaking kid replied. Flash forward four years to Knight sitting in the boy's living room in Indianapolis.

"Do you remember that question I asked you four years ago?" Knight asked.

"Yes," the kid replied.

"Is the answer still the same?"

"Yes."

And that's how Knight recruited future NBA player Randy Wittman. It's all part of his recruiting philosophy, jokes Knight. Scare a kid into making a promise when he's fourteen, then hold him to it four years later.

Trying to make small talk, I say it must be tough being a celebrity. That remark is met with a long stretch of silence. While we may have spent a couple of years in the same orbit a long time ago, we're strangers now, and it's beginning to feel like getting stuck in a car with an ex-girlfriend, trying to remember why you ever asked her out in the first place.

We end up at Assembly Hall and walk into Knight's office under a sign that says: "A man's gotta believe in something. I believe I'll go fishing." It's obviously not a working office. It's a place where he drops stuff off, an oversized closet for various and assorted stuff. There's something on every horizontal surface: red-and-white IU memorabilia, books, hats, trophies; fishing, hunting, and golf paraphernalia; basketballs that need signing, mail that needs reading, on the desk, on the floor, on shelves, on easy chairs. There are plaques, photographs, and prints propped up against wood-paneled walls already full of framed mementos. It looks like the aftermath of a tornado in a Bloomington tourist trap.

Knight moves a stack of papers so I can sit in my designated seat, a beige leather wing chair. He sits ten feet away, not behind the desk, but on the left side, in a red leather chair. I gingerly remove the tape recorder from my brief case.

I take a quick breath. "Okay if I record this?"

He looks surprised that I asked. Like, of course you're going to record this. I get the thing going, settle back in my chair. Knight has the demeanor of a man about to undergo a vasectomy.

The first question in any interview is critical, particularly with a potentially hostile subject. You want to give them an easy one, a "softball," just to get them talking. After a lot of thought, I've settled on a question that is one part interrogatory to nine parts ass-kissing.

"You changed basketball beginning at West Point back in 1965," I say. "What was it about you, the institution, and the players that set that change in motion?" The question will also serve as an ego test, a chance to see if "Knight is about Knight," as one ex-player put it.

Years ago as a TV news photographer, I shot a story on a country singer named Marty Robbins who was in the hospital recovering from some kind of surgery—heart, I think. Robbins had a string of rock 'n' roll hits back in the fifties and later morphed into a huge country-music star. Robbins was near the twilight of his career, and that and the surgery apparently had set him to ruminating about his place in music history. After some thought, he decided he was bigger than Elvis. He seemed sincere.

With my "you changed basketball" question, I am giving Knight the opportunity to tell me just how much bigger than Elvis, how much bigger than the game, he really is.

I lob the softball gently in Knight's direction, a big fat pitch with a high arc that I am expecting him to knock out of the park with five minutes of bullshit supporting my basic thesis—"You're the man!"—with maybe a few qualifications here and there for modesty's sake. What I get is twenty minutes on everybody who even remotely contributed to his early success.

The first sentence out of his mouth: "The guy that really got basketball going in the right direction was Tates."

That's Taylor Osborne Locke, the head coach when Knight arrived at West Point. You remember Locke? The renegade coach later famous for getting run out of town down at Clemson for some over-the-top recruiting violations. Remember Tree Rollins? That Tates Locke.

"When Tates took it over," says Knight, "basketball was no more important at West Point than lacrosse or track or baseball or anything else. It was one of the other sports."

At West Point, football was king. Still is.

When Tates took over, there was no basketball dressing room, no dedicated basketball trainer, a pittance of a recruiting budget, and a home floor that didn't go down in the field house until a day or two before the first game. In Tates' first year, they didn't even make that deadline, and the team played the opening game of the season at a practice gym where it was standing room only. Not because there was a big crowd, because there were maybe two hundred seats in the whole place. When Locke took over in 1963, Army was at a low point. The team had gone 8–11 the year before, including a loss to archrival Navy. What's more, while the team had made its first-ever NIT appearance in 1961, Army had gone one for thirteen in tournament play over the previous eight years and had not won a road game in almost three seasons.

So Tates is the first person Knight gives credit for his success. Then comes Mike Silliman, the *Parade* High School All-American out of Louisville, Kentucky. The 6′6″, highly recruited Silliman was averaging 18 points and 11 rebounds a game when Knight became head coach.

"Silliman or David Robinson," says Knight, "would be the two most outstanding players that ever played at a service academy." And Silliman, Knight has said, is the best college player he ever coached, and that's a group that includes NBA all-star Isiah Thomas.

So there was Tates Locke and Mike Silliman sharing credit for Knight's success. Then comes the dean of the academic board, Brigadier General John Jannarone.

Jannarone, who some call the most powerful man at West Point during that era, graduated first in his class in 1938, playing varsity basketball and baseball and scout team football. He was the epitome of a West Point cadet, a scholar and an athlete, and a man, it would turn out, who was willing to do what needed to be done.

"Jannarone was the key," says Knight, "the absolute key."

The credits keep coming: Athletic Director Ray Murphy, the guys who handled admissions, the athletic board, the military officers that looked out for the team, the head football recruiter, the hockey coach, and, of course, Al Lo Balbo, the man in the pastel, who put the "P" in "pressure defense."

We're twenty minutes into the interview now, and I've almost forgotten what I asked him. Knight has relaxed a little, propped a foot up on the desk. I move the tape recorder out of harm's way. During this whole time, Bob Knight devoted exactly one sentence to himself, and that to his days as an assistant coach. "I was there," said Knight, "and nobody would work any harder scouting and recruiting than I did."

That's it. In twenty minutes. It's like Elvis saying, "It's not me, it's the Jordanaires. It's the Colonel."

The charge that "Knight is about Knight" is not holding up. The interview will continue for another hour. I don't push him. I have documentation on the first case of chair abuse, the first showdown with an athletic director, the first player to tell him to go fuck himself. But this is just the first interview, and I'm hoping there will be many more.

We move on to specific games, and the stories I've heard are true: Bob Knight has an incredible memory. "You'll be amazed at how closely I remember this," said Knight, and ticked off an exact score from a game played thirty-five years before.

"This is verbatim," he says. "That happened on a Wednesday," he says. If it can be checked out, he is almost always right or so close it doesn't matter. If it can't be checked out, then you have to take his word for it, because as one ex-player said, nobody can dispute him because nobody else remembers anything at all.

"We get beat because the guy goes one for twelve," says Knight.

"We played 'em in the second game of the Holiday Festival, and they beat us by six."

Knight looks at his watch. "I gotta go now," he says.

I'm only halfway through my questions thanks partly to the twenty minutes he spent giving other people credit. I want to ask him about playing close with number-three Vanderbilt and Clyde Lee, about Wes Unseld and Louisville, about another basketball legend, Joe Lapchick and St. John's. Next time.

As we leave Assembly Hall, we run into Kirk Haston, Indiana's 6' 10" center. He's headed to the gym to work out, and I think of teasing him about the timing, his sucking up to the coach: "Look, I work out when I don't have to." Luckily I keep my mouth shut.

Knight asks Haston if he's called Pete Newell, Knight's coaching buddy, about participating in Newell's basketball camp.

"I tried," says Haston, cornered.

"Trying doesn't get it. Get it done today," orders Knight.

Haston says several times he only wants to do one camp. Knight says you'll do as many camps as I tell you to do. He's the coach, Haston's the player. As we continue to the car, Knight tells me Haston's had a real hard time since his mother was killed by a tornado that ravaged his home town, Lobelville, Tennessee, the year before. Always carries his mother's picture with him, says Knight.

Knight drives back to the Hampton Inn where we meet Al Lo Balbo and Mike Gyovai. Knight offers to take them to lunch before they ferry Lo Balbo to the airport. Mike and Lo Balbo have already eaten, but say they'll go to chat. As an afterthought, Knight invites me. He seems surprised when I accept. We end up at a Knight haunt, the deli inside a Marsh grocery store.

I get a smoked turkey sandwich with potato salad. Knight quickly finishes a salad and I eat hurriedly, thinking they are waiting on me. I dump my plate in the garbage to show I'm done just as they arrive with Knight's main course, pulled chicken, drizzled with some kind of dark sauce. It looks like a diet thing.

Knight asks how long I stayed in the Army. When I say "four years, one month, and thirteen days," he grins, fighting it. Smiles don't come easy. It's like they escape despite his best efforts to stifle them. He's normally dead pan even when saying something he thinks is funny.

We get started on Vietnam, and I get the sense Knight is an infantry groupie. Maybe he feels like he missed out on something, that combat is something he would have been good at. He told one interviewer he would have liked a career in the military, "but only if we were at war." I've read Patton is a hero. Surprisingly, Knight, the history buff, doesn't know how many were killed in Vietnam. He thinks it's 120,000, about double the number who actually died.

Lo Balbo fidgets, worried about his flight. His watch is still set on eastern time and he's antsy, not talking, bored. Knight tells him to take it easy.

Knight says Vietnam was a total waste, that the U.S. should have thrown in with Ho Chi Minh to rebuild the country. Gyovai disagrees, weighing in with the domino theory: if Vietnam falls, the rest of Southeast Asia follows. Nothing but commies from China, "Red China" then, to Malaysia, three thousand miles to the south. It all sounds so anachronistic and I try to rekindle my youthful passion, try to remember how it felt to be half-drunk in a Vietnam officers' club, sporting, only half-jokingly, a "Kill a Commie For Christ" button; try to recapture the feeling of paranoia we all felt about the "red scare." It was us against them, ideology versus ideology, with the whole world at stake. It was a time when ideas, political philosophies, seemed to count. Quaint.

Lo Balbo has had enough. He takes off to tour the parking lot. Short attention span, says Knight.

I tell my stock Vietnam story about the battalion commander, a lieutenant colonel, who ordered us to stage battles so he could report fake body counts and increase his chances for promotion. How I refused, effectively ending my military career. Gyovai seems skeptical.

After lunch, a pretty blonde who works in the deli starts flirting with Knight. Gyovai goes outside to chase down Lo Balbo, who has wandered to the other side of the parking lot. I soon follow. When Knight comes out of Marsh, he teases Lo Balbo, shouting, aping Lo Balbo's whiny Bronx accent. "I can't sit next to the wall!" cries Knight. "I'm left-handed." Lo Balbo loves the attention.

We stand in the parking lot and Knight gives me directions for a shortcut home that will "save a half hour." He goes over it two or three times and finally I write it down. We say our good-byes, and about fifty miles later, I make a wrong turn in Paoli after not following Knight's directions to "go three-quarters of the way around the square before turning" and end up on 150 West instead of 150 East and see a sign for French Lick, Larry Bird's hometown.

Larry Bird, NBA superstar, the one Knight let get away. I had always assumed Knight had scared him off. Turns out Larry Legend never even practiced, much less played, at Indiana. It was not Knight, but the big classes that scared Bird away. That and his roommate's wardrobe. Like Mike Noonan, who chose West Point because of the free clothes, Bird owned only "a few shirts and a few pairs of pants" when he came to Indiana. His roommate was a clotheshorse by comparison. So Bird checked out the clothes, the classes, and hitchhiked home to French Lick in the middle of the night. Much later Bird would say, "Coach Knight and me wouldn't have had no trouble." I'm guessing the same can't be said for Bird and the IU English department.

I get turned around and make it to downtown Paoli. The town square is worth the Knight shortcut, even if it didn't save time. It's vibrant, Disneyesque, shops crouched around a square-columned, white court-house looking down from the side of a hill.

The highway was four lanes all the way to Paoli, but just outside town I join a long line of cars stuck behind a dump truck going forty miles an hour. The better part of an hour later, I'm thinking this is

Knight's revenge. If so, I'm in. He only tortures people he likes. But when I reconnect with the interstate outside of Louisville, I discover I've saved the half hour Knight promised. It'll be nothing but cruise control the rest of the way to Nashville.

As I hit I-65 heading south, I rehash the weekend. I think it's odd that Coach Knight never even mentioned standing me up that first morning. But so what? I got the interview. All is forgiven. And even better, I didn't spook him. He's invited me back for a second chat when practice starts in October. As for any hope of building some kind of relationship: no progress there. He's still the coach and I'm still the player.

I worry about the wisdom of sticking to my original idea: Knight's first team at West Point. Should I really be writing about things that happened before Neil Reed was born, when all anybody wants to talk about is when, not if, Knight will throttle the next player, throw the next chair, berate the next reporter, and hop the "Woody Hayes express" to coaching oblivion? Maybe not. But I'm more interested in the "rise" than the "fall" of Bob Knight.

I'm interested in that twenty-something hothead who got thrown out of the Washington State game, who reportedly had a fistfight with Tates Locke at the old armory before the American University game in D.C., and who had the shouting match with the West Point athletic director following the Brigham Young game at Madison Square Garden, but had a special something that kept him from getting fired. Why did uptight, by-the-book West Point keep him on? What was it about him? And much as I hate La-Z-Boy psychology, I'm interested in finding the answer to one really big question. That's the question first posed by Knight's inaugural freshman team, a group which had never even heard of Bob Knight before showing up for their first surreal practice: Who *is* this son of a bitch?

Part II

SCARY GUYS

Chapter 6

Come to Papa

Blame it on the Nazis and pure blind luck. Without both, there would be no "Bobby Knight." At least not the one we know today.

In March of 1963, the twenty-three-year-old Knight stood talking to his ex-coach, Ohio State's Fred Taylor, in the lobby of the Brown Hotel in Louisville, Kentucky. Both were in town to watch Loyola play Cincinnati in the finals of the NCAA. (Loyola won 60–58 in overtime.)

Knight had just finished a year coaching the junior varsity at Ohio's Cuyahoga Falls High School, and he was ready to get on with his life. Both his father, Pat, and his maternal grandmother, Sarah Montgomery, were pushing him to go to law school, but Knight wanted to continue coaching. So he decided to split the difference and was now looking for a school where he could study law while working part-time as an assistant coach. Coach Taylor had been shopping him around, and the young Knight had entertained the notion of going to UCLA's law school and assisting John Wooden. That was a pretty good gig, even in those days before Lew Alcindor (later Kareem Abdul-Jabbar), but Knight was undecided.

Then, as Knight talked to Taylor in the hotel lobby that day, fate intervened in the form of Army coach George Hunter. A friend of Taylor, Hunter listened as the two talked about job prospects. Hunter himself was in the market for a new assistant coach and, after Knight left, told Taylor that if Knight were to enlist in the Army, "We'll get him transferred to West Point to do some coaching with our plebe team."

"Had it not been for George Hunter coming into that conversation at exactly the point he did, I probably wouldn't have gone into coaching," Knight would write in his autobiography.

Whatever interest Knight had in Army had little to do with basketball. While in his five-year reign Hunter had managed to maintain a faint pulse in a moribund Army program, he'd had two losing seasons in a row and lost four out of five to Navy. And anyway, everybody knew there was only one sport that mattered at West Point: football, a program that had gained national prominence during the eighteen-year career of the legendary Earl "Red" Blaik.

Under Blaik, Army had won two national championships in the mid-forties, and during his last season in 1958, only a scant five years earlier, the team, led by Pete Dawkins and "Lonely End" Bill Carpenter—not "lonesome" said Blaik—had gone undefeated, ending the season ranked third nationally. What's more, in 1962 the Academy had hired Paul Dietzel, the winner of a national championship at Louisiana State, in hopes of putting Army football back on top. At West Point, football was the only sport that mattered, and coaching basketball at the Academy was, at best, a painless way for Knight to fulfill a military obligation that can be traced to the Nazi's early successes in Europe a generation before.

On September 16, 1940, after the Nazi's had chased the British back across the English Channel and the bombs had begun falling in what came to be known as the "London Blitz," Franklin Delano Roosevelt would sign the bill initiating the first peacetime draft in American history. Following a three-year hiatus after WWII, the draft would be reinstated in 1948, and for the next twenty-five years, every American boy, including Bobby Knight, was required to serve two years in the armed services after he turned eighteen. Taking that into consideration, Hunter's offer had real appeal.

"I started thinking about getting my military obligation out of the way and doing some coaching too," wrote Knight.

And in the spring of 1963, Knight decided law school could wait and volunteered for the draft. No big loss.

"I couldn't understand why anyone as honest as my dad would ever want to admit he had a son as a lawyer," Knight would say.

Then fate intervened again.

A week after Knight signed up, Hunter got fired and young Bobby was left slowly twisting in the wind. He was now committed to two years in the U.S. Army with no guarantee he would ever set foot on the West Point military reservation.

"I didn't know what the hell was going to happen," said Knight.

Coach Fred Taylor went to bat for Knight again. This time he called twenty-six-year-old Tates Locke, the newly appointed Army head coach. Locke heard him out and agreed to honor Hunter's commitment. What would follow was a perfect fit, the pairing of "soulmates—two men crazy for basketball," as Knight biographer Phil Berger put it.

"George [Hunter] was a talkative guy," Knight said years later. "But a hard-core basketball coach? I'm not sure."

As for Locke? Hard-core was an understatement.

"Basketball is—it's his life, the first and single most important thing," said Locke's first wife, Nancy. "He just couldn't stand the thought of losing. He was an intense fella."

So purely by coincidence these two perfectly matched young coaches had ended up together. Not only that, the two also just happened to be at one of the few schools in America whose core values included an obsession with winning. At "there-is-no-substitute-for-victory" West Point, nobody thought twice about a couple of coaches who believed that, in basketball as in war, there were three things that mattered: winning, winning, and winning. One more thing. Year after year after year, the Big Gray Machine, the Academy, could be counted on to serve up a never-ending supply of very bright, very tough kids accustomed to receiving harsh treatment as a means to an end. For these two basketball firebrands, it was nothing less than coaching heaven.

There was one final chuck under the chin by a decidedly unfickle finger of fate. For the first time since the mid-forties, West Point had not only the will, but the way to win and win big. For the year before, in the face of astounding odds, Tates Locke had "sweet-talked" a round-ball wunderkind named Mike Silliman into coming to the military academy.

It hadn't been easy.

——➤•◄——

Spring 1962, Louisville, Kentucky. There had been a swarm of activity at the brick cape cod at 3009 Kent Road on the outskirts of Louisville. Celebrities coming and going. Strange cars parked out front. A steady stream of letters. Evenings interrupted by ceaseless phone calls back when it was considered rude not to answer the phone. Everybody *knew* you were home.

"There were so many letters coming in and phone calls," recalled sister Susan Silliman McDaniel. "It was just a crazy time."

The University of Kentucky contingent came. The legendary Adolph Rupp, "Baron of the Bluegrass," brought along an entourage.

Coach Fred Taylor from Ohio State came. He and his athletic director flew directly into the airstrip at Bowman Field and walked across Taylorsville Road to the house.

Coach John Jordan from Notre Dame came, listed second in the pecking order just behind Kentucky.

And then Assistant Coach Tates Locke from West Point came, parking his ugly, green car, stenciled "U.S. Army," out front.

All came to court a seventeen-year-old basketball phenom named Mike Silliman. In 1962, following his senior year at St. Xavier High School, Mike Silliman was named Kentucky's "Mr. Basketball," the leading vote-getter in the Louisville *Courier Journal*'s All-State team for the second year in a row. But Mike was not only the best player in basketball-crazy Kentucky, he was a first-team *Parade* All-American and, by Bob Knight's account, the best high school player in the nation.

"If there had been a Gatorade Player of the Year [back then]," Knight said years later, "Silliman would have been picked."

In March of 1962, Mike had led the St. Xavier Tigers to the Kentucky state title, beating rival Ashland 62–58 before sixteen thousand fans at Louisville's Freedom Hall. The 6′ 6″, 225-pound Silliman got twenty-three points and thirteen rebounds. For the year, he had averaged twenty-four points and twenty rebounds leading St. X to a 34–1 season and setting a new Louisville high-school scoring record. Some said he was better than Ohio State legend Jerry Lucas at this stage. Not only that, Mike Silliman was an honor student and the president of his class. Mike's only knock was the perception he couldn't shoot outside. Then St. X coach Joe Reibel admits Mike "seldom even shot from fifteen feet." But there was a reason for that.

"He didn't have to. All I had to do," recalled Reibel, "was get him the ball in the paint area and it was two points."

Reibel may have been a rookie coach, but he was a fast learner. "It didn't take me long to know I really love lay-ups."

Reibel's fondness for lay-ups led to Mike shooting a phenomenal 63 percent during the state tournament. This in a sport where hitting half your shots is considered outstanding.

Great player, great student, a genuinely nice kid, Mike Silliman was a dream recruit. Any team that had him would become a contender. And so they came.

By the spring of his senior year, Mike had narrowed his choices to six: Kentucky, Notre Dame, West Point, Vanderbilt, Ohio State, and Duke. Everybody predicted he would choose Kentucky, and Adolph Rupp had already come by the house on Kent Road to talk to the family.

"It was just an awesome feeling to see Adolph Rupp and Harry Lancaster [an assistant coach and future Kentucky athletic director] sitting in our house," recalled brother Greg Silliman.

"They were all big. They were all dressed up in their suits," recalled sister Susan. "Brown and black suits. Wasn't anything casual about it. It was very formal."

The three Silliman boys had grown up on Kentucky basketball, listening to games on the radio. Before UCLA, before North Carolina and Indiana and Duke, Kentucky was sitting at the pinnacle of the college basketball world. The school had more wins, more NCAA championships, more everything than any other school in college basketball history. In 1962, Kentucky was the place and Rupp was the man—and he wanted Mike Silliman.

"Your son," Rupp told Gus and Betty Silliman, in his distinctive twang, "is a real thoroughbred, a real horse."

While the Silliman boys might have been in awe of the legendary Rupp, Betty Silliman was not. "If you consider my son a horse," she said, "I don't want him playing for you."

The family's still talking about that one.

Rupp had been hoping for a quick decision, but he didn't get it. Mike announced he wouldn't choose a school until late May. It's unlikely Rupp was worried.

"Adolph just thought, hey son, if anybody didn't wanta come play for us, they're crazy," said Gene Rhodes, one of Mike's former coaches.

Ohio State's Fred Taylor had been working on Mike for over a year. He had the family up for a football game in Columbus that fall, and they watched as OSU routed Illinois 44–0. Fourteen-year-old Greg was impressed.

"There were eighty-five thousand fans in the stands and I said, 'Boy, this is a big place.'"

Ohio State had a lot to offer. The team had made it to the NCAA finals three years in a row, winning the championship in 1960 with Jerry Lucas, John Havlicek, and a role player named Bobby Knight. But Coach Taylor would have to wait just like everybody else.

John Jordan and Notre Dame were on Mike's short list. It seemed a perfect match. Mike Silliman, the devout Catholic, great athlete, and great student is recruited by a Catholic school known for athletics and academics. Mike gave the Irish a serious look, but according to Bill Helkie, Silliman's West Point teammate, he was put off by Notre Dame's "bully ball" style.

The Notre Dame basketball team was a bunch of bruisers in those days, recalled Helkie. "They had all these guys 6′7″, 6′8″, about 250 pounds," he said. And Coach Jordan told Mike if they could "put another thirty pounds on him, he'd be just what they wanted," said Helkie.

Already built like a tackle, Mike didn't like the idea. Anyway, he was a finesse player, relied on his basketball skills, his quickness, speed, and sound fundamentals, not muscle. Bully ball was against his nature.

"Michael was always a large child, and he never took advantage of that with the other kids, ever," said Pat Slover, who grew up across the street from Mike. She recalled a childhood run-in with a neighborhood boy who was terrorizing the other kids.

"This kid was so mean. And he used to come over and hit Michael. He hit everybody. He hit all of us." And even though Mike was "about three times as tall as this little boy," said Slover, "Michael would never hit him back. And finally Betty said, 'Just hit him. If he's being that mean to you, just hit him.'"

That reluctance to use his muscle carried over to the basketball court. High school coach Joe Reibel remembers that Mike, because of his size, was always "a little afraid he was gonna hurt somebody," and when he would accidentally knock somebody down, "he would, without question, stop and pick them up."

The most unlikely recruiter to make the pilgrimage to 3009 Kent Road that spring was Tates Locke, the sandy-haired, movie-star handsome assistant coach from Army. And charming. Joe Reibel remembered Tates as "about as likable a guy as you could ever run across." Good thing, because charm was about the only thing the twenty-five-year-old Locke had going for him.

In 1962, the Army basketball recruiting juggernaut consisted of one apparatchik, Tates Locke, pounding out letters on a typewriter missing one key. An older, wiser man wouldn't have been wasting his time and minuscule six-hundred-dollar recruiting budget chasing Silliman. Army was a school with no basketball tradition and no basketball future. It was a military school, for God's sake, a thousand miles away in New York. But still Locke had hung out at the Kentucky state basketball tournament like some pathetic stage-door Johnny. Of the fifty-five or so schools recruiting Mike (the family lost count after a while), West Point seemed the most unlikely. Still Mike hadn't said "no," so Locke persevered.

"Stubborn," he said.

Like all the other coaches, Locke had invited Mike to visit the campus. Unlike the others, he couldn't offer to pay for the trip. Academy rules prohibited that. Mike's dad balked. While Gus Silliman made pretty good money as a traveling salesman for Glenmore Distilleries, the wife and five kids meant he didn't have a lot of money left over for frivolous expenses like subsidizing the budgets of military academies.

Tates found the money.

Mike made the visit in late April of 1962. He got the normal recruiting spiel, which exploited recruits' fear of the draft.

"If we were recruiting someone and a civilian school was recruiting someone, we could remind them that after four years of education," recalled Bob Kinney, an Academy sports PR man from that era, "you were subject to the draft. You want to go in as a private, or you wanta go in as a lieutenant?"

So a cadet got a free, first-class education and avoided being thrown into Army boot camp with every lowlife on the planet. And there was more.

West Point could "guarantee everybody a job after graduation," said Kinney. "That was always a big plus for us."

And not only a job, but a job with a lot of responsibility.

"You start out as a twenty-two-year-old guy with maybe thirty people under you," said Bob Knight, recalling his West Point pitch. "I said, 'Where else can you do that? At the end of four years that may go to two hundred people that you're responsible for. You're gonna be a more desirable commodity at twenty-six years old than I would be graduating from Ohio State at twenty-six.' And that's how I recruited."

The cost of all this—the free education, the guaranteed job, the insulation from lowlifes—was two more years in the military service. It sounded pretty good. And since you were going to college anyway...

Recruits were given a tour of Thayer Hall, the main academic building at West Point, entering beneath a giant concrete rendering of the Academy crest, an eagle squatting on a heraldic shield. The newly refurbished building, once a riding hall, was humongous, featuring sixty-five classrooms, forty departmental offices, two auditoriums—one seating eight hundred, the other fifteen hundred—and the West Point museum, which claimed to have one of the finest collections of small arms in the world, including one of General George S. Patton's pearl-handled forty-fives. Inside, recruits were introduced to department heads friendly to basketball. They visited classes. One recruit recalled seeing cadets working on a ballistics problem, "figuring out the velocity of a bullet as it moved through a block of gelatin."

"Well, that's neat," he had thought. It didn't seem so neat three years later when he flunked the course.

"I was impressed with the classroom size and the academics," recalled Mike Silliman. "All the classes basically have only twelve or fourteen students, and I thought that offered a good learning opportunity."

Recruits watched cadets march to a meal and took in breathtaking views from a campus perched high on a bluff overlooking the Hudson River. One recalled eating dinner with Tates and wife Nancy in the "Duncan Hines–approved" dining room at the on-campus Thayer Hotel, which offered "complete dinners from $2.60." Nancy ordered fish.

"The fish had its head on, and she was a little aghast at that," the recruit said.

For superstar Mike Silliman and his family, Tates Locke added a few extras to his recruiting pitch.

"I told them my home would always be open," said Locke, "and that was gonna be his only solace from all that stuff."

Nobody asked, "What stuff?" And while Tates claimed he never held anything back, it would have been almost impossible for even a cadet to explain just exactly what recruits were getting into when they stepped through the stone portals at West Point; to explain the military part of academy life, the torturous process the academy employed to prepare students for "a lifetime career as an officer of the Regular

Army," as the catalog put it. Just before leaving home for the Academy that July, one of Mike's future teammates had sought the counsel of a West Point cadet home for the summer. The cadet's advice to this teetotaling recruit? "Get drunk."

———•◦•———

The highlight of any recruiting visit to West Point was the parade. Anyone who has ever stood on the edge of the Plain, the West Point parade field, on a lovely spring afternoon and watched the Corps of Cadets march by to the strains of some catchy Sousa tune cannot fail to be caught up in it. The precision, the spectacle, the history, the glamour, and the uniforms, my God the uniforms: gray swallowtail coats, white pants, black tar bucket hats with matching iridescent plumes, flashing sabers and brass breast plates sparkling in the sunshine, rifles perched on squared shoulders. What boy wouldn't want to be a part of that band of brothers?

Forget about the world-class education, the guaranteed job, and the pristine campus; it was the parades promising a glamour as glossy as Marilyn Monroe's nails that pulled a recruit in, seduced him. Few thought about what it took to get a couple thousand sex-starved, wild-ass, pubescent boys to march in perfectly straight lines; the discipline behind each thirty-inch step, behind those spotless, perfectly aligned white gloves clutching the butts of immaculate, inspection-ready M-14 rifles; what it took to get the brims of those tar buckets positioned precisely two fingers above twenty-five hundred noses. Nobody thought about that, and the recruiters weren't reminding them.

And so a boy watched as the Corps of Cadets marched by, thinking he could be a part of that in a couple of months. He didn't have to wait four long years to be somebody, eons for an eighteen-year-old. *Step right up.* He would be a West Pointer the instant he walked through the gates. *Sign right here.* Would join the ranks of Eisenhower, MacArthur, Patton, Grant, and Lee. Not bad company for an ambitious teenager. *Have some candy, little boy.* So what if the free West Point education they were promising him would be earned one heartache at a time? *Come to Papa.*

—————

On May 9, less than two weeks after his recruiting visit to West Point and just four days after his eighteenth birthday, Mike Silliman announced the decision that would slingshot his life into an entirely new orbit. Pending the outcome of a physical in mid-June, Mike told the *Louisville Times,* he would be going to West Point.

Even Tates Locke was surprised.

"He basically shocked the world," said Locke. "I never believed we were gonna get him. Never in a million years."

Chapter 7

Beast Barracks

West Point, New York. July 2, 1962. The boy stepped off the olive drab U.S. Army bus and looked around. Lots of gray stone and gothic arches. "Candidates Report Here," the sign read. Off to the left, at a distance, shouting.

"Go through the sally port," someone said.

"Whatever that is," the boy thought as he hoisted his suitcase and followed the guy in front of him under one of those gothic arches and through a short tunnel, a "sally port," that led into Central Area, the very bowels of West Point. One step on the other side of that tunnel and he entered a brain-scrambling maelstrom.

There were people scurrying here, there, and everywhere propelled by shouting and more shouting and the echoes of shouting that ricocheted off the granite walls and concrete floor of the four-story quadrangle of dorm rooms known as Central Barracks. At a glance, he saw boys with contorted bodies standing in lines, marching, being accosted by boys in gray uniforms.

"Why so angry?" the boy wondered before that thought and any possibility of thought was drowned out by the first words heard by every "New Cadet."

"Drop that bag!" screamed the boy in uniform.

He dropped it.

"Pick it up!"

He picked it up.

"Drop it!" "Pick it up!" "Drop it!"

At West Point only five seconds and the New Cadet had already learned his first lesson: instant, unquestioning obedience.

Welcome to Beast Barracks.

A second lesson began immediately in the "Fourth Class Position of Attention": shoulders back; thumbs along the seams of the trousers or "trou" (never "pants"—girls wear pants); feet at a forty-five-degree angle. And the chin? It was to be pulled back until it disappeared, creating a laminate of wrinkles where there once was a neck. "Bracing," it was called.

"Suck that chin in, Dumb John!"

Then came an important clue. Not that the New Cadet noticed. It was July 2, the height of summer, T-shirt weather, and the cadet a foot in front of his face, the one with the gaping maw, the one screaming, was wearing a heavy wool jacket, gray wool hat. Only a pair of starch-stiffened, white cotton pants made a nod at summer. Odd. Dress gray over white the uniform was called.

"What are your three answers, Dumb Guard?"

"Yes sir! No sir! No excuse sir!"

Tags were attached to a belt loop on the New Cadet's left side, always the left. "USMA Form 2-176," one tag read, "1st Day Process Check Card for New Cadets." It was a checklist for the day: "First Trip Cadet Store," where gnome-like men with thick foreign accents would measure him for one of those tailor-made, gray wool jackets, the ones with the tight clerical collar and the black stripe running from breast bone to mid-thigh; "Haircut," where barbers would assault him with electric clippers; "Shown room and sinks," where the New Cadet would tour the dorm and "sinks," the community shower; "First Drill Period," "Second Drill Period." On the back of the tag, a list of things the New Cadet would learn during drill: "position of attention" (bracing, as if any of the boys in uniform would overlook that one), "Parade Rest," "Hand Salute."

Tagged like a prize steer at a charnel house.

"Report to 'The Man in the Red Sash!'" barked the gaping maw.

Behind the first picket line of scowling upperclassmen was a second. This group wore the same gray jacket, but with chevrons on the shoulder, seniors, "firsties," waists cinched with a swath of crimson wide as a fist.

"Get those beady eyes off me, Mister!" screamed a short cadet holding a clipboard.

"We can't even gaze around or they holler to keep your eyes straight ahead," one New Cadet wrote home that night. "So far the only thing that I've seen clearly is my room."

"Suck that head in!"

From "The Man in the Red Sash," the New Cadet moved to the barber shop. Standing in line, still bracing, he saw a boy pass by, shaved head bleeding from a gash made by errant electric clippers.

The clues were all right there if only the boy could have seen. Had a chance to mull it over. Examine the evidence. Might have too, if it weren't for the screaming. One guy did see. Five minutes of hazing and he shouldered his golf clubs and headed back home.

"If any time had been provided to sit down and think for a moment," Dwight D. Eisenhower said of Beast Barracks in 1911, "most of the 285 of us would have taken the next train out."

"Drop that bag! Pick it up!"

The letter welcoming each of the more than eight hundred boys accepted by the academy in the summer of 1962 warned that West Point existed only to churn out Army officers and "without strong determination to achieve such a career, many of the demands of cadet life will be irksome and difficult."

The letter didn't say anything about screaming "Move it, Dumb Guard!" or freedom.

Within seconds the New Cadets had experienced as absolute a loss of freedom as any inmate interred on death row. Their every waking and sleeping hour would be pre-planned, monitored, accounted for, filled with new adventures. From here on out, for the next four years, that precious freedom would be doled out an hour at a time under the moniker of "privileges." And during the next eight weeks, most of their "free time" would be spent either polishing, cleaning, or memorizing.

Polishing: shoes, hat visors, all things brass, the sharp odor of Brasso stinging their nostrils.

Cleaning: rooms, equipment, that bulky rust magnet known as an M-14 *rifle,* never "gun."

> This is my rifle.
> This is my gun.
> (Grab crotch.)
> One is for fighting.
> The other's for fun.

Memorizing: the nonsensical trivia known as "Plebe Knowledge."

"How is the cow?"

"Sir, she walks, she talks, she's full of chalk, the lacteal fluid extracted from the female of the bovine species is highly prolific to the nth degree."

There were seven hundred official lines of "Plebe Knowledge," but unofficially plebes could be made to memorize anything that struck an upperclassman's fancy. Like officer ranks—for the Navy.

"Sir, Naval ranks. Ensign, lieutenant j.g., lieutenant, lieutenant commander..."

Army branch insignia.

"Sir, infantry, crossed muskets..."

This intermingled with the mundane day-to-day plebe knowledge.

"How many lights in Cullum Hall, Dickhead?"

"Three hundred and forty lights, sir."

"How many gallons in Lusk Reservoir?"

"Ninety-point-two million gallons, sir, when the water is flowing over the spillway."

"What's the definition of leather, Dork-head?"

"Sir, if the fresh skin of an animal, cleaned and divested of all hair, fat, and other extraneous matter, be immersed in a dilute solution of tannic acid, a chemical combination ensues: the gelatinous tissue of the skin is converted into a non-putrescible substance, impervious to and insoluble in water: this, sir, is leather."

All this "knowledge" to be spouted on command at any time of night or day, but especially when a plebe had attracted the attention of an upperclassman with some infraction—say, a dusty hat visor.

"Crank that chin in, Mister!"

At West Point in 1962, none of this—the yelling, the forced recitations, the "drop it, pick it up" harassment—qualified as hazing. The definition of hazing had been refined and redefined over the years so that now "hazing" meant the physical stuff. Push-ups were hazing. Yelling was not. At West Point in 1962, hazing was placing a coin at the base of a New Cadet's skull and making him sweat it against the wall. Hazing was making a New Cadet drink a helmet full of hot water and then run up and down four flights of steps until he threw up. Hazing was throwing a laundry bag, a "laughing bag," over a smirking New Cadet's head and making him do squat jumps until cured of his sense of humor.

"Somebody would be punching you on the outside and you couldn't see who it was," recalled one veteran of the laughing bag.

That was hazing. And it would happen out of sight of the tactical officers, the regular Army types, who thought they were running the place.

The shenanigans the new Class of 1966 was subjected to in Central Area were institutionalized, a long-accepted part of the Fourth Class System, the traditional way freshmen at West Point were treated.

By the time the clock tower in the middle of Central Area read 10 A.M., all of the 807 new cadets in the Class of 1966 were present and accounted for. Now on every square inch of concrete, the boys in the heavy wool jackets were teaching small groups of New Cadets how to march, salute, and do an about-face only a few yards away from the dorm rooms where cadets Douglas MacArthur and John J. Pershing had once slept.

On the right, a group of ten New Cadets marched by, five of them "out of step," some still in civilian clothes, some wearing half a uniform: heavy wool pants with a black stripe, black web belts with shiny brass buckles, and black military oxfords topped by a white T-shirt with plastic name tag, white on black, last name only.

"Parade rest!" barked a boy with chevrons at his wrist, and on the word "rest," a dozen left feet snapped to the side, shoulder-width apart, hands clasped at the base of the spine, thumbs intertwined.

Although the New Cadets had been here only a few hours, they were already totally beaten down, eagerly answering to their new names "Dumb Guard!" and "Dumb Crot!" and, out of earshot of the hovering tactical officers, "Dumb Fuck!" and "Dipshit!" Forget the B-movies and the pulp novels—there was not a rebel to be found in this bunch. For if a New Cadet should so much as let a cloud of anger darken his countenance—strike "anger," strike "darken." If a New Cadet should so much as give even the slightest hint that the long-range emotional forecast might threaten to alter the tint of just one freckle in his ashen, death mask of a poker face, the single gaping maw would first become three: one in his face and one in each ear, all shouting, then four, five, six screaming banshees each with his own set of indecipherable demands. Deep six all those fairy tales about rebels. Nobody made it through plebe year without the largesse of upperclassmen. Nobody.

And if a New Cadet quit, so what? The Academy actually took pride in its high attrition rate. A few days into Beast Barracks the West Point second in command, a brigadier general named Richard G. Stilwell, appeared before an assemblage of the entire Class of 1966. He asked about a third of the New Cadets to stand.

"That's how many of you will be gone by June 1966," he boasted.

West Point's high attrition rate was a nightmare for athletic recruiters like Coach Tates Locke.

"We probably lose three freshman players a year and more fine ones leave than stay," Locke once complained.

Locke was determined that super recruit Mike Silliman not fall victim to the system. And before Beast Barracks was over, the coach would go to extraordinary lengths to protect the franchise player who would contribute mightily to both his and Bobby Knight's success over the next four years.

Meanwhile many of Silliman's classmates would fall victim to the hazing that was not hazing. And to hear the old grads tell it, that was all part of a grand plan.

"The plebes come to West Point all puffed up," one grad told historian Stephen E. Ambrose. "For in their own towns they generally were the best athletes and smartest students and, in addition, had just won the coveted appointment to the Academy. The cockiness had to be suppressed."

This sentiment from 1949 was in response to still another in a long line of attempts to stop hazing. More than fifty years later, another grad would express a more universal argument in support of the practice. Seems during a battle in the Gulf War, circumstances combined to ratchet up the degree of difficulty for this West Point grad. He was functioning on no sleep, was fighting a bout of diarrhea from hell, and was being pounded by "friendly" artillery. All this in the midst of a rainstorm. Still he managed to keep his head. He would credit his calmness under fire to a Fourth Class System he described as a "priceless gift" whose "goal was not harassment, ridicule, or punishment" but "to train the neural network to deal with an overwhelming amount of disjointed information, quickly process that information, categorize it, and make rapid, sound decisions."

So the hazing, the argument went, helped West Point turn out efficient killers who would not be panicked by the chaos of war. Or as another grad indelicately put it: "West Point trains you not to lose it at the sight of a helmet full of brains."

Got it.

"West Point is tough! It is tough in the same way that war is tough," General Stilwell would tell the Class of 1966.

But this was not by design. Not at first. Whatever the modern rationale, there was nothing high-minded about the origins of hazing. According to historian Stephen E. Ambrose, what little hazing there was prior to the Civil War was confined to "harmless pranks" during summer encampments. And without the benefits of the Fourth Class System the academy managed to turn out a few decent soldiers.

In 1846, without benefit of hazing, the five hundred-some Academy graduates who fought in the Mexican War made such an impressive showing that honcho General Winfield Scott credited the West Pointers with vastly shortening a war which was won without losing "a single skirmish." The Academy also distinguished itself during the "late unpleasantness" of the Civil War, not only offering up Confederacy President Jefferson Davis, Ulysses S. Grant, and Robert E. Lee, but providing generals on *both* sides for all but five of the sixty most important battles of the war. Again without benefit of hazing.

According to Ambrose, hazing developed after the Civil War not as a conscious effort to train anybody's "neural network," but as a response to a cutback in extracurricular activities that left a pack of mischievous boys with too much time on their hands.

"The cadets turned to hazing with such enthusiasm that it soon came to be associated with the spirit of West Point," Ambrose reported.

Pandora's box was open.

During an early version of what was to become Beast Barracks, upperclassmen forced plebes to perform "exhausting physical exercises" sometimes resulting in "permanent physical damage"; they devised creative plebe menus featuring entrees like rope ends and soap; they even resorted to torture, dropping hot grease on the feet of their charges. All this accompanied by the singsong recitations the Academy would become famous for.

"How are they all, Dumb Smack?"

"They are all fickle but one, sir."

For the tormentors of the nineteenth century, as in the summer of 1962, the *raison d'etre* for hazing *was* humiliation. For them, the intent *was* "harassment, ridicule, or punishment," not to mention payback for what they had gone through. Any less would cheapen "the West Point experience." If I had to put up with it, the thinking went, so would these guys. While generations of grads have argued that it is through hazing cadets become familiar with panic and learn to control it—a handy skill in combat—the fact remains, any good that ever came out of hazing began as a happy accident.

———◆———

Around noon on their first day at the Academy, the New Cadets of the Class of 1966 were marched into the southeast wing of Washington Hall, the cadet dining room. On the command "Take seats!" the plebes at near a hundred tables plopped down in chairs and the yelling resumed. At each table, what was supposed to be a sit-down dinner for ten was the luncheon version of a three-meal-a-day haze-fest choreographed by the "table commandant," the upperclassmen sitting at the head of the table.

During the year, the twenty-five hundred members of the Corps of Cadets would gather here in Washington Hall *en masse* three times a day to share a meal. It was a spectacular setting. Dark wood wainscoting rose head high beneath stone walls adorned with oil paintings of former West Point superintendents. Stained glass gothic windows flanked by flags from all fifty states soared twenty feet toward the massive exposed timbers of the ceiling. On the south wall of the wing where the New Cadets sat, a colorful thirty-by-seventy-foot mural, egg tempura on plaster, celebrated the "twenty most decisive battles of the world." Hannibal was depicted along with Napoleon and Joan of Arc in a piece meant "to inspire loyalty and courage" said artist T. Loftin Johnson, a Yale graduate.

It was here in Washington Hall that General Douglas MacArthur had delivered his stirring, valedictory address to the Corps, his famous "Duty, Honor, Country" speech only a month before.

"Duty, honor, country," the old soldier had rasped. "Those three hallowed words reverently dictate what you ought to be, what you can be, what you should be."

On this day, as every day, the food was served family style, steaming bowls passed around. At a table beneath the mural, one plebe took care of the table commandant's "beverage preference," iced milk in this case, as his table-mates spooned modest helpings onto their plates. Little of the food would actually be eaten, and the plebes' crisp linen napkins would remain all but spotless.

The New Cadets sat on the front six inches of their wooden chairs, backs straight, chins pulled back in a brace. They quickly forked bites the size of a thumbnail into their mouths, hands returning to their laps as they chewed. Then the New Cadet sitting at the foot of the table glanced up.

"Sit up!" the table commandant screamed.

The New Cadet dropped his fork, metal clanking on china, hands flying to his lap. After "suggesting" the plebe might want to keep his eyes on his plate, the table commandant seemed to be finished.

"Rea-dy... eat!" he cried, and the New Cadet sprang for his fork.

"Too slow! Sit up!" screamed the table commandant.

The boy dropped the fork.

The table commandant glared at the boy over the top of a pair of regulation, plastic-framed glasses that made him look like a youthful Trotsky. "You wanta eat, Smack Head?"

"Yes sir!"

"Then you move when I talk to you, Mister! When I say eat, you eat!"

The boy tensed. Around him, classmates took advantage of the distraction he was creating to shovel it in. A blur of forks flew from plate to mouth. Better him than me.

"Rea-dy... sit up!"

The boy sprang for his fork.

Trotsky came out of his chair. "Did I tell you to eat?"

"No sir!"

"Suck that head in, Dumb Guard! You don't eat until I tell you to eat—EAT!"

The boy was slow.

"Sit up! Suck that stupid goddamn head in!" Trotsky eased back in his seat. "Do you want to eat?"

"Yes sir!"

"Sound off!"

"YES SIR!"

After a while Trotsky tired of the game and, glancing at his watch, allowed the boy a few hurried bites before the meal ended.

Much has been made of the rigors of eating one of these so called square meals. But the real issue was not how you ate; it was *if* you ate. For at a time when starving New Cadets was a popular upperclass diversion, the plebes were happy to be eating anything, square or not.

It shouldn't have been an issue. For in the summer of 1962, the folks in charge had ordered that the New Cadets get "full and sufficient" meals. To make sure that directive was being followed, they asked the civilian wait-staff to weigh the leftovers from each table. But the waiters tipped off the table commandants, the food deprivation continued, and, just like in years past, the New Cadets would end up filling their stomachs with cold water and toothpaste back in the barracks. In an acknowledgment of their lack of control, the men supposedly running Beast Barracks eventually set up special tables for plebes who were losing too much weight and, in a final, unconditional surrender to reality, ordered that all the New Cadets be fed an evening snack of a half-pint of milk and a piece of fruit. The cadre jumped all over that one, rewriting the class motto. Out of earshot of the tactical officers, "Fame Will Mix with '66" became "With fruit and milk we get our kicks, 'cause we're the boys of '66." The teasing, most agreed, was well worth it.

Chapter 8

Scary Guys

Late afternoon, July 2. Time to take the oath, and Mike Silliman along with the rest of the Class of 1966 used his rudimentary marching skills to move out of Central Area. They tromped by Cullum Hall—completed in 1898 to honor "West Point's famous sons"—moved past the parade field known as "the Plain," and continued on to Trophy Point, stopping in front of Battle Monument, a towering cylinder of granite that memorialized soldiers who died in the Civil War.

By now the New Cadets were unwilling converts to the all-wool, all-the-time theology of the Academy, outsweating the cadre (still in dress gray over white) in their charcoal gray, long-sleeved wool shirts, heavy wool pants, black wool ties, and white gloves.

They were met at Battle Monument by a coterie led by the West Point commandant, Brigadier General Richard G. Stilwell, Class of 1938. A veteran of World War II, the CIA, and Korea, the general was all done up in a summer tan uniform with gold buttons, his left breast nearly overrun with colorful ribbons, a shiny silver star perched on each shoulder. Stilwell had reportedly loved West Point from the first day of Beast Barracks and was the prototype for a certain type of officer found in great supply at the Academy: "the scary guy." According to Rick Atkinson in *The Long Gray Line,* the forty-five-year-old general made "lesser men squirm" with his "penetrating gaze." While in private the general could have been a master of the fox-trot and chocolate soufflé, his stern, unyielding public persona snarled "I'm tough," (make that "I'm *really* tough") "and you're not." It was a variety of balls-to-the-wall intimidation that made quavering junior officers and New Cadets all but pee in their pants. And that, of course, was the whole idea behind the bona fide, West Point scary guy. Another bona fide scary guy around that summer was one Colonel Robert M. Tarbox, the titular leader of Beast Barracks, and a man whose mere photo can still be used to fumigate closets.

"Just thinking of the guy makes me shudder," said a former New Cadet almost forty years later.

Ole Robert, recalled that cadet, "would glare at you like he was unhappy to be sharing the same planet, like he'd 'out' you in a second, vaporize you with those laser-beam eyes if it weren't for all those god-damned rules." If Tarbox ever smiled, no cadet saw it. In fact, among the regular Army tactical officers—the keepers of all things military, the scary guys—smiling was so rare as to be, literally, something to write home about.

"Contrary to most officers," a cadet once wrote of a new tactical offi-cer, "he smiles every once in a while."

In his Trophy Point speech, scary guy Stilwell welcomed the New Cadets into "the noblest of professions, the military service" and promised they would be "tested, retested, tested again" to make sure they were worthy. And in case anyone had in mind to question the "Drop the bag! Pick it up!" malarkey from that morning, he sounded a familiar West Point theme. "If you can't learn to obey orders, explicitly," intoned the General, "you will never be able to give orders properly."

An order is an order is an order? Not really. Beast Barracks was a monument the size of Mount Rushmore to cadets disobeying orders. Efforts to stop hazing began about the same time as the hazing itself, and over the years the Academy had been successful in putting a stop to many over-the-top hazing practices. For example, cadets stopped forcing plebes to drink Tabasco after the unfortunately named Oscar L. Booz died of "tuberculosis of the larynx." (Doctors denied there was a connection.) Still, lesser forms of hazing became an accepted part of the system. Not because the big cheeses liked it, but because attempts to stop it were futile despite the rare death or suicide.

This defiance of authority was dependent upon a collusion of plebes and their tormentors. The upperclassmen saw hazing as a legitimate part of the system and plebes seemed to agree, refusing to rat on offenders, even lying to protect them. (This in the face of the fabled West Point Honor Code that said a cadet "will not lie, cheat, or steal.") Irony of ironies, Beast Barracks, a system meant to teach New Cadets instant obedience, was founded on disobedience: a brazen defiance of orders stretching back almost a hundred years.

"My constant theme, sirs," continued Stilwell, "is that the history of the United States of America and the history of the United States Army and the United States Military Academy are so closely intertwined as to be inextricable, one from the other. As goes the Army, so goes the nation."

Nah.

"Raise your right hand," said Stilwell, and led the boys of the Class of 1966 in an oath dating to just after the Civil War. Only when the chanting was done would General Stilwell and company be able to rest easy, knowing that even if "the South should rise again," none of these Academy graduates would be fighting on the wrong side.

"I, Michael Barnwell Silliman," chanted Mike along with the rest of the New Cadets, "do solemnly swear that I will support the Constitution of the United States and bear true allegiance to the national government; that I will maintain and defend the sovereignty of the United States paramount to any and all allegiance, sovereignty, or fealty I may owe to any State, county, or country whatsoever."

With the taking of the oath, it was done. As of about 1800 hours on July 2, 1962, a New Cadet's heart might still belong to mama, but his ass was now property of the United States Army, West Point chapter.

It was "a day none of you will ever forget," Stilwell had told them, making it sound like the day was over. Not quite. Something was waiting in the basement.

That evening the bracing New Cadets were marched downstairs into the "sinks," a basement locker room, and lined up against the wall. They were about to take part in a "shower formation," the strangest ritual in a place known for strange rituals. At its height, it would involve two distinct groups of boys: the first in uniform. And the second? They would be naked.

"Suck that head in, Fuck-face!"

It was close quarters down in the sinks and, with nowhere to escape, the sound was deafening.

"I said suck it in!"

Inches from the New Cadet's face, the familiar gaping maw, now under a white hat with black visor topping a crisp, short-sleeved white cotton shirt with gray epaulets, gray wool pants with a black stripe, and spit-shined black shoes. The capper: spotless white gloves at the end of hairy arms.

"Dressed as fussily as any prom queen," observed one critic.

"Sweat, Mister!"

The New Cadets were wearing their prescribed uniform: regulation lightweight summer bathrobes, pale blue cotton with black and gold piping, name tags pinned over the left breast pocket. In the palm of each New Cadet's left hand, a plastic soap dish, open for inspection. A white towel was draped over each boy's forearm in the manner of a waiter in some swanky restaurant.

The object of this game was simple.

"You can't take a shower until you sweat through your bathrobe," one New Cadet would explain to his mother.

The cadre was willing to help out, and so the hazing that was not hazing continued in earnest, the shrieking rising to new heights. The cadre yelled at the New Cadets because two years before they too had been yelled at. Just when the "neural transmitters" threatened to overload, select sweaty plebes were trotted to the showers.

That was no relief. The New Cadets were lined up and, on cue, shed their robes and marched into the shower where they were allowed thirty seconds of hot water to shouts of "Soap down, Mister! Move it! Move it!" before rinsing with cold.

The pace quickened and clouds of steam roiled out of the tile showers to a soundtrack of more yelling as dozens of buck-naked teenagers, all wet willies and glistening white butts, were herded around by white-gloved boys in spiffy gray and white uniforms.

One would think that when some brave soul finally sits down and writes *Bulging White Trou: The Startling but True History of Gay Cadets at the United States Military Academy*, this shower formation thing is going to be in the first chapter.

Amazingly none of the Army officers in charge—men five, ten, even twenty years out of the Academy, men with at least a splash of maturity and experience—stepped forward and said, "Uh, excuse me. Tell me again what we are trying to accomplish with this de Sade–worthy, homoerotic fantasy?"

Back upstairs, almost time for "night night," but the squeaky clean New Cadets were forced to perform one last chore on this, their first day at the United States Military Academy: write a letter home. "Am fine, must polish equipment," wrote one. Another thought he was prepared for such an assignment, had even crafted a catchy phrase before leaving Palookaville. "It's hell, but I love it," he imagined he would say, echoing Sherman's "War is hell." Years later, he couldn't remember what he actually wrote, but this grad, this combat veteran, had by then jettisoned the melodramatic "hell" in favor of a more earthy metaphor: Beast Barracks, West Point, war—each, he had decided, was like a carbuncle, a cluster of festering boils, located in a particularly delicate spot.

Meanwhile back in Ohio, the newly-graduated Bobby Knight was pondering his future. Fresh out of Ohio State, he was not ready to give up on basketball. Not yet.

"I had a point to prove," Knight would say later. "I was just coming off a playing career during which I didn't do as well as I'd hoped."

His career had begun well. In 1958, Knight had started on an undefeated freshman team dubbed "The Fabulous Five" along with three future NBA players including Jerry Lucas and John Havlicek. But during his varsity years Knight was only a role player.

"He didn't amount to a hill of beans," wrote Frank Deford of Knight's playing days.

It wasn't quite that bad. Although Knight started only two games, he was often used as the sixth or seventh man, and he would play in seventy-two of the eighty-four games in his three varsity seasons. His high point came in the 1961 NCAA Finals when he hit the basket that sent the game into overtime. (Ohio State would end up losing by five to Cincinnati.) But in the Finals his senior year, Knight wouldn't even get into the game.

"I always thought I should play more," he said.

Didn't happen. The problem? Ironically, he couldn't play defense.

"A hacker," said Coach Fred Taylor.

"The worst defensive player on the team," said Havlicek.

Knight's lack of playing time led to friction with Coach Taylor, who reportedly nicknamed him the "Brat from Orrville." Taylor denied that, but did say Knight "probably set the NCAA record for the number of times to quit the squad."

While on court Knight was not as successful as he wanted to be, off court he was making quite an impression. From the first, Knight cultivated an image as a tough guy, telling gullible teammates "that back home in Orrville, I was a member of a motorcycle gang called 'The Dragons.'" Even after teammates found out the truth, they continued to call Knight "Dragon." The nickname stuck, speculated Knight, because of his on-court demeanor: "the idea of a fire-breathing dragon," he said.

According to Frank Deford, tough guy Knight also tried to impress teammates with what Deford called "brash hijinks" and the rest of us would call "larcenies." While on a trip to New York, Knight "stunned his wide-eyed teammates" when he "boldly swiped a couple of bottles of wine from Mamma Leone's restaurant," reported Deford. He then shoplifted "a few ties from a midtown shop" and topped that off by chatting up the security guard. John Feinstein claims he got nailed for stealing the wine. No word on the ties.

While Knight's criminal career met with mixed success, the success of his basketball career was never in question. Averaging only 3.8 points and 2.1 rebounds per game over three seasons, Knight himself would admit to being "a very average player." And on a team that went to the NCAA Finals three years in a row, winning once, there was no place for average.

All in all, Knight's college career had been a real comeuppance for a kid who had averaged twenty-four points a game his senior year in high school.

"I'm sure that when Bob went to Ohio State, there was no doubt in his mind that he was going to be a regular," said Harold "Andy" Andreas, Knight's boss at Cuyahoga Falls High School. "Then he had a disappointing experience there, and I think that made him want to prove something. Several of his teammates went on to play pro ball, so he had to do something to compensate. I really think he felt he had to prove he could be just as successful in basketball as his teammates."

Knight would leave Ohio State with "failed hopes," ending what John Feinstein would characterize as "the most frustrating four years of his life."

"I very early realized I wasn't good enough to play after graduation, so I'd better figure out something I could do," Knight once told *Indianapolis Monthly.*

And in the summer of 1962, the basketball-obsessed kid who had taken a ball on dates in high school, who had practiced his block-out moves on a bedpost in his Ohio State dorm room, was left to choose between coaching offers from high schools in the small Ohio towns of Celina and Cuyahoga Falls. At Celina he had been offered a job as head basketball coach if he would agree to moonlight as a line coach in football. Knight balked.

"I thought, if I'm going to be a basketball coach, I can't be diverted," Knight said. "I wanted vertical concentration."

So Knight would end up "vertically concentrating" in Cuyahoga Falls, not as a head coach but as an assistant. And that fall as bosom buddy John Havlicek set out for the big-city lights of Boston where the Celtics were just coming off the fourth of eight straight NBA championships, Knight accepted his exile in stop-light-challenged Cuyahoga

Falls where he would teach freshman history and serve as junior-varsity coach. Talk about "failed hopes." It was enough to humble even a tough guy like Dragon.

———————

19 July 1962

Dear Mr. and Mrs. C. A. Silliman:

I am the Tactical Officer of the New Cadet Company to which your son, Michael is assigned. As you may know, he is presently undergoing treatment in the hospital for a knee condition that, according to the doctors, probably resulted from some activity last April.

Michael was admitted to the hospital on 11 July 1962 and after careful consideration the doctors have decided that an operation is necessary to repair a torn ligament. He is scheduled to undergo the operation on 19 July 1962 and will probably remain in the hospital an additional two weeks. He will also be required to wear a cast for approximately five weeks.

Sincerely yours,
Richard L. Hunt
Major, CE, Tactical Officer, 1st NC Co

Mike Silliman first hurt his knee playing baseball for Saint Xavier High School back home in Louisville. Sliding into second base, his Uncle Jerry said. Thinking it was just a sprain, Mike continued playing, never missing a game, and in the second week of June was even able to pass the strenuous physical-fitness test required for entrance to West Point. He returned home just in time for the "World Series of High School Basketball," the annual doubleheader between all-star teams from Kentucky and Indiana. But he would aggravate the injury in practice and end up sitting out both games. Doctors now described the injury as a "pinched cartilage."

"It feels like a needle sticking in it," Silliman told the Louisville *Courier Journal.*

Silliman was advised the knee would take two weeks to heal, but not long after, doctors decided there was ligament damage and they would have to operate.

Tates Locke took the news calmly. Where most coaches would have seen disaster, Locke saw opportunity and immediately began hatching a plan to protect his star recruit from the savagery of Beast Barracks.

"I loved beatin' the system," Locke said.

It was vintage Tates.

The coach had always affected a kind of "rebel-without-a-cause" image dating at least to his college days. Former wife Nancy first met Tates at Ohio Wesleyan College in the late fifties.

"He was sorta a rebel for his time," said Nancy.

Back when people used to dress up in a suit and tie just to go to the movies, Tates took Nancy to a Louis Armstrong concert wearing jeans and a white T-shirt, sneakers, no socks. He wore the same outfit to meet Nancy's parents, with predictable results.

"My parents thought Tates was awful," said Nancy in Tates' book *Caught in the Net.*

Odds are they weren't too crazy about his "snowman" car either: a black '57 Chevy with red interior.

"He used to race that car," said Nancy. "Thought he was big time, too."

Locke had come to Ohio Wesleyan after failing to make the basketball team at Miami of Ohio. He would end up captaining the 1959 Wesleyan squad and after graduating became an assistant coach at the school. A year later, Tates enlisted with the guarantee he would spend his two years in the Army as an assistant basketball coach at West Point. When his military commitment was complete, Locke decided to stay on to coach the plebe team, a team that would be built around one Mike Silliman. And in the summer of 1962 Tates was intent on doing everything he could to make sure Silliman "didn't have to really go through Beast Barracks."

The plan was to postpone Mike's knee operation until he got to West Point. By the time he got out of rehab, Tates figured, Beast Barracks would be over.

As "part of the recruiting," he said, "we were gonna operate on his knee as soon as he got in the service."

It's a great story, part of team lore for more than thirty years, but it doesn't add up.

First, Mike committed to West Point on May 9, about six weeks before anybody knew his knee injury was more than just a sprain. So the recruiting was long done before doctors decided an operation was needed in mid-June. Second, even if Louisville doctors had operated immediately on what they thought was a torn ligament, the prognosis would have had Mike missing more than half of Beast Barracks anyway. So at best, Locke would have gained only two weeks by delaying the operation. In the meantime, Mike would have had to limp onto a plane to New York, change doctors in midstream, and his dad would have had to foot the medical bill. So it just made sense to do the operation at West Point.

On Wednesday, July 11, Mike checked into the West Point hospital. "I don't fear missing out on things in Beast Barracks," he wrote home, "but I do fear missing the constant pressure of discipline," adding that "life in the hospital is quite easy."

The operation was performed on July 19, 1962, and the injury proved to be less severe than expected: no torn ligament. "Just a cartilage," Mike wrote home. He was left with a three-inch scar and after a couple of weeks on crutches was back in business. He would miss only half of Beast Barracks, but even that was too much.

During Beast Barracks a New Cadet learned everything he would need to become a full-fledged member of the Corps of Cadets in September. It was in Beast Barracks that the New Cadet learned how to march, how to do the manual of arms, how to spit polish shoes, how to execute a "spot weld" when firing an M-14 so that the rifle's kick wouldn't produce a knot on his cheek. He learned that dress gray "under arms" didn't mean showing up with a uniform tucked into your armpit, as one New Cadet had done; it meant "bring your rifle."

So Tates Locke was lucky Mike Silliman was absent for only half of this cadet "basic training." Any more and Tates might have outsmarted himself. For every day Mike spent in the hospital was a day he missed something he would need down the road, all the minutia that would keep him from attracting the attention of pesky upperclassmen with little patience for plebes who didn't know how to execute a perfect about-face.

Chapter 9

Second-Class College

In late August, the United States Corps of Cadets, twenty-five hundred strong, reunited on campus for "Reorganization Week." The sophomores, "yearlings," returned from nearby Camp Buckner where they had spent the summer in combat training. Some of the juniors, "cows," and seniors, "firsties," returned from Europe where they had spent a month as "third lieutenants" with active Army units and others from staff positions at Beast Barracks and Camp Buckner.

The Corps was organized into two regiments, each with twelve companies of about a hundred boys lettered A-1 through M-1 and A-2 through M-2, respectively. There was no J company, a practice dating back to 1816 because of possible confusion (in the nineteenth-century handwritten rendering) between the letters "i," "j," and possibly "f." During "Reorgy Week" the New Cadets, now promoted to "Cadets," were integrated into the companies that would sustain them for the rest of the year as everyone geared up for the beginning of academics.

Plebes now had more or less free run of the place as long as they kept bracing, and those from the nether regions would soon be introduced to prejudices they didn't know existed. They would hear "Guinea" jokes, Irish jokes, and Polish jokes, all totally meaningless to boys from homogenous small towns in the Midwest and South who knew of only two "ethnic" groups: "white" and "Negro." Weaned on Elvis and rock 'n' roll, the plebes would also hear evidence of the cultural isolation of the Academy coming from the stereos of upperclassmen. Marching about campus at the prescribed thirty steps per minute, arms swinging nine inches forward and six inches back, they would hear the favorite artist of cadets trapped here since 1959: Julie London, a fifties torch singer. Her rendering of "Cry Me a River," a heart-wrenching ballad about love gone wrong, echoed through the granite canyons. But there was hope. While in that atmosphere it was hard to imagine ever dancing again, the plebes were happy to learn that the twist was no longer outlawed at cadet dances.

With the upperclassmen back on campus, the plebes were outnumbered about three to one and, for the brief period before academics began, the hazing rivaled the first few weeks of Beast Barracks.

"If Beast Barracks was tough," Mike Silliman wrote home, "then Reorganization Week is living hell."

Over in the notoriously loose Second Regiment, the influx of upperclassmen didn't mean as much. But in Mike Silliman's regiment, the First Regiment, in companies such as H-as-in-"Hell"-1 and the even more notorious I-as-in-"Inquisition"-1 (the latter washing out twelve of thirty-one plebes before the end of January), the so-called "Fourth Classmen" were wise to lay low. For some that was impossible because of high-profile "plebe duties." Among them, "letter carrier,"—essentially the company mailman, who in delivering the mail would in twenty-four hours make a hazing-acquaintance with all of the seventy-some upperclassmen in the company—and, the worst plebe job of all, "minute caller."

At the sound of the first bell signaling assembly for the next formation, the minute caller stood at a midpoint in the company (on the second-floor landing in Central Barracks, for example) and counted down the minutes left until the upperclassmen had to be in ranks. This happened at least four times a day before assemblies for reveille, breakfast, dinner, and supper. Woe be it to the plebe who screwed it up.

"Sir, there are five minutes until assembly for reveille formation," the minute caller might shout. "The uniform is dress gray over white. Five minutes, sir."

During Reorgy Week, foul-tempered upperclassmen were often less than overjoyed by their recent return to the Academy. As one wrote his girlfriend: "It's all West Point and gray buildings and the Hudson River and uniforms and bells and books and lonely days and nothing but men, men, men."

And after pouting through a few choruses of "Cry Me a River," ("I cried a river over you"), the cadets were looking for someone to take it out on, and any minute caller would do. A couple of days into Reorganization Week and Mike Silliman was second-guessing himself.

"I woke up this morning resolved to resign. I hated West Point not as a plebe, but as any individual. It demands so much of you. I had decided to attend Notre Dame since they have discipline and academics near the scale the Academy has. Many, many times I wished I had not come, but it's done now. I can't resign because of fear of losing faith in myself. It's a personal challenge and no one can help."

Actually, it had been "done" a long time before Reorganization Week. The gates had closed quietly behind Mike Silliman and the rest the moment they walked through the stone portals of West Point. They were trapped. They couldn't walk away without letting down their family, community, church, school, themselves. To walk was to have a flaw in your character. West Point, a hallowed and revered institution, was always right. You were always wrong. To leave was to spend the rest of your life explaining yourself.

West Point was established in 1802 to create a corps of professional army officers qualified in artillery and engineering. That was radical in a day in which higher education meant the classics, the "dead and deadening" Latin and Greek, as historian Stephen E. Ambrose put it. The academy got off to a slow start, partly because of rather broad admission standards. To get in, an applicant had to be male. That was it. Things got so loose, according to Ambrose, that the academy was admitting twelve-year-olds and, in one case, admitted a "one-armed boy from Pennsylvania."

The academy limped along—not even making a splash during the War of 1812—until the arrival of a soldier-scholar by the name of Sylvanius Thayer in 1817. A graduate of West Point and Dartmouth, "at the top of his class," this Napoleon-worshipping, peacock of a man would soon transform the academy. After a trip to Europe to observe what the French and Germans were doing with military education, Thayer came home with some new-fangled ideas that explained much of what Mike Silliman and the Class of 1966 would face when they entered the classrooms of Thayer Hall, named after you-know-who, in the fall of 1962.

At the École Polytechnique, "the most famous scientific military school in the world," reported Ambrose, Thayer would find his ideal curriculum: heavy on math and engineering. At West Point, there would be no Latin, no Greek, and no electives. And as in both the German and French schools he visited, students would "be taught in small sections, divided according to ability."

Professors in Thayer's academy would not teach but, like professors at the Harvard of his day, direct the work of classroom instructors who were recent graduates. At West Point in 1962, that translated into classes taught by Army officers with their masters-degree diplomas still at the framers.

Finally, Thayer was determined that all cadets, whatever their station, would be treated alike.

"All submitted to the same discipline, wore the same clothes, ate the same food, slept in the same rooms, studied in the same classes, and were graded by the same teachers in the same manner," wrote Ambrose.

Under the guidance of Thayer, who came to be honored as "the father of the military academy," West Point would soon become not only the best, but the only engineering school in America. Early graduates, wrote Ambrose, would gain more fame for building "great canals, railroads, and public buildings" than fighting wars.

In 1962, the approach to education fathered by Thayer had changed little since its inception. While 40 percent of the curriculum was now social sciences, subjects such as economics and Latin American studies, most cadets considered those bullshit courses to worry about after the heavy lifting was done. For the plebes, the backbreaker was mathematics, mostly calculus, six days a week, eighty minutes a day, followed by more than a week of exams at the end of each semester. For sophomores, the math burden fell off to three days a week, but they now had chemistry and physics to worry about. Juniors were required to take a staggering load of introductory engineering courses: mechanics of solids, electrical engineering, nuclear physics, thermodynamics. That made it clear why the West Point degree was in something called "general engineering." In comparison, seniors were slackers. Civil engineering and ordnance engineering were the only math-saturated courses on the schedule, and they were allowed to choose two electives in their final year at the Academy.

Why all this engineering? It was the Thayer way. And while West Point coaches of that era were forever hoping for an overhaul of the curriculum that would, as Bob Knight said, make the education "a little more inviting," it never came, and they were left to echo a criticism often heard among the cadets themselves.

"I mean nobody—MacArthur could not have convinced me that an engineering degree was a necessity to be an Army officer," said Knight.

The only crib courses offered during the four years were occasional forays into no-brainer military subjects such as "Military Psychology and Leadership" (or "Leadersleep," as cadets called it) and "Tactics." While the mandatory physical-education classes did not require any brain power, nobody would ever describe them as "easy." The first year alone, cadets were subjected to swimming, boxing, wrestling, and gymnastics taught the West Point way. In swimming that meant paddling around in freezing water while wearing fatigue uniforms, boots, and a backpack full of bricks. No hanging on the sides of the pool. "There are no walls out there!" snarled Robert E. Sorge, the only civilian then at West Point who qualified as a bona fide scary guy. (Knight would begin his bid a year later.) In all, the cadet academic load was heavy, about twenty-one hours a week. All required, of course. No drops. No adds. No excuses. Attendance was mandatory, on time, "properly shaven," with shoes shined or face the consequences.

And the atmosphere?

Imagine student Albert Einstein at the blackboard feverishly working out the last few kinks in the theory of relativity. Squeaky white chalk on black slate. Behind him stands a starched-colon martinet in Army green.

"Mr. Einstein!" he roars. "When's the last time you got that hair cut?"

Contemplation? Forget it. Scholarship? No time. Memorization? That's the ticket. The cadets even had their own word for it: "spec," as in "spec and forget," to make way for the next wheelbarrow load of facts, data, and theorems.

"I have to see if I can guess what to memorize to pass the tests," one cadet wrote home. "Thinking lost out somewhere in the academic program. It is the man who can accumulate the most relevant facts in his cranium who wins out in the end. Maybe that's what knowledge is, but I don't think so. Not too much incentive in memorization. I guess the problem is that the material is so difficult they don't feel they have time to really teach us 'why?', but just 'what.'"

That winter, writer David Boroff would skewer the West Point academic program in a critique that appeared in the December 1962 issue of *Harper's*.

"The faculty isn't good enough," wrote Boroff. "The students are overloaded and have little or no time for the kind of contemplative activity that alone can make an educated man. The program, by virtue of its military coloration, tends to reward precision far more than critical ability."

After taking a long look at the test scores, the curriculum, the faculty, and the atmosphere, Boroff concluded, "West Point is a second-class college for first-class students."

They're still grumbling about that one. They shouldn't be. It was like criticizing Harvard for not being a good school of ballet. West Point's mission was to turn out soldiers, not scholars. And the quality of its graduates, their degree of mastery of the fine art of killing people and blowing up things, was to be measured not in ivory towers, but on the battlefield.

Chapter 10

Prize Recruits

In September the plebes were allowed off the grounds of West Point for the first time when the entire student body traveled to the Polo Grounds in New York to cheer on Paul Dietzel's first Army football team. Following the 9–2 win over Syracuse, basketball recruit Bill Helkie's roommate drained deep the chalice of freedom and "threw up all over the goddamn place." Counseling ensued.

"Everybody just started harassing the hell out of him," said Helkie.

The screaming tormentors dropped by before breakfast—"Let's hear the Code of Conduct!"—after breakfast—"Why isn't that underwear folded properly?"—after class—"Suck it in, Mister!"—and Helkie got caught in the backwash. This went on for days.

Helkie had stayed in touch with the soon-to-be-legendary Davidson basketball coach, Lefty Driesell, and that was in the back of Bill's mind when he went to visit the A-1 Company executive officer.

"I came here to study and play basketball," Helkie told the exec. "And I'm willing to do this shit. I'm willing to do all this shit. But these guys just made me memorize the West Point band's chain of command. I did not come here to memorize the fucking West Point band chain of command. And I didn't come here to take a bunch of shit because my roommate is an idiot."

"If these guys keep fucking with me like this, I'm gone after Christmas," continued Helkie. "I'm not threatening, I'm not doing anything else. It's just not what I signed up for."

And that's how Mike Silliman and Bill Helkie came to be roommates in the unofficial jock wing of Company A-1. The two prize basketball recruits were now surrounded by friendly faces: upperclassmen like Bob Foley, the captain of the basketball team; John Ritch, another basketball player; the West Point heavyweight boxing champ; two hockey players; and the exec himself, who had played B-squad basketball.

"We were just about the only plebes on the floor," said Helkie, adding, "It wasn't by accident."

While Silliman and Helkie performed the usual menial plebe duties, things like delivering mail and hauling laundry, "We were more like fraternity pledges," said Helkie. "There was no bracing for a half-hour and all that crap."

Helkie had ended up at West Point almost by accident. All-state in Indiana in both football and basketball, Helkie could have had a scholarship to any school he wanted, but not in basketball.

"My high school coach said I could play anywhere in the country in football," said Helkie. "All I had to do was tell him where."

But Helkie's first love was basketball even if he was being recruited by only three schools: Army, Davidson, and Oklahoma. Oklahoma had also offered him a math scholarship.

"In basketball, I think some people were scared off by my SAT scores," recalled Helkie. "They were too high."

Too high.

"So a lot of bandit schools bailed out."

Helkie had been leaning toward Lefty Driesell and Davidson until he met Mike when both traveled to the Academy in June to take the physical-fitness test.

"He was really an impressive guy," said Helkie.

So impressive, Helkie would end up basing his college selection on what Mike did.

"If he would have gone to Notre Dame," said Helkie, "I would have gone to Davidson. When he committed, I committed."

That commitment meant West Point would end up with two really smart kids who could play basketball: "too high" Helkie and Mike Silliman, a brainy kid sister Susan described as "a real thinker."

How brainy was Silliman? As an adult, Mike would read his way through a shelf full of leather-bound "great books" in only three years. At his home, a nosey visitor would happen upon underlined and annotated copies of Stephen Hawking's *A Brief History of Time* and Dante's *Inferno* in a closet.

Underlined and annotated.

Still no one ever mentioned the "i-word." Not then. And certainly not in the early sixties when Mike was being recruited. For in the middle America of that era, being an "intellectual" was suspect. Not quite manly. Back then you were either an athlete or you were smart. And while boys like Silliman and Helkie might routinely make the dean's list, outside of school that was always a secondary qualification: "a great kid *and* a good student," "a great athlete *and* a good student."

So intellectual or not, nice, middle-class boys from middle America were about as likely to join the *corps de ballet* as go to one of those sissified Ivy League schools. That was a place for "effete intellectual snobs," as Vice President Spiro Agnew would later call them, and while nobody outside of Princeton knew exactly what that meant, it sounded right. But there was one academically elite school back east that met with almost universal approval: West Point.

West Point was a school that offered an acceptable way to be smart. It was the perfect place for one of those "and a good student" kind of boys. A place for men of action who also had brains. While there may have been towers at West Point, they weren't ivory. They were stone and bristling with machine guns.

Then Superintendent William C. Westmoreland would shore up that macho mystique when he told the West Point student body, "Speculation, knowledge, is not the chief aim of man—it is action." (This might explain Vietnam.)

But in fact, Westmoreland to the contrary, the average cadet's twenty-one-hour-a-week academic load was "awesome," as Academy critic David Boroff pointed out in his 1962 *Harper's* article. So for a West Pointer to claim he was solely "a man of action" was like a bisexual claiming he liked only girls. To make it at West Point, you had to swing both ways.

Mike Silliman and Bill Helkie qualified. They were both jocks and scholars, and so was virtually everyone else at West Point. About a third of the cadets had been high school team captains, and about a fifth made all-state in their sports. To qualify for admission, incoming cadets not only had to have outstanding SAT scores (reminding Boroff of a Harvard freshman class), they also had to pass a rigorous physical-fitness test. At West Point, everyone was an athlete and, if not a scholar, at least an outstanding student.

This was a brainy bunch. Too brainy for some.

On a road trip during his junior year at West Point, brainiac Bill Helkie sat in the back of the team bus poring over a political philosophy text from a class taught by a cigar-chomping Rhodes Scholar named Dale Vesser. After a while Helkie started a discussion with a teammate taking the same class.

Coach Tates Locke heard what was going on and started stewing. A few minutes later he stood up abruptly and stomped midway down the aisle. He had a tortured look on his face. Then, for the first and perhaps last time in basketball history, a major college coach proceeded to lambaste his team for being "too intellectual." They needed to be spending more time thinking about basketball, said Tates, and less time worrying about things like political philosophy.

They were "men of action" after all.

Tates may have been right. Years later a survey of the thirteen players on the bus that day would turn up two college professors, a Rhodes Scholar, a neurosurgeon, a lawyer, a journalist, and a senior staffer on the Federal Reserve Board, Helkie himself, who by then had a Ph.D. in economics from Purdue. In all, this one West Point team would end up with well over a dozen advanced degrees. Not exactly the typical profile for a college basketball team. Yet for Silliman and Helkie the situation was ideal. West Point offered a testosterone-infused intellectualism that conformed to the values of middle America and gave them a chance to hang out with teammates both manly and smart that the two would find in short supply in locker rooms at Kentucky, Davidson, or even Notre Dame.

Basketball practice began in October, and all the plebes on the basketball team and all the other budding "Corps Squad," nee "varsity," athletes were now assigned to tables in the jock section of the Washington Hall dining room. Here they would escape scowling upperclassman and the three-meal-a-day hazing since these tables were presided over by athletes. No bracing. All you could eat.

And while basketball practice was tough, "It wasn't as tough as Beast Barracks which we had just gone through," said Neal Hughes, a player in later years. And even if it had been, "that was more than compensated for by the fact we were able to eat. I'd run through the walls to do that."

One player escaped company tables just in time. Only a week before, the table commandant had put him in charge for "three seconds." Traditionally a plebe given this power shouts "Fall out!" meaning the three plebes at the table could eat the rest of the meal without bracing or other harassment. In what the player would later characterize as "the dumbest move in four years of dumb moves," he turned to the table commandant and screamed, "Suck that head in!"

No extra dessert that night.

"More balls than brains," the player would say.

The five recruits—including Silliman, Helkie, and Bobby Seigle—plus a slew of walk-ons identified in tryouts during Beast Barracks made the roster. The number of actual basketball recruits was lower than normal, thanks to Congress.

In the spring of 1962, Louisiana Senator Russell Long was unhappy with West Point football coach "Pepsodent" Paul Dietzel. Not only had the man with the dazzling smile just deserted Russell's beloved Louisiana State University to take a job at the Academy, the coach, said the senator, was trying to "steal away" all the potential All-American players in the country, going so far as to recruit players already signed with other teams.

Not so, said then Athletic Director Ray Murphy.

"Hell, we had like three hundred high-school football captains, but none of them weighed over 120 pounds," Murphy recalled. "Statistics-wise, it looked like we were getting a hell of an influx of athletes. And this is what a lot of people grabbed when they wanted to fight you."

In late May, a little more than a month before the Class of 1966 was to report to West Point, Congress passed what was dubbed "the West Point football bill," limiting the recruiting of athletes, and then, for good measure, passed a second bill increasing the military obligation following graduation to five years to "minimize career possibilities in professional sports."

Before this bill, Tates Locke could recruit an unlimited number of athletes.

"He could get anybody who could qualify," said Bobby Seigle.

The bill did end up cutting down on the number of athletes recruited, but not in football.

"They didn't take away anything from football," recalled basketball recruit Billy Platt. "They just pared down the other sports."

Around the time he was trying to pass the SAT for the fourth time, Seigle got a heads-up on the cutback from his brother, who was teaching at the Academy.

"My brother somehow got wind of that at West Point," he said.

Seigle was worried, thinking he might have been recruited under false pretenses. Tates had first heard about the Mt. Healthy, Ohio, guard through a Cincinnati sportswriter who had seen Seigle play once and billed him as a fierce defensive player. Maybe that night.

"Guy stuck a finger in my eye," said Seigle, "and I came back in the game and apparently was all over him, because I was just rabid on defense."

Seigle's brother was afraid Bobby might not make the final cut and advised him to write the superintendent.

"I've dropped everything else based on acceptance of coming to West Point," Seigle recalled writing to General Westmoreland, "and my options are zero to go anywhere else."

The ploy worked and Seigle got the appointment. Meanwhile recruits Billy Platt and a hotshot named Bob Deluca would get the ax. Later, in a "fit of anger," Tates would blame role-player Seigle for costing him Deluca, who ended up being a big star in the Ivy League.

Billy Platt got word of his rejection in late June, only days before he was to leave for West Point. His high school coach would help him wrangle a track scholarship to Indiana State, and Platt would end up starting on the freshman basketball team there before entering the Academy the next year.

But even without Platt and Deluca, Tates Locke had a powerhouse team.

"I bet we had eight Division I–caliber guards," recalled Helkie, at least five of them walk-ons. One, an Arkansas native named Jerry Edwards, made the highlight reel during the first practice, showcasing a nifty between-the-legs dribble he had perfected during a stay at the Sewaneee Military Academy in Tennessee. That hot-dog move was soon banished from his repertoire.

Shortly before practice began, the nation had moved to the brink of nuclear war when Soviet missiles were discovered in Cuba, only ninety miles off the coast of Florida.

"Nuclear catastrophe was hanging by a thread," said one Soviet general of the conflict that came to be known as the Cuban Missile Crisis.

There were rumors that all or part of the Corps would be called up or that the seniors might be graduated early like during the Civil War and World War II. Plans were announced to inoculate some cadets against tropical diseases. But the Soviets backed down, agreeing to dismantle the weapons. And after what amounted to a mere tap of the brake pedal, the Big Gray Machine rumbled on, unslowed by intrusions from the outside world.

Christmas came and went. In those days plebes weren't allowed to go home for the holidays, and one player complained of upperclassmen who "made us sing 'I'll Be Home for Christmas.'" Meanwhile, the plebe basketball team was on its way to making history.

In the first road game ever for a freshman team, the squad would beat St. John's 69–51. Without asking permission, Coach Locke had put the team up at New York's swanky Waldorf Astoria, where the football team traditionally stayed. That was the last time that happened.

"We violated some rules there," said Locke.

Led by Mike Silliman, the plebes would go undefeated in seventeen games with an average winning margin of almost twenty-three points. Mike led the team in both scoring and rebounding. The team was so talented that before a scrimmage against the varsity, Locke told his players to "let the varsity win." Not likely. Owing to Locke's aggressive recruiting and a plethora of talented walk-ons, the plebe team was stocked with a different kind of player.

"We set our sights really on some outstanding kids," said Locke.

Before he got there three years before, the talent level was not what it should have been. And decades later, Tates would tell one of the walk-on players from that plebe team, "You were better than anybody who was there when I got there, skillwise. Cause you could shoot it. You were an athlete. You weren't a mechanical person. So many of the guys when I got there were just mechanical."

Stiffs. Klutzy white guys with overactive pituitary glands. There were exceptions, of course, but not enough to overcome Silliman and company. The plebes ended up winning. It was the ultimate humiliation for a varsity team that ended a dismal 8–11 season by losing to Navy for the fourth time in five years. That spring Tates Locke would replace George Hunter as head coach, taking over a team that had suffered two losing seasons in a row and had not won a road game in almost three years. Locke's first hire was an obscure junior-varsity coach from Cuyahoga Falls High School in Ohio: a twenty-three-year-old kid named Bobby Knight.

Chapter 11

The Summer of 1963

Tates Locke didn't actually hire Bobby Knight, of course. George Hunter did. When Hunter was fired, Tates just let the agreement ride. And after Knight finished basic training at Fort Leonard Wood, Missouri, he was assigned to West Point with the guarantee that he, like past and future enlistees Tates Locke, Bill Parcels, and Don Devoe, would spend his two-year military commitment as an assistant coach at West Point. Knight's pay? A private first class's eighty-nine dollar a month, about twenty bucks a month less than the cadets themselves were making.

Knight's father was amused.

"When I told him I was going to join the Army to coach at West Point," Knight told *Playboy* in 1984, "he really thought then he'd raised an idiot."

An *idiot savant* maybe.

While Knight's Army peers were staring down the commies across the Thirty-Eighth Parallel in Korea, freezing their asses off at Grafenwuhr training area in Germany, or crawling through mud at Fort Benning, Georgia, Knight would be getting a leg up in his chosen profession. It was about as good a way of fulfilling the draft obligation as could be found.

"I never wore a uniform," Knight would brag years later.

Not true. But, he wore a uniform so seldom that when he did, he needed help getting dressed.

"He came running in one day and said, 'How do I put all this stuff on?' He had his two weeks active duty and he had to wear his uniform," said a Knight pal. "He didn't know how to put all that brass [insignia] on. He hadn't worn it since he'd been there."

In or out of uniform, Knight—whose Ohio State degree was in history and government—felt a special affinity for West Point.

"I had enjoyed reading military history, and I ended up majoring in history in college," said Knight. "What more historical institution than West Point is there in America?"

Knight had to know he was in the right place when he walked into Central Gym for the first time and saw the quote from Douglas MacArthur chiseled over the door, the one about victories on the "fields of friendly strife" leading to victories "upon other fields." He would soon become acquainted with another MacArthur quote: "There is no substitute for victory." That seemed right.

Although only one season into his coaching career, Knight had already developed a reputation back in Cuyahoga Falls. After losing his first junior-varsity game on a last-second shot, the rookie coach had totaled a clipboard, the first of many.

"I guess he set a record for broken clipboards," Knight's boss, Harold Andreas, told Knight biographer Phil Berger.

Following that first loss, Knight decided his players needed some extra work. The practice went on for six hours.

"You're going to kill these kids," cautioned Andreas.

Later in the year, a player was having trouble catching the ball.

"You couldn't catch Marilyn Monroe in a phone booth," Knight told him, then pummeled the boy with pass after pass until he showed some improvement. Must have worked. The boy ended up playing for Knight at West Point.

And even in that first year, Knight was developing habits that would come back to haunt him thirty-some years down the road. Habits like insisting young people treat their elders with respect, and another one: manhandling players.

A woman who was a student at Cuyahoga Falls High back in 1963 wrote to the *New York Times'* Ira Berkow years later telling him that Knight used to "rant and rave" in the hallways.

"One particular time, I had the misfortune of being in the hall when he was throwing a student up against a locker," she wrote. "I couldn't equate this behavior with being in sports or being human. It scared me to death."

———◦◦———

After a month's vacation following plebe year, the Class of 1966 had returned to the Academy for two months of military indoctrination at Camp Buckner, a 16,400-acre training area located on the grounds of the West Point military reservation. Weekdays began at 5:15 A.M. when the new "yearlings" donned gym shorts and combat boots for a little exercise and "reveille run." All before breakfast.

"Every morning we do calisthenics and then run two or three miles with rifles," Mike Silliman wrote home.

After a year of pomp, ceremony, and differential equations, Buckner was a dose of the real Army. During the week, the cadets shed their fancy-pants, tailor-made cadet uniforms in favor of baggy, olive drab Army fatigues.

"We fired machine guns and some bazookas," wrote Mike in mid-July. "The noise was terrible. Today, we ran the obstacle course and in the afternoon we have gas mask practice."

Following a lecture on bacteriological and chemical warfare, the cadets slipped on the black rubber masks for their second go-around with tear gas. During Beast Barracks the New Cadets had been marched into a tent filled with the stuff and then ordered to remove their masks so they could experience the nose-running, eye-stinging misery firsthand. This time the plan was for the cadets to be exposed out in the open air.

"First they used plain smoke to check which way the wind was blowing so we'd get the full effect," one cadet wrote home, "but when they lit the tear gas bomb, the wind shifted and the officers got a face full. I didn't get hardly any. You should have seen the officers run."

Over the summer, the trainees manned bulldozers, tanks, and armored personnel carriers; fired .45 caliber pistols, 105-millimeter howitzers, and mortars; built pontoon and trestle bridges; set and disarmed booby traps; and sampled a variety of C-rations, including ham and lima beans, a vomitous concoction that, it would turn out, only the Viet Cong would eat. For sixty days, they would learn what the real Army was all about.

"They have a number for everything," one cadet wrote home. "Pliers are TR 133, batteries are BA 30's, rifles are M-14's. M-13's are gas mask carriers. M-79's are grenade launchers. M-14 A's are bayonets. M-60's are machine guns. 2-1's are 'Delinquency Reports.' I'm C66372."

"Tomorrow morning about 3:30 A.M., we leave for Recondo," Mike Silliman wrote home in early August.

"Recondo," a combination of "reconnaissance" and "commando," was the brainchild of West Point Superintendent William C. Westmoreland, the action-is-the-chief-aim-of-man guy. The course was an introduction to guerrilla warfare and sleep deprivation (only ten hours sleep in five days) that Westy had brought with him from the 101st Airborne Division.

"It's pure hell," one cadet wrote home.

Cadets learned hand-to-hand combat in a sawdust pit where on the command "On Guard!" they delivered "simulated chops and blows to the killing zone." There was mountain climbing, patrols in the dead of night, map reading, and, at the hands of a cadre from the 101st Airborne Division, an introduction to harassment, infantry style. But unlike the rigors of plebe year, "What we are doing makes a little sense," wrote one cadet.

The night before his Recondo training was to begin, Mike Silliman's life flashed before his eyes.

"More and more each day I believe I made a mistake coming here," he wrote home, "[but] it's too late to quit. There is too much social pressure on anyone here to quit. It would be hard to face people and even yourself if you quit."

Despite his misgivings, Mike was a star during Recondo, making a name for himself as "King of the Pit." He got the title by being the last man standing following a free-for-all with around forty classmates in hand-to-hand combat class.

To end Recondo, the weary cadets were put through two "confidence courses." In the first, cadets climbed to the top of an eighty-foot tower, grabbed a pulley, and slid down a cable before dropping into the lake below—the "slide for life" it was called. In a second, they climbed another tower, then battled their fear of heights as they walked across a log suspended thirty-four feet above the water. Both of these "courses" taught the cadets to function while facing paralyzing fear, one of the realities of war.

By sheer happenstance, the cadets would be introduced to another reality of war: violent death. One afternoon, during a demonstration by the Special Forces, a helicopter hovered over an open field as the entire Class of 1966 looked on from the viewing stands. As a narrator described what was happening over the PA system, ropes were dropped from the belly of the chopper and two men rappelled down them in a blur. One stopped with a jerk, just short of the ground, feet dangling, before settling softly to the grass. The other misjudged the distance and slammed into the turf, breaking his rifle in half. He bounced so high, some cadets thought they were watching a dummy, thought they were seeing another cheap trick for shock effect. Who would think the human body would bounce like that? They had already seen a man bite the head off a live snake in survival training and another kill a rabbit for sport with a drop of nerve gas. As the medics hauled the lifeless young lieutenant away, the narrator went on talking as if nothing had happened.

One cadet in the audience admired the narrator's cool under fire. "What a man!" he recalled thinking in *The Long Gray Line*, Rick Atkinson's definitive history of the Class of 1966. "I'd like to be just like that."

But Camp Buckner was not just an incubator for nascent sociopaths. At times, in this gathering of some seven hundred of America's finest boys, there could be found a sort of joyous tumescence.

At night, after taps, with the cadets tucked snugly into their bunk beds, a deep, haunting baritone would sometimes be heard wafting out over the wooden barracks, coming from a top bunk over in Fifth Company. By request.

"Last night, I stayed up to masturbate," the boy sang with gusto. "It felt so good. I knew it would. Last night, I stayed up late to masturbate, I used my hand, it felt so grand." He then moved quickly to the opening lines of the chorus—"Wham it! Bam it! Slam it on the floor!"—before closing with a sentiment that surveys in later years would prove neigh on universal: "Some people say that fucking is so grand, but for pure enjoyment, I would rather use my hand."

Not that there weren't opportunities to move beyond the pleasures of self-abuse. On weekends, beautiful girls flocked to Camp Buckner to dance with the boys in their dashing all-white, Good Humor–man uniforms: white hats, white jackets, white pants, gold buttons. And there were opportunities for privacy of a sort. Camp Buckner boasted Yearling Walk, an off-campus replication of Flirtation Walk, West Point's version of the "no-tell motel." There, in the spring, observant boaters on the Hudson River might spy starched white cotton pants hanging in the trees. At Camp Buckner, as on campus, these trysting places, these trails through the woods, were off-limits to tactical officers, scary guys, who only an erection away (okay, two or three) would write up cadets for merely holding hands, an infraction known as PDA: "Public Display of Affection." Not that these particular regulations stopped anybody. Cadets with dates who had an aversion to rolling in the dirt would boast of romantic encounters in a variety of exotic locations including the baseball dugout at Doubleday Field (yeah, that Doubleday, he's a grad) and on the steps of the main auditorium at Thayer Hall. One cadet even made a virtue out of the all-male environs of the Academy when, one weekend, he set up housekeeping with his girlfriend in a seldom-used Thayer Hall ladies room.

When Camp Buckner finally ended, the last machine gun fired, the last grenade exploded, the last reveille run a memory, the class would return to West Point in triumph. Sure one classmate had flattened a jeep with a tank, but, unlike a previous class, nobody had lobbed any artillery rounds into the surrounding communities. And, anyway, this feeling at the onset of their second Reorganization Week had nothing to do with performance. Its source was more elemental. They were no longer plebes.

"It's really something not being a plebe anymore," wrote Mike Silliman the day the Class of 1966 returned to the main campus. "To hear the upperclassmen hollering at someone else besides you is a great feeling."

For Mike Silliman it had been a successful year. He'd led the plebe team to an undefeated season, he was ranked in the top fifth of the class academically, and not only had his company been named the best at Camp Buckner, he'd won the class golf tournament easily and come in second in tennis doubles. The loss in the tennis finals had prompted a private and rare display of temper as he tore the strings out of his racket. Yet despite all his success, the two months of Army 101 at Camp Buckner had not convinced him.

"I don't care anything about the military," he wrote home, and he was even thinking of a career change.

"I've thought of the priesthood," he wrote his dad, "but there again is another problem. I don't know if I could put up with the isolation."

A new year meant new basketball recruits. Among them, Jocko Mikula. So far Jocko was not having a good time. The night before Beast Barracks began, he and Billy Platt had stayed with Tates and Nancy Locke. The next morning Nancy drove them to the front gate. On the way down the hill, Jocko asked Nancy to stop the car, and he threw up on the lawn at the Catholic Chapel.

It was the beginning of a long summer. Jocko recalled "standing in formation and watching these guys cutting the lawn on the Plain" and thinking he would "trade places in a heartbeat."

A product of parochial schools in Dayton, Ohio, Jocko had not adjusted well to the more secular environment of the Academy.

"I remember going to Tates Locke after Beast Barracks and saying, 'I don't like it here. I'm really disappointed with the upper-class and the way they talk to us, the foul language. I've never heard "fuck" used so many times and in so many different ways,'" recalled Jocko. "And Tates rolled his eyes. 'What the fuck is this guy talking about?'"

The summer over, rookie coach Bob Knight jumped into his job scouting, recruiting, and coaching the plebes. Knight would set the tone early. At the first practice, Ed Jordan, a skinny kid from Alabama, trotted in sporting a set of nifty knee pads.

"Knight ate me alive," Jordan recalled.

"Nobody's playing on my team with knee pads," Knight said.

"That's when I learned a sign of valor was skinned knees," said Jordan.

Knight showed no mercy to the browbeaten plebes. One prize recruit, who was "constantly in trouble plebe year," showed up at an early practice after not sleeping for a couple of nights. Exhausted, he kept sneaking to the back of the line during a drill.

"Knight caught him and sat everybody down," said Jocko. "And he went into a tirade. Kicked the basketball and was screaming. And the guy whispered to me, 'Who is this son of a bitch? Tates Locke recruited me. And they bring in this fucking guy. Why should I listen to him? I know as much as he does.' A lot of people had that point of view at that time."

———◆———

Five weeks after basketball practice began, the cadets would be sobered by the sight of a riderless horse passing in front of the White House, a beautiful woman shrouded in black, face hidden by a wispy veil, a tiny boy saluting a passing coffin.

"A fallen leader," one caption said.

There were solemn ceremonies. The morning after the assassination, the entire Corps had assembled on the Plain in a drizzling rain, wearing full dress gray, the most formal uniform, to hear the official announcement of the president's death, just as they had assembled at the passing of Abraham Lincoln almost a century before.

They stood in memory of the man who three years before had challenged, almost dared them to come here.

"Ask not what your country can do for you," John F. Kennedy had said, "but what you can do for your country."

And so they had come, these boys from Saginaw, and Indianapolis, and San Francisco. Ready to serve.

"When you are asked by a President of the United States or any other American what you are doing for your country," Kennedy told the Corps of Cadets in 1962, "no man's answer will be clearer than your own."

The boys of West Point had done their part. Answered the call. Come here to do something for their country.

Now what?

Chapter 12

Showing Signs

The Army football team had its own private dressing rooms. All the other varsity sports were thrown together in the "same old damn locker room," as Tates Locke put it. "So we wanted to separate." That made sense. The "damn locker room" was in Central Gym, and the basketball team practiced in the field house a couple of hundred yards down the bluff toward the Hudson River.

"The team used to dress up in the gym," recalled former West Point trainer Jim Wallace, "and then they would get a bus down to the field house."

Tates snooped around the field house and found a small abandoned room up a couple of flights of metal stairs.

"That was a mess up there," he said.

The renovation began immediately, without asking permission, of course. "We just did it," said Tates. He rounded up a bunch of custodians and "gave them as much liquor as I could come out of the PX with," and bit by bit the room was transformed. Bobby Seigle helped to paint.

"They had a little shower in there and everything," said Wallace.

The renovation done, Tates made arrangements for Wallace to tape ankles at the new location.

"I said, no problem," Wallace recalled.

Tates had already relocated the basketball office, moving away from Coach Dietzel and the football team, and the new locker room would be as much symbolic as practical.

"We wanted to institute some pride and some individuality," said Locke.

Locke wanted his players to think of themselves as an athletic elite, to recognize "they weren't just part of the cadre, weren't just part of the athletic department, that they were Division I basketball players."

When practice began, Bob Knight started working with Mike Silliman immediately. The reserve from Ohio State was going to teach a kid who had always played center how to play forward. It would require Mike to turn his game "inside out." As a center, he had played underneath with his back to the basket. As a forward, he would play outside facing the rim. Mike was less than enthusiastic.

"I actually do not see how I can play forward," Mike wrote home. He even worried he might not start. "I can't stand the thought of that."

Locke had big plans for the varsity squad. He would scrap George Hunter's shuttle offense in favor of something he called "a driving offense involving a lot of forward and pivot play." Translation: get the rock to Silliman. But for Locke the offense was secondary. The emphasis would be on the new pressure defense.

"Tates believed in defense first," Knight would write in his autobiography, "and he had a lot to do with my feeling in that regard."

"The [first] week and a half of practice has been devoted to the fundamentals of our defense," Tates wrote to the parents of players. "For most of the boys, this has been a new experience."

It was a new experience for Locke too.

"I wanted to do some things and I didn't have a system to do it," said Tates. For that he turned to defensive guru Alfred Anthony "Al" Lo Balbo.

Locke and Lo Balbo first met while scouting a Rutgers–New York University game. It was a real New York moment. Lo Balbo was sitting up in the balcony of one of those old-fashioned gyms and, according to Al, Tates walked up, prompting this exchange.

"Hey, Coach Lo Balbo, what are you doin' here?"

"Who the hell are you?" Lo Balbo replied.

"I'm Tates Locke."

"Oh, Tates Locke. Yeah, that means a lot to me."

"The next thing I heard, he was the West Point coach," said Lo Balbo.

Locke soon came calling, asking Lo Balbo for tips on how to design and teach pressure defense.

"He already had a system in place," said Locke.

It was a system Lo Balbo had perfected while winning a bushel of state championships, seven says Bob Knight, at St. Mary's High School in Elizabeth, New Jersey.

"We were able to get into his head and we learned a lot from him," said Tates.

What exactly did Locke learn from Lo Balbo? The same thing the eighty-something coach was preaching almost forty years later.

"You gotta jump to the ball," said Lo Balbo. "You can't be a girl waitin' for the ball to hit you in the mouth. You gotta go after the ball, because, if you don't, they have all the time in the world to go their way."

"The defense on the man with the ball has gotta be right up in his face," continued Lo Balbo. "He's gotta make him turn his ass to the basket."

That done, said the coach, the man can see only half the court, has only half the options. The next step is to play three-quarter defense on the ball side of the post man.

That eliminates another option. While the guy with the ball may be able to pass it, he can't pass it to his big man.

"All we wanted was to prevent an inside pass," said Lo Balbo.

There was more, much more, on rebounding, blocking out, the importance of defense.

"If they weren't playing defense, I yanked 'em," said Lo Balbo. "I didn't care how good they were on offense, I just yanked 'em out of the game and yanked 'em out of practice."

A team playing the Lo Balbo pressure defense would contest every pass, challenge every shot.

"Some of the boys are having trouble making the adjustment to [the] punishment of playing good defense," Tates wrote to Mike Silliman's dad in late October.

The team would come around as Locke taught his "boys" how to play the stingy defense Army would soon become famous for. Years later Knight mythologizers would say that "his approach to defense revolutionized the game." More thorough reporters would trace the defense to Locke and then Lo Balbo. But pressure defense had been around long before Al.

While Lo Balbo had "really worked at it, refined it, and did a lotta things with it," said Knight, "pressure defense was way, way before Al."

In *Hoopla,* a history of college basketball, Peter C. Bjarkman credits New York City teams like Nat Holman's City College of New York; Joe Lapchick's St. John's; Manhattan; and NYU with pioneering the "tough-minded defense" at least a decade before. So it was nothing new. Neither was Army's controlled, slow-down offense.

In the midtwenties at CCNY, Coach Nat Holman was running the so-called "Holman Wheel," reported Bjarkman, "a patient offense in which all five players cut and swerved through endless loops around the basket until the uncontested shot could be found."

By the late twenties the St. John's "Wonder Five" was the talk of New York City with its "patient offense and air-tight defense," wrote Bjarkman, playing an "almost error-free ball control game." In one game against Clair Bee's Rider College, St. John's held the ball "for eleven minutes before earning an easy shot."

Meanwhile, a different philosophy of how to play the game was developing in the Midwest.

"The team that makes the most mistakes will most likely win the game," said Ward "Piggy" Lambert, the Purdue head coach who pioneered the "racehorse, fast-breaking style." At around the same time, Forest "Phog" Allen, who took over at Kansas from James Naismith, the inventor of the game, was pioneering zone defenses—and sports-speak. Allen called one of his defensive schemes the "Stratified Transitional Man-for-Man Defense with a Zone Principle" and told sportswriters he picked his starters based on whether or not he could detect a "victory light" in their eyes.

In 1963 rookie coach Tates Locke was looking for more than a "victory light" since the upcoming schedule was, in his words, "without question the toughest an Army team has ever encountered."

The team would start strong, 6–1, including a 92–71 victory at Colgate, Army's first road win in almost three years. The team then traveled to Washington D.C. to face American University and generate an early Bob Knight story.

After a pregame practice at the "old armory," Tates and Bob faced off on the empty court.

"He and I used to play one-on-one after practice all the time," said Tates.

They were playing to twenty-one baskets, had to win by two, and the game was nearing an end with one of them trying to hang on to a one-basket lead by hacking the other whenever he got an open shot. It was a time-honored dirty trick.

"Whoever was ahead, I forget, wouldn't let the other one get a shot. Fouling 'em every time," said Tates.

After a while whoever was getting hacked took exception and, by the time the team made it out of the locker room, "We were standing there toe-to-toe swinging," recalled Tates, "and they had to come out and break it up."

Picture it: a raging Bob Knight, standing at midcourt, swapping punches with his B-O-S-S over a less-than-meaningless one-on-one game. Good God Almighty, is that a great "Bob Knight story" or what?

I asked Knight about it. Knight doesn't discount many of the tales told by old friends. For example, he admits that he might have gotten into "a little scuffle with the tennis coach," as trainer Jim Wallace put it, during a heated intramural basketball game. That was West Point head tennis coach Bill Cullum, to be precise.

"I always liked Bill, and Bill was a good basketball player," Knight told me. "I mean he and I may have gotten into a hassle playing basketball sometime, but jeez, it's not anything I even remember."

But Knight does remember playing one-on-one against Tates after the practice at American University and said it was possible either one of them could have been systematically hacking the shit out of the other and that there might have been some jawing going on. But as for a fist-fight broken up by players: "That's absolute fucking bullshit."

Whatever happened that afternoon, it was all in the family.

"We're like brothers," Tates would say.

The two men had a lot in common. Both were from Ohio, both were only children, both had hot tempers, both had an us-against-them fox-hole mentality, and both possessed an almost insane desire to win basketball games.

"He is so obsessed with the whole thing," one player said of Tates. "I sometimes wonder if he isn't just a little off."

"It was fun. We kind of rode around like Butch Cassidy and the Sundance Kid," said Locke. "I don't think I could have enjoyed it with anybody but Bobby cause he had the same [attitude of] defiance as I did."

While the two "fought and argued," when push came to shove, "It was like two guys always watching out for each other," recalled Locke.

After rolling over American University 100–70, the team continued south to Miami for the Hurricane Classic. They would lose to Miami by eight in the first game, but Mike Silliman would hold future NBA great Rick Barry (who would average thirty-two points a game that year) to only seven. In the consolation game, Army would beat Princeton with consensus All-American Bill Bradley for the team's first tournament win in seven years. While in Miami, teammates claim Silliman taught ROTC cadet Bradley how to spit shine his shoes. Coming out of the Hurricane Classic, Army was showing some signs. So was Tates.

During the undefeated plebe season the year before, Tates had little opportunity to show his temper, and he was making up for it. One day during practice he had hurled a ball at Dick Murray. It hit Murray in the head and knocked him off his feet, no small task since Dick was 6′ 4″, 190. Originally in the Class of 1965, Murray had been recycled into the Class of 1966 after severely injuring a hand playing intramural football. Plebe year, he had spent so much time at Walter Reed Hospital in D.C., he ended up playing on *its* basketball team.

Before the ball that knocked him on his ass had rolled to a stop, Murray "walked out of practice and was gone from the team for two or three games." When he returned, he was held out of the starting lineup.

"He was mad at *me*," explained Murray, "because I walked out of practice."

Like most major college athletes and coaches, Tates absolutely hated to lose. The difference was he couldn't hide it whether coaching or playing. One day after losing a game in West Point's notoriously competitive Noontime League, an intramural league for staffers, Tates stomped off the court. The gym door had a one pane, wire-reinforced glass window about the size of a steno pad at eye level. Tates aimed a haymaker at the door, missed, hit the glass.

"I shoved my hand through a glass window," said Tates.

"Hell, I can see it like it was yesterday," said Bob Knight. "That glass had wire in it and it didn't really break it. He just ripped the hell out of his arm. God, he must have had twenty-five stitches."

The reason? "Tates got beat," said Knight, matter-of-factly, as if no further explanation was needed.

"I still got two horrible scars on my arm from that," said Tates.

Tates would also mix it up during pick-up games with players.

"We used to play during the off-season," said onetime player Walt Piskun.

Fouls?

"Unless you drew blood, it didn't count," said Piskun. "That's how I broke a bone in my shoulder: guarding Tates Locke."

Doctors would operate the fall of Piskun's senior year.

Tates also had a habit of kicking things. Ball racks. Doors. Lockers. Bathroom stalls. It would be almost twenty years before Locke, by his own account, "learned to cope with defeat. Cope with it. Not accept it." But this was 1963 and he was not there yet.

At halftime on the way to a six-point loss at Duquesne University that first year, Locke aimed a kick at the bench where the players were sitting. He missed and hit Bill Helkie.

"Didn't that hurt?" team manager Brian Ashbaugh would later ask Helkie.

"Yeah," replied Helkie, "but I didn't dare say anything."

Despite or maybe because of Locke's "passionate" leadership, the team had compiled an 11–5 record through sixteen games. Silliman had successfully made the transition to forward, and newspapers started mentioning him as an All-American candidate, given his per-game averages of 19.6 points and 11.75 rebounds. Meanwhile Knight was starting to make a name for himself, but not as a coach.

"I remember the analysis and the scouting report we used to get from Knight on the opponents," said Murray. "I always felt it meant six to eight points a ball game for us."

A Knight scouting report contained more than just the obvious things like "the team plays a 2-3 zone" and "the point guard is left-handed," Murray recalled. It included little details like, the guy "will stop and pick up his dribble, take the jump shot before going all the way to the basket" or "he'll take his eyes off you on the defensive end of the court, you can back-door him" or "he's not physically strong and this is how we oughta exploit it."

By the time the Navy game rolled around to end the regular season, Army had a 15–6 record and, after beating teams like Princeton and St. John's, the players weren't much worried about the [insert cheap shot here] Midshipman. The same can't be said for Tates. The team was on its way from the hotel to the gym, recalled Tates, when he stopped the bus, "got up, and started raising hell."

"I was walking down the aisle and I get to Silliman," said Tates. "He looked at me and he says, 'What's this all about?' Here I thought I was giving a seven-hundred-dollar speech and he says, 'What's this all about?' I went and sat down."

Tates was right to worry. While Army would win by nineteen, it was only the second victory against Navy in six years. After rolling over Navy, Army received an NIT bid, the second in Academy history. In the opening rounds, the team would beat St. Bonaventure and avenge its earlier loss to Duquesne (winning by two in overtime) before losing by fifteen to eventual winner Bradley. In the consolation game, Army beat NYU by one (a team that had routed Army by twenty points earlier in the year) and took third place in a twelve-team field. Army ended the season 19–7, the most wins in Army history.

Meanwhile Mike Silliman had led the team in scoring (20.5) and rebounding (12.3). He would make the Converse All-American Team (honorable mention), the All-East, and All-Metropolitan (New York) teams. Nationally, Army would end up nineteenth in team defense, allowing only 63.4 points per game, and tenth in rebound percentage. Army basketball was on its way.

—————•◦•————

That spring Knight would take time out of his busy recruiting schedule, about an hour and a half to be exact, to get married.

"I swear to God he recruited me on his wedding day!" said 1964 recruit Paul Heiner. "Tates stood up for him."

"I went down there the night before. I spent the night at the Thayer Hotel," said Heiner. "I had breakfast with both those guys."

"I had to take a medical in the morning and then I had to take the physical in the afternoon," continued Heiner. "And during the interim Tates Locke and Bobby Knight ran off and Bobby Knight married Nancy. He recruited me on his wedding day! There was only an hour and a half window I wasn't with him."

Sounds like so much bullshit, right?

About forty years later, Knight didn't remember it specifically, but he wouldn't rule it out either.

"What class would Heiner have been in?" Knight asked.

"Class of '68."

"That could be very possible," he said. "I recruited him in the spring of 1964 and so that's very possible."

The "rushing" bride was a girl named Nancy Falk from Orrville. Knight had known her since high school although they didn't begin dating until after his freshman year at Ohio State. That summer Knight had made his move on lifeguard Nancy at the local swimming pool.

"Well, now that you've grown up," said Knight, always the smooth talker, "would you like to go out?"

Nancy said "yes," but only because she'd had her eye on the hotshot athlete since her junior year in high school. The two were married five years later in between schmooze sessions with Heiner, a skinny shooting guard from Schenectady, New York.

"I remember working out with the team," said Heiner. "And then I got in the car and drove back home. But that was his wedding day."

I was afraid to ask about the honeymoon.

Chapter 13

Single-Minded Roughnecks

ummer for the rising juniors of the Class of 1966 would begin with "June Encampment," where the cadets learned how to pass along the military knowledge they'd gained so far.

"All we do is teach classes or attend classes taught by our classmates," one player wrote home. "It beats running through the woods yelling 'Kill! Kill!'"

When June Encampment ended, the class would be separated for the first time. Some would join the Beast Barracks cadre while the lucky ones would be dispatched to Europe to spend time with real Army units in what was called "Army Orientation Training." Most of the cadets assigned to Europe took advantage of the free airfare and flew in early, shoehorning in a few weeks vacation before they had to report to their assigned units. They camped out, piled themselves into tiny rooms in funky, no-star hotels with bathrooms down the hall. Not exactly the Grand Tour, but it didn't have to be. Hell, they were twenty and in Paris.

"It's such a great feeling to be free, irresponsible," one wrote home.

They roamed the Paris side streets on Bastille Day, and, stumbling upon neighborhood block parties, stayed up all night drinking French wine, dancing with comely strangers before rising in midafternoon to go to the Paris Officers Club for a buck-and-a-quarter steak dinner.

Then off to the Riviera, a café in Nice, where a couple of cadets spotted a winsome blonde sitting at a back table, a fluffy, faux dog at her heel. The proprietor, a cynical American doing his best Humphrey Bogart, sat scowling behind the bar. The blonde crossed her legs. The boys flirted. Will you be mine? Yes. For thirteen dollars. Figure about a buck a second.

Word got around to the other cadets swarming through the back streets of Nice, and many followed the girl's near-perfect derriere up the narrow stairs of a nameless hotel. Notes were taken. Confidences shared. On a slow day she would take eleven dollars. She'd ask for more to take off her bra. She spoke no English. She had little tufts under her arms. She might show you pictures of her baby. One cadet was so enchanted by the girl that, *flagrante delicto*, he forgot himself, made a U-turn south, and later confessed to his pals, suffering merciless teasing.

Vacation over, the spent cadets linked up with real Army units for a stint as "third lieutenants."

"I haven't had a bath in seven days," one wrote home. "I'm infantry all the way."

In an August dispatch from the Grafenwuhr training area, a budding soldier waxed poetic about the pleasures of playing war.

"We got all four tanks as they came over the rise. Just as we finished them, the infantry came out of the woods. We turned the machine guns and wiped them out. How beautiful it was."

One "older" officer, maybe twenty-four, escorted a third lieutenant to the "Yacht Club" in Hanau, Germany, to further his education. There were no yachts at the Yacht Club, of course, no boats at all, not even water, just a blonde in a G-string who had a way with a telescoping cigarette holder and a brunette who made the beast with one back with "the wall, a chair, a pole," before resorting to traditional methods in her simulated masturbation scene.

The "shocked"—not to mention clueless—third lieutenant decided to share all this with his girlfriend.

"I think whores are more respectable," he wrote. "At least they don't make a public display."

Sigh.

Meanwhile Mike Silliman was serving his time with an artillery unit near Frankfurt. While he acknowledged German girls were "cute," he was not about to let them get in the way of his first love: "fraulein stein." Mike had developed a taste for beer while still in high school and, after departing for West Point, told a friend who worked for a distributor, "Now that I've left Louisville, you can take one of those beer trucks off the street."

And only weeks after his arrival in Germany, Mike had spent so much money on beer that he was about to go broke.

"I shall reduce my consumption of beer, which was pretty much. It is so good!" Mike wrote to his father. "By saving every little thing, I think I'll manage."

That same summer, Air Force General Curtis LeMay, the all-time scariest of the scary guys, had to be thrilled when, on August 7, 1964, Congress signed the Gulf of Tonkin resolution. Three months before, Lemay had weighed in with his solution to the Vietnam problem: "Bomb them back into the Stone Age," the General suggested. The Tonkin resolution would grant President Lyndon Johnson permission "to take all necessary steps, including the use of armed force" to protect the freedom of "the peoples of southeast Asia." The "peoples" at West Point didn't get it. For like the War on Poverty announced in January and the Civil Rights Act signed only a month before, it all seemed kind of remote, especially since American participation in Vietnam up until that point had been limited to a handful of "advisors." The only cadets who thought much about Vietnam were the "Gray Hogs," the gung-ho types, who were worried Johnson would beat Barry "Extremism-in-the-Defense-of-Liberty-Is-No-Vice" Goldwater in the presidential race, and the war would be over before they could get their ticket punched. As for the impact on basketball recruiting: who would have thought the damn thing would last four years?

When Mike Silliman returned from Europe, he was showing the effects of that "so good!" beer, weighing in at around 250, thirty pounds over his playing weight. Tates was upset, but it was not like he had ever discouraged Mike's drinking.

Since cadet drinking was banned not only on campus, but within a fifteen-mile radius (check the West Point annals to see the DUI toll exacted by that policy), Tates had made special provisions for Mike.

"Every now and then he'd come over to the house by himself," said Tates. "I'd just let him go in the basement and drink beer. I kept saying, 'God durn, don't you get busted when you go back in.'"

To lose weight, Mike took to wearing a rubber suit on court, leaving puddles in his wake. By the third week of October he'd lost twenty pounds, but not without cost. After a scrimmage with Long Island University in which he shot only six of twenty-three, Mike complained to his father: "I could not hit, play defense, or even run. My legs felt terrible—like lead. I guess I'm still not in shape. Germany really had an effect on me."

All the while Tates was pushing hard, not satisfied with Army's good showing the year before. Following a lackluster practice, he called a team meeting to talk about his hopes for Army basketball.

"He kept saying he wanted to be the best," one player wrote home. "Not the best Army team or the best team in the East, but the best team in the nation. I've never seen anyone who wanted to win so badly."

In the opener against Lehigh, Mike got twenty-five points and eighteen rebounds in the win, and the team was 5–2 before departing on a Christmas trip.

"I hope we can continue representing the Military Academy in the midwest as successfully as we have here in the east," wrote Tates in a letter to parents. "We intend to come prepared."

Not.

The team lost to Dayton by eight, and the only thing to make the highlight reel in Ohio was the Christmas Eve celebration in the basement of Jocko Mikula's boyhood home complete with cabbage rolls, polka music, and pretty dancing partners. The team moved on to Salt Lake, suffering a twenty-two-point drubbing by Utah, then to Portland, Oregon, for the Far West Classic, losing in the first round to Oregon State. The team was now 5–5.

"This season is aging me rapidly," Locke told a reporter for *The Oregonian*, "about five years per loss."

The accelerated aging would end as the team won the next two and took third place in the tournament.

Christmas over, the team returned to the Academy facing the worst part of the year. The next scheduled escape was spring break and first semester exams were looming. It was so bad cadets had a special name for it.

"The three months after Christmas," one cadet wrote home, "are called 'Gloom Period.' The weather is bad, academics are bad, and your disposition is bad."

Exams started in the last week of January, but over in company G-1 the studying got off to a slow start as a couple of volumes of required reading, *Lesbian Roommates* and *Lesbian Gym,* passed from man to man.

Meanwhile, Silliman was still complaining about his weight, and his scoring average was off a couple of points from the year before to 18.4.

"My speed still is much too slow and my weight is still too high," he wrote.

While the team may have been only 9–5, it was not for lack of team chemistry.

"Everybody likes everybody else. It is the most closely knit team I've ever been on," remarked one bench warmer. "Too bad we can't play basketball."

Mike was worried about the "pretty stiff competition" coming in February: Penn State, St. John's, NYU. He should have been worried about the end of January. The team barely slipped past Hofstra, winning by two, and then lost to Fordham by seven before righting itself for an 8–1 run, including wins over St. Johns and NYU. The one loss was to Penn State by fifteen.

The team ended the regular season with a ten-point win over Navy and, now at 18–7, received an NIT bid, the second in as many years. This renewed one of Locke's battles against the windmills of officialdom.

"The only time the cadets got to go anywhere was the Army-Navy game or if there was a big football game," said Tates.

So Locke had been lobbying to get cadets to Madison Square Garden to support the team. After a protracted struggle, Tates thought he had it done for the first NIT game against St. Louis. But as game time approached, the cadet cheering section remained empty.

"Where the hell are the damn cadets?" Locke asked. "And all of a sudden we hear 'em whistling and singing, coming down the aisles."

The reason for the delay?

"They were out at the concession stand getting all the beers," recalled Locke, "and I'll bet you every one of them had two full beers, one in each hand."

Army would beat St. Louis and Western Kentucky in the first and second rounds before losing to the eventual winner, Joe Lapchick's final St. John's team. In the consolation game, Army would best NYU for the second time that year and take third place in the fourteen-team field.

The success of the 1964–65 team proved that the previous year was not a fluke. Army had gone 21–8, breaking the previous year's record for wins and compiling the best two-year win total in school history, a record that still stands.

What had turned it around for Army? Mike Silliman, of course, who was named an All-American again that year, and Tates Locke.

"Tates had a really strong determination to succeed and a strong will," said Bob Knight, "and I think to a degree imposed that on his players."

Locke had also come up with a style of play ideally suited to the raw material provided by the Academy. The pressure defense and controlled offense were tailor-made for boys who were smart, disciplined, and tough physically, emotionally, and mentally.

"I think we were able to put together the toughness and the intelligence," said Locke.

"I'm the first one to recognize that both Tates and Bob were good for those times, for the kind of talent that we had," said Dick Murray, "but I do believe the players and their character and to a certain degree their individual talent were contributing factors to why we were successful."

The Academy did turn out a unique variety of athlete. While across the board the talent was often midlevel, the players weren't quite "the single-minded roughnecks who chopped their way to victory" that Frank Deford once described. Owing to a witch's brew of Beast Barracks and Recondo and brain-boggling academics and ball-shriveling scary guys, the cadets had a special something—call it "steel," heart, whatever— that enhanced the talent they had and made them absolutely relentless.

"We just never quit," said Bob Knight.

Ever.

"We were hard to play against," said Tates.

Army "never met a team," Knight would write in his autobiography, "that had an edge on them in [Vince] Lombardi's 'heart power' or Napoleon's 'power of the spirit.'"

Those who didn't believe it were invited to ask St. John's and NYU and Princeton and any of the other major teams that underdog Army had upset in the past two years. And to look at Tates Locke himself, a basketball nobody who became a somebody on the backs of those "single-minded roughnecks."

———•◦•———

On March 7, 1965, six days before Army played St. Louis in the NIT, 525 U.S. citizens, mostly of African descent, began a march for voting rights in Selma, Alabama. They didn't get far. As the marchers crossed the Edmond Pettus Bridge, named after a Confederate general, they saw a "sea of blue"—Alabama state troopers—waiting on the other side. This contingent of Alabama's finest would disperse the crowd using tear gas, batons, and men on horseback. Soon after, the day of this march for one of the basic rights due all Americans would become known as "Bloody Sunday." Within forty-eight hours there would be civil-rights demonstrations in eighty U.S. cities.

More demonstrations were just over the horizon.

During the 1964 presidential campaign, Lyndon B. Johnson had promised to not "send American boys" to fight an Asian war. And in his inaugural address on January 20, Johnson had not said even one word about Vietnam. He made up for it nineteen days later when on February 8, the U.S. began bombing North Vietnam. Exactly a month after that, on March 8, thirty-five hundred Marines would go ashore in Danang. The graffiti was on the wall. The times "they were a changin'" and the era that came to be known as "the sixties" was now cleared for takeoff.

Chapter 14

Too Much of What He Was

In the spring of 1965, things were looking good for Tates Locke and West Point basketball. In just two years, "basketball had kind of emerged as at least the second most important sport there," recalled Bob Knight.

"Our record at that time was 40–15," continued Knight. "We'd won nineteen and twenty-one games, and we're gonna win twenty games the next year. So Tates was gonna have three years at a school that had never done anything in basketball. And he's gonna have three years with three really good teams, and this team should be the best."

There was reason for optimism. On paper at least, the 1965–66 squad would have the best talent in Army history. The team boasted one returning All-American in Silliman and two future All-Americans in Bill Helkie and New Jersey phenom Billy Schutsky ("that wonderful son-of-a-bitch Schutsky," as Joe Lapchick called him) from that year's plebe team. The squad would likely rival Army's undefeated 1944 Helms Foundation national-championship squad and the three teams in the early twenties that had posted a thirty-three-game winning streak.

In short, twenty-seven-year-old Tates Locke was on the verge of making history. It was the next step up for an ambitious young man whose goal was to coach "the best team in the nation."

So what did Locke do? He quit.

"After sleepless nights, much inner turmoil, and long deliberation," as Locke put it in a May 5, 1965, form letter to the players' parents, he had decided to accept "a coaching position at Miami University in Oxford, Ohio." Under the deal, he would be the assistant coach the first year, then take over as head coach the next. Locke broke the news to Knight during a wild ride on the back roads of the West Point military reservation.

"Oh, he ate my ass out," said Locke.

"We only ever even got into it one time, a real argument," said Knight. "And that's when he went to Miami and left West Point. I didn't think he should do that at all. I didn't think he should go to Miami, number one, and I certainly didn't think he should go to Miami as the assistant coach."

The reason Knight was so upset, said Locke, was that he wasn't privy to the real reason for the move. Locke wasn't leaving because of Miami's reputation as the "Cradle of Coaches," the progenitor of such coaching greats as Earl "Red" Blaik, Woody Hayes, and Ara Parseghian. And he wasn't leaving, as some speculated, because the job offered Tates a chance to make a triumphant return to a school where he couldn't make the team as a player. He wasn't even giving in to an impulse "to git, while the gittin' was good." He was leaving because of Nancy.

"My wife was really going through it," said Locke. "Eventually she had a nervous breakdown."

So Locke was going to Miami "to try to get her back on track." She could cool down during the year off before he took over as head coach.

When Knight eventually heard the Nancy rationale, he didn't buy it.

"He went to Miami because he wanted to go back to Miami to coach," said Knight. "That's why he went to Miami."

On Sunday, May 2, Locke called the team together and broke the news.

"We were all in shock," recalled then plebe Paul Heiner.

And angry. Not even Silliman had been consulted.

"He got pissed off at me when I left. I know that," Locke said of Mike.

"I was really upset," said Billy Platt, a second-year guard. "I didn't wanta stay there anymore."

Soon after the announcement, Locke would make an appearance in the Washington Hall dining room to give a farewell address to the Corps.

"I just told them, y'know, they were the best five years of my life and that it was with deep regret that I was doing this, but y'know I felt it was in the best interests of my family and so on and I really loved 'em, I loved what the place stood for."

Speech over, Locke left the dining hall and started walking back up the hill toward his quarters. He was doing fine until he heard them singing, twenty-five-hundred strong.

"The Army team's the pride and dream of every heart in gray," the Corps sang.

It was the Army fight song: "On Brave Old Army Team." A song Locke had heard at every step along the way in his five years at the Academy. During the 1964 win over St. John's, the 1963 loss to Princeton.

"I could hear 'em singing," Locke said. "It echoed everywhere."

Echoed off the granite walls of Washington Hall and Central Barracks and North Barracks and Central Gym, following him, stalking him, all the way up the hill.

> On brave old Army team,
> On to the fray.
> Fight on to victory,
> For that's the fearless Army way.

"I cried all the way up," Locke said. "I mean I really did love that place. I loved what it stood for, and I loved beatin' the system and doing things that no one else had ever done in basketball there."

Later Locke would come to believe that leaving West Point was the "biggest mistake" he ever made.

To hear Tates Locke tell it, before the engine had cooled following his car-ride argument with Knight, he had already organized "an attack force" to get Bob named his successor.

"I went to Bob and said, 'Hey, this is what I'm gonna do and this is what has to be done. You just kinda sit back and let it go. Let it happen.'"

To hear Athletic Director Ray Murphy tell it, he had his eye on Knight all along.

"As soon as Tates left, I knew who the coach was gonna be," said Murphy, then a forty-five-year-old Army colonel.

"Murphy didn't know what the hell was going on. Okay?" said Locke. "General Jannarone's the one that made the call."

That's Brigadier General John Jannarone, the dean of the academic board, chairman of the athletic board, and at the time, by several accounts, the most powerful man at West Point.

"He's the one that made the decision," said Locke. "Without Jannarone, we wouldn't have got that done."

As for Murphy?

"He rubber-stamped it," said Locke.

Maybe so, but Locke did send players in to lobby the athletic director.

"I remember him calling me in and saying, 'Hey, look, you gotta go to Colonel Murphy,'" said Dick Murray. "'You gotta go in and tell him that Knight is the guy you want.'"

The success of the last couple of years, Murray would tell the athletic director, had been founded on a tough defense and controlled offense. "Bringing in someone else," Murray continued, "could change that dramatically."

That was preaching to the choir as far as Murphy was concerned.

"I really think that from day one, I was Murphy's choice," said Knight.

Not that there weren't concerns, even then.

"Some people on the athletic board thought he was too . . . too much of what he was," recalled Ann Jannarone, wife of the late dean. "Too tough. Too volatile."

As for more specifics from Mrs. Jannarone about how Knight came to be coach, forget it. In that era, men didn't discuss work with their wives. Take the visit of the premier of Vietnam.

"Marshal Ky comes up to West Point to visit. I learned about it from the hairdresser. My husband never told me," said Ann Jannarone.

Knight had earned the "volatile" label for his play during staff intramurals in both basketball and softball.

While Knight denies Locke's claim that he and Tates were once kicked out of intramurals for "beating the shit out of some guy," contemporaries do remember Knight as "a hell of a competitor."

"He played one hundred percent, one hundred percent of the time," said Bob Kinney, a one-time intramural opponent and sports PR guy at West Point. "Very intense player. Very physical. There were a few times when blood was shed."

"He had a reputation as a fireplug," recalled old pal Rich Cardillo, then the military "handler" of the basketball team. He remembered Knight as "a very intense player" who "was gonna win no matter what it took."

While Murphy recalls others arguing that Knight was "too young, too inexperienced" and a "little, sometimes, volatile," he says he "didn't hesitate at all." The AD viewed Knight as a "disciplinarian" and was impressed by his determination to "press people to do the best that they can."

While either Locke or Murphy or both were trying to engineer Knight's elevation to the head coaching job, Knight himself was looking for other work. He had about two months left in his Army enlistment and no firm offer. He went to see Murphy.

"I said, 'Colonel I've got to know where I am with this,' because [son] Tim had been born by then and I said 'I've got a family that I gotta take care of and,' I said, 'I don't have a job.'"

"He got on my ass about have a little patience, just wait," said Knight. "And I think that they had to convince some people."

By that time Knight had turned down freshman coaching jobs at Navy and Cincinnati over loyalty issues. He couldn't see himself coaching for the archrivals of either Army or Ohio State. On the recommendation of friend Chuck Daley, who would later win two NBA championships with the Detroit Pistons, he had interviewed with Vic Bubas of Duke at the Manhattan Hotel in New York. That, said Knight, was "the best [assistant's] job that I could have anywhere in the country," a stepping stone.

"You're gonna leave there as a head coach somewhere," said Knight.

About two weeks after Tates announced he was leaving, Murphy had the decision.

"On a Friday morning, Ray Murphy called me in to his office and his exact words were, 'Well, we have decided we're going to make you Army's head basketball coach.' And I said, 'Well, I really appreciate that and I'll give you an answer on Monday.'"

Murphy was not pleased.

"He looked at me and I thought for a moment he was going to withdraw the offer," said Knight. "I'm thinking maybe I went too far."

Knight's gambit was inspired by Ara Parseghian who, according to the newspapers, had walked out when a snag developed in negotiations with Notre Dame about a year before.

"Parseghian is saying to them 'Look, I'm gonna do this my way and if you don't like it, then get somebody else,'" said Knight. "And I thought that was a great move."

Was Knight stunned that they offered the job to a twenty-four-year-old with no significant college or high-school head coaching experience? Nah.

"I was cheap," said Knight. "I was there and I could do it. I had no reservations about whether I could do it or not."

What's more, Knight was a carbon copy of the departing coach. "Tates had done well and come from the same situation that I did," said Knight. "He was there two years in the Army and then one year as a civilian. He was there one more year than I had been [when named the head coach]. Now here comes essentially the same kind of guy."

And, like Tates, Bob understood the coaching obstacle course created by the West Point system. He understood "what you're gonna have to put up with as a coach."

"So I'd been there for two years and I'd fought the recruiting and the practice schedules and the whole thing," said Knight. "You just can't tell a kid I want to meet you in my office at ten o'clock, we're gonna look at film. You can't do that."

Knight spent the weekend pretending to think it over.

"Then Monday I came in and told him I wanted to be the coach, y'know, very much," said Knight. Then, pushing his luck, Knight asked if he had to finish up his Army enlistment.

"I said, 'Hell yes! You're gonna stay in the Army,'" recalled Murphy. "He only had a short time to go on his enlistment. People say I got a coach for a PFC's [private first class's] salary."

Not everyone was thrilled with the choice. Rumblings came from players who had played for him as plebes.

"Nobody knows what you're getting into with him," said Billy Platt.

Knight had been so tough, there were rumors going around that he and Tates had decided Knight should really slam the plebes so when they moved up to the varsity it would seem easier by comparison. Knight and Locke both deny that.

Still that year's plebe team wasn't exactly elated by the news. Just when they thought they were finally rid of the son of a bitch . . .

"Bob wasn't that popular," said Dick Murray. "Some of the plebes didn't think he was the nicest guy in the world."

"I would bet that Noonan—some of those guys didn't want three more years of what they had on the plebe team," said Knight. "I think that may have been kind of an attitude that they had."

Years later, Noonan, acting like the lawyer he is, would let that one slide. Although he admitted things went on with the plebe team when Knight was hired, he won't say what.

"I don't want to get in trouble with the coach," he said.

However Noonan did admit that, for him personally, it had been a rough plebe year. First, he was very young, not turning eighteen until the first of December. Then there was the body.

"I was 6'6½" and like 170 pounds and I mean, just absolutely no upper-body strength," said Noonan.

His first practice with Knight was a shock.

"Unbelievable. Never experienced anything like that in my life," said Noonan. "The tone of it. It was scary. It was just the energy level that was expected of us to go through that practice."

It was a long way from that trailer park in Elgin, Illinois. Not that Noonan hadn't been forewarned.

"I had a film session on my recruiting trip up there," recalled Noonan. "Knight's there and Tates plays this film."

The film showed a couple of big stiffs standing around, then suddenly this little guy takes off at half court and dives for the ball. A real floor-burn special.

"Tates, Knight, somebody in the room goes, 'That's the kind of players we recruit. Can you be that kind of player?' And I thought he meant the ones standing there watching the guy dive for the ball. I said, 'Hell yeah, I can be that kind of player!' Come to find out he wanted me to dive for the damn thing. What a shock that was to my system."

Noonan was a decent prospect. "I was like all-state Illinois, third team or something." But the future of Army basketball didn't exactly ride on his scrawny shoulders. That honor belonged to plebe Billy Schutsky, the high school All-American out of Hillside, New Jersey. Unlike Noonan, the first practice hadn't shocked him.

"Rollie Massinino was my high school coach," said Schutsky.

Schutsky doesn't remember, but fellow players say he was unnerved when he heard Locke was leaving.

"I remember that Schutsky was really upset with Coach," recalled Neal Hughes.

So upset that Mike Silliman and Bill Helkie were dispatched to talk him into staying at the Academy. It was easy for Silliman and Helkie and Murray and the rest of the Class of 1966 to go to bat for Knight. They really only knew him as a scout.

"You guys hadn't played for him," said Billy Platt, who played on Knight's first plebe team. Platt thought about leaving, but stayed because of his dad.

"He never got the chance to do anything," said Platt. "He was so excited about it, I couldn't have left there if I wanted to."

"Knight Succeeds Locke As Coach of Army Five," read the May 20 *New York Times* headline.

"Bob Knight, who coached the Army plebe team to a 11–7 won-lost record last season," continued the *Times,* "was named today the head basketball coach at Army."

And with that, the deed was done.

Part III

BOBBY BALL

Chapter 15

Jug of Booze

On the night of Saturday, September 18, 1965, Captain Thomas L. "Moon" Mullan was the Officer in Charge—the scary guy of record—at the United States Military Academy, West Point, New York.

"It was quite an evening. I used to get lost in those evenings," recalled former cadet Bruce Philip "Cousin Brucie" Auer.

"I don't remember how we came to get this—to come up with this jug of booze. A fifth of something or other," said Auer. "Probably was Maker's Mark, because he was partial to that. His dad used to sell it."

At 6' 4 3/4", Captain Mullan was the only tactical officer at West Point who could look Cadet Michael Barnwell "Barney" Silliman straight in the eye.

"Anyway we consumed quite a bit of it up there in his room and we were going over to the hop [dance] at the gym," recalled Auer. "[On the way over] we set fire to a dumpster, busted some windows out of a sally port where the grades are posted—stuff that was relatively unheard of. I never heard of that happening there before."

"So you kind of left a trail?"

"Yeah. Havoc. We never got nailed for that. I'm sure they knew where it came from, but nothing was ever said about that."

Despite his size, Captain Mullan was never an athlete. "Asthmatic," said wife Elizabeth.

"I remember Barney going all over the place with his dress coat unzipped," said Auer. "That was kind of shocking stuff for the atmosphere, the environment at the time."

"Tom says, 'Liz, stay put, I'll be back,'" recalled Elizabeth Mullan.

Cadet Silliman was doing pull-ups when Captain Mullan arrived at the dance in Central Gym. He wrote up cadets Silliman and Auer.

"Dumb," said Bob Knight years later. "They could've just run their ass out of there and let it go at that. Y'know, just got them the hell out of there."

> Our star basketball player got caught drinking the other night and it is doubtful whether he will play ball this year. It was kind of a shock, needless to say...He has been doing this stuff all along and he finally got caught. I really don't see how he could do something so selfish. The team really needed him, but he was just a little too cool.
>
> He might be in confinement for six months. The least he will get is two months plus a group of punishment tours in a bundle of eighty-eight or more plus at least forty-four demerits.
>
> — Teammate's letter, September 19, 1965

A "punishment tour" was an hour wasted walking back and forth across Central Area with a rifle on your shoulder.

"Once you get confined, you can't play Corps Squad," said team captain Dick Murray.

"I was surprised. I didn't know he drank," said Bobby Seigle. "Everybody else afterwards says, 'Good Lord, you didn't know he drank? We didn't know he did anything else.'"

"Remember General Jannarone? He called me and he said, 'What are we gonna do with your boy?'" recalled Tates Locke. "And when he called me, I thought he was talking about Knight, because I had to work so hard to get Knight the job. I said, 'What did Coach do now?' He said, 'No, I'm not talking about Coach, I'm talking about Mike.' 'John,' I said, 'what are the options?' He says, 'Really, there aren't any. But I gotta go to war for him.'"

"I think there was a deal that might have precluded him from playing basketball at the time," said Knight. While claiming he was not involved, Knight said that "somebody was smart enough to eliminate that. Now that would've come from, uh, y'know, Jannarone would've got that done."

Silliman and Auer got off relatively easy, each receiving twenty demerits, forty-four punishment tours, and two months confinement, the penalty usually assessed for mere possession of alcoholic beverages. What's more, during his confinement, Mike would be allowed to practice with the team.

"It was handled so quietly," said Auer.

"He could've been on probation or kicked out, I guess," said George K. Maertens, who at the time was the colonel in command of the First Regiment. "He got 'slugged' instead and got through it all right."

"Considerably less than I expected," said Auer, "because basketball was coming up. So they couldn't afford to lose Mike."

"I went all the way through that place not knowing anybody got any special privileges," said Seigle. "I really did. I didn't know Mike got any special protection or anything. I thought he was in there slugging it out like everybody else."

"It was really handled delicately," said Auer. "I just remember being very thankful Barney was there. If it had been anybody else, I think we would have been hung up by the yardarm."

"The confinement is not too bad except on weekends," Silliman wrote home.

"My husband's favorite sport was basketball," said Ann Jannarone.

Chapter 16

Bobby Ball

The red brick monstrosity overlooking the Hudson River looked like a two-bedroom rancher on steroids. Sure the architect had tried to dress it up by slapping some gothic touches on the outside, an arch here and an arch there, but even that didn't help. The building was so butt-ugly that nobody even bothered to name it. They just called it "the field house." But what the building lacked in beauty, it made up for in utility. The seventy-thousand-square-foot facility was the home of the indoor track and basketball teams and served as a rainy-weather practice field for the football squad. Back when it opened in the thirties, one writer had described the building as "the greatest thing of its kind ever built." But for the basketball team, there was a catch.

"The field house is yours when you want it," West Point officials had told Red Blaik when he was hired as football coach in 1941. "We're not interested in other sports."

The "field house is yours" policy was still in effect a generation later. And when the administration said "yours," they meant "yours." Football had dibs on every square inch of the building from September until the team departed for the Navy game in late November.

"They wouldn't start putting that [basketball] floor down until the buses had departed West Point to drive to Philly," said Bob Kinney, then in the sports information office.

That meant the basketball team didn't get to practice on its home floor, shoot at its home baskets, until a few days before the season started. So early in the year, the team was playing on what physically amounted to a neutral floor. The field-house policy was the kind of thing that could make even a seasoned coach crazy and, when offered the head coaching job, Knight had only one request.

"I wanted the field house to start practice in," he said.

Athletic Director Ray Murphy said he would fix it and did—belatedly. That first year there was a ten-day delay before the team began practicing in the facility.

"From then on, all our practices were in the field house," said Knight.

And if the football team needed to move indoors? They would have to make do with the other sixty thousand square feet.

In 1965, basketball practice began on Friday, October 15, the day before a hundred thousand Vietnam War protesters marched in eighty cities across the nation. While practice time during the week was limited to about two and a half hours a day by a rigid Academy schedule, there were two-a-days on Saturday and Sunday. Coach Knight took full advantage.

"He was so meticulous in his preparation for practice," recalled Bob Kinney, "it was geared to the second, to the minute."

"You almost felt like you never stopped moving the whole time you were there," recalled Dick Murray. "You were like running for the whole two and a half hours. That's what it seemed like. You were moving, moving, moving."

"I can remember having to hold myself up by the shower head, you were so tired after practice," recalled Paul Heiner. "I can remember going to that mess hall so thirsty you drink water, you drink milk, you couldn't tell the difference. I was so tired, I couldn't taste."

Knight had put his "new sheriff in town" stamp on the program in early September when he called a team meeting to announce a preseason conditioning regimen, an early version of today's so-called "voluntary workouts."

"We're all, like, in shock," said Heiner.

"My idea was, at the time, that you run for three weeks," said Knight. "Run five days and don't run on weekends."

"Knight was really taking the position that he's a real stern disciplinarian and this is what we're gonna start doing," recalled Heiner.

Knight had asked golfing buddy Joe Palone, the soccer coach, to put the whole basketball team on the roster for B-team soccer. That got the players excused from mandatory intramurals, a move unheard of at the time. Then every weekday afternoon the team donned combat boots, olive drab fatigue pants, and T-shirts and jogged from Central Gym up the hill by the Cadet Chapel and on to Michie Stadium. Once there, they would run up and down the steps of the football stadium eight times and do fifty- and hundred-meter sprints.

"All we do is run, run, run, run," one player complained in a letter home. "God, it's bad, but I guess it's necessary."

"I increased it as we went along," said Knight, "so at the end of three weeks, you weren't running eight [sets of] stairs, you're probably running twelve."

The conditioning gave the team a head start on the season, and when practice began three weeks later, Knight would have more time to teach players the finer points of "Bobby Ball."

"I didn't know a hell of a lot about basketball," Knight told *Playboy* eighteen years later, "but I knew how I thought the game *should* be played, and I knew I could coach it the way I thought it should be played."

One player got a taste of what would become Bobby Ball when he saw Knight in action at an Ohio State–Wichita State game several years before.

"I do recall this guy comin' off the bench and just being a kind of kamikaze on the court," said Neal Hughes. "He went for rebounds. He went for the loose balls."

"Your intensity [should be] as great as it can be as long as you're in the game," Knight would say.

Bobby Ball did not come naturally for most players of that era. Knight forced them to do things they didn't want to do on a basketball court.

What things? "Dive on the floor for a loose ball," Knight told *Playboy* in 1984. "Get down in a defensive stance and just scratch and scramble and work like hell to keep the guy from getting the basketball. Block out on every shot. Take nothing but good shots. Make good passes."

And Knight had drills to teach every facet of the game.

"He had a zillion different blocking-out drills," said Billy Schutsky. "One-on-one, two-on-two, three-on-three, five-on-five."

Blocking or "boxing" out, where one player keeps another from getting a rebound, is the second roughest play in the game. In one classic drill, Knight would stand at the top of the foul circle and toss the ball toward the basket. When the ball was in the air, each defensive player would get between his man and the basket. Then, all in one motion, the player would pivot 180 degrees, crouch, make contact, and back his opponent away from the rim. It was one of the few occasions on the basketball court when having a really big butt was a good thing.

"You've gotta sit on their legs and sit in their crotch," said defensive guru Al Lo Balbo, "and then use your elbows a little bit."

The resulting pushing and shoving would be overlooked by officials. All part of the game.

"They'll let little things go," Lo Balbo said.

"Then we'd do the defensive drills," said Murray. "They'd point and we'd be down in our defensive stances," sliding left and right, forward and back.

"Don't cross your feet!" Knight would yell.

There were dribbling drills, passing drills.

"Never leave your feet to pass the ball!" yelled Coach Mike Schuler, Knight's new assistant. A 1962 Ohio University grad, Schuler would be named NBA Coach of the Year while at Portland in 1986–87.

Fundamentals, fundamentals, fundamentals.

"Before if you had the ability and the size, you just overran the other people," said Mike Silliman. "I think Bob took the necessity for sound fundamentals to a new level."

And Knight contributed to the development of a whole new category of fundamentals with the invention of something called "the loose-ball drill."

"That was war! That was war, right?" recalled Dick Murray.

A "loose ball" is any ball up for grabs other than a rebound. Knight had tried out the drill on his junior-varsity guinea pigs at Cuyahoga Falls before exporting it to West Point. The idea, said Knight, was "just to get guys going after the ball."

The drill was also a quick way to find out who was naughty or nice. (Hint: naughty was better.) In Bobby Ball, nice guys didn't finish last. Nice guys didn't make the team.

The drill was simple enough. The players formed two lines. Knight would then point out three baskets, designate them red, white or blue— "just to make you think," he said—and roll the ball on the floor. Both players would dive for the ball and the battle was on. It was like a football fumble without pads, helmets, and the dampening effect of grass. Naked flesh on hardwood.

"If you happened to get the ball and I hollered red," said Knight, "then you had to take it to that bucket as quick as you could to score, and the other guy had to defend."

There were no fouls.

"I got to the ball first and Schutsky pulled the shirt over my head," said Ed Jordan.

"First time we did a loose-ball drill, I said 'Are you kiddin' me?'" recalled Mike Noonan.

"I got to the ball first," recalled Billy Platt. "I didn't hang onto it too long because I was out of bounds bouncing off the damn wall."

"There were a lot of guys who would kind of reach into the pile," said Noonan. "They'd lead with their hands instead of their nose. He wanted guys who would lead with their nose."

"Most of us volunteered for Vietnam to get away from the loose-ball drill," quipped Bobby Seigle.

"The fundamental thing you have to know about getting a loose ball," said a Knight-trained loose-ball expert, "is you're not going after the ball, you're going after the other guy. First you knock him on his ass and then you get the ball. The trick is to time it just right so the refs won't call it. The contact has gotta look incidental."

As for the ensuing lay-up, players learned to get the ball off despite the inevitable blow about the head and shoulders.

With the loose-ball drill, Coach Knight was teaching the kind of head-knocking play that had led to a rule change in the early days of the college game. At one time regulation basketball courts were surrounded with wire cages (hence "cagers") to "protect players from ornery crowds," according to historian Peter C. Bjarkman. As an added benefit, the cages also kept the ball in play. So when the cages were removed, there was a need for new "'out-of-bounds' legislation."

The rule makers decided to give the ball to the first team that touched it after it went out of bounds. Bad move. This led to so many "violent scrambles," reported Bjarkman, that it renewed concerns about violence in the sport. A few years earlier, Harvard President Charles Eliot had called for a ban on basketball since it was "even more brutal than football." So in 1913, the out-of-bounds rule was changed to the one still in effect today: the team that touches the ball last loses possession.

So far there has been no rule change in response to the wholesale muggings that can be traced to Knight's loose-ball drill, and the battle for a loose ball is the roughest legal play in basketball. Meanwhile the drill has become a part of the repertoire of coaches all across the country. So whenever the subject is Bob Knight's contributions to the game, it is at least worth speculating that his invention of the loose-ball drill marked the moment when modern basketball began evolving into a full-contact sport.

Those who doubt the game is rougher today than a generation ago should try to recall the last time they heard anyone characterize one of today's hardwood heroes as a "finesse player." (That's what old-timers called a silky smooth guy who didn't so much run as glide around the court, never making contact with anyone.) They should recall the now nostalgic class struggle between those *real* basketball players and the ham-handed galoots recruited off the football team who mixed it up, crashed the boards. They should channel surf on a snowy February afternoon trying to find just one example of this endangered species.

They would have better luck checking out the backyard birdbath for a homing pigeon. Finesse players have gone the way of short pants and the sweeping hook shot, and Bob Knight is at least partially to blame.

Bob Knight fashioned his rough-and-tumble teams from his own image, and later, when his Indiana teams won and won big, they were replicated by coaches all across the land. This assimilation was hastened by Knight's generosity in countless coaching clinics and by a platoon of Knight disciples scattered at colleges all across the country.

So today guys who would have been the finesse players of the past are gobbling "dietary supplements" and bench pressing three hundred pounds. All this because of the loose-ball drill, or at least that's the theory. But even if the loose-ball drill doesn't explain this wholesale change in the way the game is played, it does help to explain Bob Knight and Bobby Ball.

For it was a drill made in the very image of Bob Knight the player. Bob Knight the man. High intensity. High contact. High colonic. A drill that required more will than skill, the ball going to the man who wanted it the most, the guy who played the hardest. And in the Bob Knight pantheon of values, "playing the hardest" is the ultimate accolade; he has always pushed his teams to play as hard as the rules allow. That may help clear up one mystery still surrounding the 1965–66 team.

In March, following the 1965 NIT and spring leave, Tates Locke had called the team together to vote for the next year's captain. The leading candidate, obviously, was All-American Mike Silliman. But after the votes were counted, Tates announced that Dick Murray had won the job. Silliman, the man who would end up captaining the 1968 Olympic Team, had seemingly been rejected by his college teammates. Even Murray was shocked.

"I think the first thing that went through my mind was surprise," said Murray. "Mike had been the center cog of the team for two years."

So how did Murray end up captain? While nobody can remember the actual vote count, it's likely the election was rigged.

"We'd have a team vote, and if it didn't turn out like we wanted, we appointed them," said Locke.

While Knight didn't remember any of this, it sounded right.

In ensuing years, "I let 'em vote and then I picked the captain," continued Knight, choosing "the hardest-playing guy we had. Not necessarily the best player."

"Murray was more emotional," continued Knight. "Murray was more outgoing. Murray was probably more in tune with being a cadet than Mike was."

And Silliman's theory? He believed the coaches blackballed him for being late to a team meeting following a weekend in Ocean City, New Jersey.

"I held no grudge for that," Mike said.

If "hardest-playing" was really the criteria, as Knight asserted, then Murray was an excellent choice.

"He's the toughest guy I've seen on a basketball court," said teammate Neal Hughes. "Just the toughest."

"I know that Tates liked the fact that I played tough defense," said Murray, "and did a lot of the dirty little jobs."

It would be a while before Murray learned that being captain was another one of those "dirty little jobs."

Chapter 17

Wrong on Both Counts

It was a pet Bob Knight theory peddled to dozens of gullible listeners in one form or another over the years. The secret of his success at West Point, Knight would claim, was being harder on the cadets than the Academy itself.

"We've got two hours of practice," Knight said in one version. "Instead of a kid coming to the field house and saying, 'Hey, I can relax now,' the kid on the way to the field house has to gird himself for what's gonna take place. 'Damn, this is gonna be harder than anything I've had all day.' And that was my approach from day one."

In another version, Knight gave his take on discipline, complete with a set of practiced hand gestures. He would begin with a forearm leveled in front of his stomach. "With their demands here, my demands had to be up here, had to be higher than the Point's," he said, raising the forearm up to his chest. In a variation reported in *Sports Illustrated* in 1973, there were three levels: civilian discipline, West Point discipline, and Bob Knight discipline. Throughout his career, Knight has always aspired to be "the toughest guy from a standpoint of the demands."

So by Knight's reckoning, when practice began at 4 P.M., Army basketball players would face the toughest part of their day at the mercy of the toughest son of a bitch at West Point.

Wrong on both counts.

For starters, basketball under Coach Mussolini would have been a cakewalk compared to ordinary life inside "Hell on the Hudson." At West Point, by design, the demands were coming at cadets from all sides twenty-four hours a day. One day, it would be the T.D., Tactical Department, crawling a cadet's ass for "room totally unprepared for inspection"; the next day, the O.P.E., Office of Physical Education, would offer up one of its biannual physical fitness tests; and the third day, the folks over in Thayer Hall might issue the latest eight-by-thirteen-inch, spiral-bound, fun read from math department head Charles P. Nicholas: "Special Topic Memorandum No. 26, Differential and Integral Calculus, Chapter 13, Physical Applications of Integral Calculus." This one jacketed in bright red, the color of fresh blood. While at most colleges there was only one way to flunk out, West Point offered three: academics, physical education, and military aptitude. In comparison to that ongoing three-pronged attack, the multifaceted pains-in-the-ass routinely offered up by the Academy, basketball had little chance of being the hardest part of the day.

So the idea that cadets approached the field house on an average day quaking at the thought of another afternoon with Bob Knight was just so much rhetoric. Practice was the *only* situation the cadets faced all day, including the walk up and down the hill to the field house, where they didn't have to worry about some green-uniformed geek "writing them up" because their belt buckle, shirt placket, and fly were not "properly aligned." No player ever got a single demerit for taking a bad shot.

As for Knight's claim on the title of "the toughest son of a bitch at the Academy," the competition was fierce. His role models in this category were the West Point scary guys, fright-night ghouls like Brigadier General Richard G. Stilwell and "The Fumigator," Colonel Robert M. Tarbox. Bob Knight didn't have a chance in a head-to-head with that bunch.

Knight was hot. Scary guys were cold. Knight was desperate for you to do well. The bona fide West Point scary guys were itching for you to fail. "That's how many of you will be gone by June '66," General Stilwell had boasted. Underneath there somewhere Knight was on your side. Scary guys were on the side of some kind of martial righteousness.

What's more, down at the field house, things generally made sense. Suffering through the loose-ball drill meant that the team would come up with more loose balls during a game. Box-out drills meant more rebounds. Meanwhile, on the other side of the Plain, the scary guys ordered that all window shades in the barracks be "displayed at half-mast," pulled halfway down the window. Why? They said so.

There was another reason Knight couldn't compete in the scary-guy sweepstakes. The players wanted to be there.

"I loved basketball," as one player said. "So whatever it took, whatever it took, that's what I was gonna do."

So while the tough-guy role models provided by West Point would influence Knight, he would never realize his ambition to become the scariest of the scary guys. Truth is, the man was simply lacking.

"I've never been sadistic," he said.

"All I know is he scared the shit out of me," said Jocko Mikula.

Still, even from the first, even at the Academy, there were those who didn't approve of Knight's methods.

"People would get upset with me because they thought I was too hard on cadets," said Knight. "I heard that a lot."

Too hard on cadets? Would that be the cadets who suffered through shower formations and Recondo while those same critics stood mute? The cadets whose future "training" included systematic starvation and, in some cases, torture—literally—at the United States Army Ranger School? The cadets who would be propping up dominoes in Southeast Asia in a little more than a year? Those cadets?

Too hard or not, Knight's ultimate goal was something much more basic than teaching players anything so mundane as how to execute a perfect two-hand chest pass. The goal, said Knight, was to "take the talent that you have available and get the absolute most out of it."

"So I pushed and pushed and pushed," said Knight, "trying to get the most out of what we had, and I don't think I ever changed from that."

To get the most out of his players, said Knight, required nothing less than a triumph over human nature.

"Human nature dictates to us that we do what we have to to get by. So we got to beat human nature's ass, first of all," Knight told *Playboy* in

1984. "Then the next thing I got to do is get these players to play harder than they think they can play. I got to get them to work harder than they think they can work. Get people to be better than they think they can be."

Under Knight, "the coach's reach exceeded the players' grasp," and, like all good teachers, his ambitions for his students often surpassed their own. He was convinced he knew what they were capable of, and he was determined they realize that potential one way or another. That was not lost on players like Bobby Seigle who saw in Knight "the commitment, the passion burning in his body to make us as good as we could be." Even St. John's coach Lou Carnesecca took notice of Knight's dedication.

"Kids are ready to lay down their lives for him," Carnesecca told *Newsweek* in 1975, "because they watch him bleeding his life out for them."

This determination to push players to their limit was one of the legacies Knight would take away from his West Point experience and the source of much criticism over the years. For when Knight pushed players to the limit one day so he could push them past it the next (to paraphrase Knight hero Red Blaik), it looked and felt a lot like what's called abuse these days. For it to work, players had to trust their coach, believe there was a reason behind their suffering. In Knight's first year, most did, some didn't as the coach straddled that fine line between doing something for the players and to them, as Joan Mellen phrased it in *Bob Knight: His Own Man*.

"He [Knight] believes that if even one of them starts to think he's doing something *to* them rather than *for* them," Mellen wrote, "he can no longer coach them."

During the 1965–66 season, the "for them" group was led by Mike Silliman, the best player in West Point history, while the "to them" group started with Billy Platt, a little-used junior guard, and ended with the team captain, a tall, hawk-nosed senior by the name of Dick Murray.

One November evening a month after practice started, Mike Silliman was sitting in the audience in South Auditorium, Thayer Hall, listening to a lecture.

"I felt a sharp pain in my side," said Silliman.

Alone, "doubled over" with pain, Silliman hobbled to the nearby West Point Hospital.

"They operated immediately," said Knight.

Appendicitis.

The operation would accomplish what the drinking bust could not: keep Silliman off the basketball court.

"We had to play Princeton without him," complained Knight.

And Worcester Tech. Don't forget Worcester Tech.

Chapter 18

Firsts

On Saturday, December 4, 1965, the Army team less Silliman traveled to Princeton, New Jersey, for Bob Knight's first game as a head coach. Bill Bradley, the 1965 Player of the Year, had graduated, of course, but Princeton still had Butch van Breda Kolff, the 1965 Coach of the Year, and the remnants of the previous year's Final Four team.

"Princeton was awfully good," recalled Knight.

Just before the 8 P.M. tip-off, the team, dressed in black "away" jerseys with gold numerals and matching black short-shorts with gold trim, recited the Lord's Prayer in the locker room. On the way out to the floor, head trainer Ed Pillings cozied up to Knight. "For whatever it's worth, I just don't think you and praying mix," he said. Knight took Pillings's advice to heart, and even though the prayer seemed to work for a while (there were seven lead changes and the score was tied at twenty-five at the half), that would be the first and last time anybody prayed out loud in a Bob Knight locker room.

"God couldn't care less if we win or not," Knight would say.

With or without divine help, Army was still in the game well into the second half.

"We played pretty well. Probably thirty-two or thirty-three minutes, we hung in there," Knight said. "And we got down into the last few minutes and they just hammered us."

The problem? "We couldn't score," said Knight.

That might have had something to do with Princeton's smothering full-court press. With things out of hand, Knight decided to give sophomore guard Paul Heiner a look and put him into his first college game with 1:16 left on the clock. The first time down, Heiner got the ball on the wing and did what the set offense called for: waited for the center to set a pick and watched for the cutter coming across the lane from the weak side. Seeing the guy wasn't open, Heiner kicked the ball back outside.

Next time down, same thing. Heiner took the pass, and the center went to set the pick, but this go-around, with only thirty seconds left in a blowout, neophyte Heiner didn't wait for the cutter.

"I'm wide open from fifteen, sixteen feet," recalled Heiner. "'Fuck this!' I take a jump shot. Boom! Around the rim and out. So the game ends."

Army was routed 70–49 and the postgame festivities began.

"We got thumped and you know how he used to yell and scream when we got beat," said Heiner. "So we're all sittin' there on the bench in the locker room and I'm at the far end. I played one minute, sixteen seconds, so I'm, like, tunin' him out."

"There are three things that piss me off!" Heiner recalled Knight screaming.

Heiner didn't catch the first thing that pissed Knight off and didn't do a whole lot better on the second. But the third thing that pissed Knight off? Heiner remembers that one vividly.

"He comes marching down. I look up. The fuckin' guy's face is about an inch from mine," recalled Heiner. "And he goes, 'Goddamnit, Heiner, when I put you in the game, I expect you to run the fucking offense!' I went 'Holy shit! Holy shit!'"

When you were playing for Bob Knight, whether it was the first or last thirty seconds of the game, whether you were up twenty or down twenty, you "ran the fucking offense."

"You talk about discipline!" said Heiner.

Discipline had not been enough against Princeton, and so after one game as a college coach, for the first and last time, Bob Knight had a career losing record.

As locker-room tirades go, the one inspired by the Princeton loss was mild. Perhaps the most infamous Knight exorcism on record can be found on the so-called "cult recording" made following a 1991 Indiana practice. In one fifty-four-second stretch, Knight managed to use twenty obscenities, one every 2.7 seconds. "Fuck" or one of its variations appears fourteen times, including four times in this one sentence alone.

> I had to sit around for a fucking year with an 8–10 record in this fucking league and I mean you will not put me in that fucking position again or you will goddamn pay for it like you can't fucking believe!

An audio version of this "oration" can be found at Salon.com, where writer Eric Boehlert calls Knight "an angry, vulgar, violent creep."

Over the years many mainstream sports reporters have pretended to be shocked by Knight's language and tone and have done the kind of in-print "tsk-tsking" that would be expected in publications that describe themselves as "family newspapers." Meanwhile a couple of pages over in the entertainment section, fellow reporters are lauding the 2001 Emmy Award–winning *Sex and the City.* That's the sitcom that once featured four beautiful women sitting around at lunch having an "in-depth" discussion of anal intercourse.

It's enough to make Bob Knight blush.

Following the Princeton loss, Army would face "small college" and, since 1973, Division III Worcester Tech.

"We beat them at West Point pretty easily," said Knight.

"That was supposed to be an away game," said team captain Dick Murray. "The president of Worcester Tech was a former West Point guy, and they were building a field house, and we were gonna go up there and open it up."

But the arena wasn't finished on time, and the game was moved to West Point. It was the only game all year in which the Cadets would physically overpower an opponent. Leading 38–15 at the half, Army cruised to a 71–62 victory in Knight's first win.

Mike Silliman would be back for the NYU game on Saturday, December 11. This was a day after the *New York Times* reported that 190 professors from seventeen New England colleges, including Harvard and Yale, had announced their "full support of the Administration's Vietnam policy." Silliman scored twenty-one points and snagged about a dozen rebounds in a 76–68 win.

"This is like with one day's practice," said Knight.

The Associated Press called it an "upset" although Army had beaten NYU in the consolation game of the NIT the previous spring on two late baskets by Murray. This time around, Bill Helkie led the scoring with twenty-six.

Two days later Army would blow a fifteen-point lead with about eight minutes left but hang on to beat Cornell 76–74. Cornell's top scorer, with eighteen, was All–Ivy League Bob Deluca, the guy Seigle bumped off the West Point recruiting list with a well-timed letter to the superintendent three years earlier.

Knight later said Cornell and NYU "were the first good teams that a team of mine ever beat." Not *that* good. Cornell would be 15–9 and NYU 18–10 for the season. But Army would next face a genuine, poll-certified "good team" at the third annual Vanderbilt Invitational Tournament in Nashville.

Army would play Vandy in the first round on Friday, December 17. Fifteen-point favorites, Vandy was an undefeated Southeastern Conference powerhouse then ranked third by UPI and fifth by AP. Clyde Lee, an All-American 6′9¹⁄₂″ center, had led the team to an SEC championship the year before.

"Vanderbilt is a great basketball team," said Knight.

The trip to Nashville would begin on a bizarre note. First a driver ferrying some of the players the nine miles from the airport to Vanderbilt managed to get lost. Then, after the team had finally checked into the Holiday Inn on West End Avenue, things got really strange.

"We walked down the hall and this guy was sitting in a West Point gray jacket with pictures on his desk of West Pointers," recalled Jocko Mikula. "So you think he's affiliated. Turns out he wasn't."

But this guy, West Point's biggest fan or something, kept showing up. When the team went to dinner, the guy was there.

"Knight finally had him thrown out of the restaurant," said Jocko.

When the team played Vanderbilt, the guy was there.

"He was yelling in the stands and they finally threw him out of the arena," said Jocko.

And the guy was still there three years later.

"This is 1969—I'm assigned to the Mountain Ranger Camp and there were some West Pointers there," recalled Mikula. "They had rented a big house in Dahlonega, Georgia, and I went over there one time, rang the bell, and this guy, who got thrown out of the restaurant, was their butler. He was their butler. And he answered the door with a towel on his arm. He would shine their boots, press their clothes."

Now that's a fan—or something.

For the Vanderbilt game, Knight would start Silliman, Helkie, Murray, Mikula, and Danny Schrage, a solid, 6′1″, 190-pound junior from Breese, Illinois. Schrage was a jumping jack who Knight once described as "his best defensive player ever," and, as usual, defense was Knight's first concern.

The Vanderbilt team was built around All-American Lee, who had averaged twenty-seven points in the team's last three outings and had led the SEC in rebounding and scoring the year before. Stop Lee and you stop Vanderbilt, Knight figured.

The game plan called for Murray to "sag" off Jerry Southwood, a 6′2″, 190-pound guard to double-team Lee. Sounded like a good idea at the time. Southwood was billed as a "defensive specialist"—often code for "can't shoot"—and had averaged only 2.2 points the previous year, shooting just 34 percent. So leaving Southwood open to double up on Lee didn't seem to pose much of a risk. Nobody told Southwood.

Army got off to a bumpy start.

"I had three fouls on me in the first eight minutes," said Silliman.

So Silliman sat down and at the half Vandy led by eight, 36–28. Credit one of those points to a Knight technical, his first as a head coach. Seems Knight didn't think Southwood was really fouled while driving for a lay-up.

In the second half, Vandy would lead by as much as fourteen, but with 3:48 to go the score was 61–59. Then Vandy scored the next six, including four by Southwood, before sealing the 71–63 win with clutch foul shooting. The second half had ended up a tie, each team scoring thirty-five points.

Knight's game plan had worked well enough against Lee, who missed ten of thirteen shots and scored "only" eighteen points. But nobody could keep him off the boards, and he grabbed fifteen rebounds. As for Southwood, he scored twenty-three points on better than 50 percent shooting.

"Southwood hurt us bad," Knight told the *Nashville Banner*, in a gross understatement. "He had shot only eighteen times in four games so we decided to let him go and try to jam up the middle."

Southwood had realized immediately that not only was nobody guarding him, nobody was blocking him out. So he would add eight rebounds to his team-high scoring, and the junior guard's play would end up being the difference in the game. Knight had bet against Southwood and lost. More than a generation later Knight had another take.

"We get beat because Murray goes one for twelve. Murray had just all kinds of shots," Knight said with a hint of bitterness. "Got one basket and three free throws."

While Knight was sometimes off a point or two in his recollections, he was dead right on this one after thirty-five years. That's a long time to carry a grudge.

The next day in the newspapers, for the first time, reporters would remark on Knight's animated style on the sidelines.

"Perhaps the most frustrated person among the eighty-six hundred in Memorial Gymnasium Friday night was Army's coach Bob Knight," read the lead to Edgar Allen's story in the *Nashville Banner*.

Knight's continuing antics had led to a second technical, the last coming in the final seconds with the game out of reach. When reporters asked about the officiating, Knight "wouldn't broach the subject" wrote the *Banner*'s Allen; "had no comment," said *The Tennessean*.

"Vanderbilt Slips by Army," read one headline the next day. "The fifth-ranked Commodores fought off numerous Army rallies and finally beat the Cadets," the Associated Press reported. Army had given

Vanderbilt a scare and proven they could play with one of the best teams in the country.

In the consolation game the following night, Silliman was "virtually the whole show," reported *The Tennessean*, scoring thirty-two points, twenty in the first half, as Army beat Southern Methodist University 64–51 to take third place in the tourney. The team was now 4–2. Vandy would beat Western Kentucky 72–69 to take the title. Three MVPs were named: Silliman, Lee, and Clem Haskins from Western Kentucky. There should have been four.

"Haskins, Silliman, Lee tie for MVP, But Southwood Real Key in VIT," read *The Tennessean* headline. While Southwood had almost single-handedly scuttled Army's game plan from the opening tip, in the Western Kentucky game his heroics came in the second half.

"All Jerry did was score two key baskets, make a vital steal, and hold Haskins scoreless for the final ten minutes of the game," reported the *Banner*'s Dudley Green.

"Southwood did a job for us," said Vandy coach Roy Skinner.

———

That same day in *The Tennessean*, next to the picture of Jerry Southwood, Vanderbilt's "New Offensive Star," there was some big news from the Associated Press. "SEC Rivals Calmly Accept Negro Signing," read the headline.

"Southeastern Conference athletic officials accepted with little comment the signing yesterday of the first Negro to an SEC grant-in-aid. Nat Northington, Louisville Thomas Jefferson football tailback, was signed by the University of Kentucky."

With that the SEC became the last major conference to integrate.

"Georgia Coach Vince Dooley said he 'is not surprised,'" the article continued.

"'I am sure it is bound to come in the Southeastern Conference,' he said. 'But it would be hard to say how long it would be before there are Negro athletes at Georgia.'"

It would be five years.

"'Auburn has played against colored football players before so it won't be anything unusual,' said Coach Ralph Jordan. 'We might as well play against them on the Kentucky team as anywhere else.'"

"Florida Coach Ray Graves and Dooley both said their teams had opposed squads that included Negroes before so it would make no scheduling problems."

"'Right now we are not actively recruiting colored boys,' Graves said, 'but if a qualified one comes up we will offer an athletic grant-in-aid. We have nothing against it.'"

A "qualified one" first came up in 1968.

"Alabama and Mississippi officials could not be reached for comment."

Alabama and Mississippi State would find a "qualifier" in 1969, the University of Mississippi in 1970.

The recruitment of black athletes in the SEC was another step toward ending a long history of discrimination by the league. Early on, as indicated in the Associated Press story, many SEC schools not only would not recruit blacks, they wouldn't play against a team that did. While at most schools this was an unwritten rule, in the mid-fifties legislators in both Louisiana and Mississippi had passed laws that prohibited state colleges from competing against schools fielding "Negro players" to avoid, as one newspaper reporter would put it, "the switch-blade society that integration spawns." As a result, SEC basketball champion Mississippi State had turned down bids to the NCAA Tournament in 1959, 1961, and 1962. Finally, in 1963, Mississippi State Coach Babe McCarthy had had enough, and the team managed "to sneak out of town in the middle of the night" just ahead of an injunction. In the game at East Lansing, Michigan, Mississippi State would lose to eventual NCAA champion Loyola of Chicago, a team that started four "Negroes." That starting lineup violated another one of those "unwritten rules," this one prevalent north of the Mason-Dixon Line, where the discrimination was more subtle. The rule said that a team would "start no more than two African Americans at home, or three on the road."

It would be almost thirty years before Mississippi State again made it into the NCAA tournament. "When it did, in 1991," reported author Frank Fitzpatrick in *And the Walls Came Tumbling Down,* "ten of its thirteen players were black."

For the record, Bob Knight recruited the first black basketball player to West Point in 1964.

"Tommy Martin was a black cadet in our class," recalled Mike Noonan. "He never made the varsity, but he was recruited."

Technically, West Point had lifted the ban on black intercollegiate athletic competition in the early fifties. But unless the black athletes were "passing" or absent on picture day, a quick perusal of team photographs from 1965–66 demonstrates that a decade and a half later, Academy coaches still weren't exactly busting their asses to recruit African Americans. At a time when, for example, around six out of ten major-college basketball teams included at least one black player, there were no blacks pictured on the West Point basketball or football teams, only one on the baseball team, and two on the track team.

"West Point was trying to increase the minority representation at the Academy," said Athletic Director Ray Murphy of the era. "And that applied to athletes and non-athletes alike."

Maybe so, but minority recruitment was obviously not a high priority in those days before affirmative action. Flipping through the 1966 *Howitzer* (yes, the West Point annual is named after an artillery piece), black faces are hard to find. For example, there are only three black cadets in the Class of 1966. There are no black tactical officers pictured, no black professors or instructors, and no blacks in the physical education department. By today's standards this seems astonishing. West Point was then as now a showcase for the United States Army, an institution that President Harry Truman had ordered integrated in 1948.

Not that African Americans were turning down a flood of offers from other institutions across the country. Despite the Supreme Court–ordered desegregation in 1954, resistance to integration continued to be fierce in the mid-sixties. So much so that Congress had been forced to pass the

Civil Rights Act in 1964 and the Voting Rights Act in 1965 in another attempt to guarantee rights that African Americans supposedly had been granted by a pair of Constitutional amendments dating from the Civil War era. So now in the mid-sixties, a hundred years down the road, African American "firsts" that should have had nineteenth-century datelines were popping up all over the social landscape.

———————

Coming out of the Vanderbilt Invitational Tournament, Army would next face Louisville, where two of the first three black players ever recruited by the school were still on the squad. Louisville was about a four-hour drive up the road from Nashville, but instead of loading up the bus and heading out, the team was flown back to West Point to catch a couple of sessions of civil engineering, history of the military art, and mechanics of solids before turning around and flying back to Kentucky. By the time the team reached Freedom Hall in Louisville on December 22, the players were suffering from jet lag and a second malady unique to the West Point athlete.

Bob Knight started his head coaching career with players whose schooling included hand-to-hand combat and exposure to tear gas. In comparison, his practices were a welcome relief.

All photos courtesy of the United States Military Academy unless otherwise indicated.

"Scary guy" Col. Robert M. Tarbox (right), the head of Beast Barracks. "Just thinking of the guy makes me shudder" one cadet said years later.

New cadets learn how to salute properly. The author is first from the left in the deep background, standing at attention.

Bob Knight and Tates Locke, the head coach when Knight arrived at West Point.

The 1965–66 West Point basketball team. Jack Isenhour kneels at far right.

Coach Knight instructs his team before a game.

Coach Knight stands with future Duke coaching great Mike Krzyzewski, a point guard on the plebe team during Knight's first year as head coach.

Forward/center Bill Helkie was at his best in the 1966 NIT, scoring a then-season-high 27 points in one game and opening the next shooting 11-for-12 on his way to a new career high of 34.

All-American forward Mike Silliman, who would go on to captain the 1968 Olympic basketball team.

Forward Billy Schutsky poses with Coach Knight.

Mike Silliman, on crutches after tearing ligaments and cartilage in his knee, is honored at halftime of the Navy game for his outstanding career.

Forward Mike Noonan ties up Vanderbilt's Clyde Lee.

Guard/forward Eddie Jordan
puts up a shot against Navy.

The (Louisville) Courier-Journal

Mike Silliman drives around Louisville's Wes Unseld, two
former Kentucky "Mr. Basketballs" going head-to-head.

Norvelle Kennedy/Texas Tech University

Texas Tech fans cheer the arrival of Coach Knight in 2001.

Knight speaks to the crowd at Texas Tech.

Norvelle Kennedy/Texas Tech University

Chapter 19

Frightful Shoulders

At West Point early on, it was not just the gray stone walls and strict regimentation that brought to mind a monastery. Beginning with the reign of Sylvanius Thayer in the 1800s and continuing for more than a century, the only time in four years cadets were allowed to leave the Academy was for a ten-week "furlough" following their sophomore year. While this forced, almost monastic seclusion was long gone by the mid-sixties, the tendency remained, and, by the standards of the day, cadets still didn't get out much. They were allowed only a month off in summer, a couple of weeks at Christmas, and a few days at spring break. Upper-classmen who had earned "privileges" were also allowed a weekend off here and there. So if a cadet was not from the greater New England area, the only time he was able to go home was during those Christmas and summer vacations. Then there was the basketball team.

While the rest of the Corps went home to mama at Christmas, the 1965 basketball schedule called for the team to play the Louisville Cardinals on Wednesday, December 22, then return to West Point for practice on Sunday the twenty-sixth before beginning play in the Holiday Festival at Madison Square Garden on Monday the twenty-seventh. That left only three "Honey-I-shrunk-the-vacation" days for players to celebrate Christmas with family and friends. So when the team got to Louisville, the players' minds were more on those precious three days off than on the task at hand. It was a textbook case of the "Christmas doldrums," a unique West Point affliction.

"Everybody was thinkin' 'Let's get done with this game and get on a plane,'" said Mike Silliman. "'Let's go home for three or four days.'"

"A lot of cadets go on Christmas break a little earlier in their minds," said Billy Schutsky. "So everybody is thinking warm and fuzzy about Christmas."

The game was billed as Silliman versus Unseld. That's Wes Unseld, an early black recruit at the University of Louisville, who a generation later would be honored as one of the NBA's top fifty players. The two hometown phenoms had a lot in common.

After Silliman's St. Xavier team had beaten Unseld's Seneca on the way to a state high school championship in 1962, Unseld and company had won the championship two years in a row. There were other similarities. Both played center, both had been named Kentucky "Mr. Basketball," both were high school All-Americans, and both had led their college freshman teams to undefeated seasons.

The matchup had the Cardinals expecting their biggest crowd of the season. Those expectations were met as 13,010 showed up to see a game played in the midst of a thirty-hour cease-fire in Vietnam.

At 6'7" and 240 pounds, Unseld was bigger than the 6'6", 230-pound Silliman.

"He was huge," said Billy Platt.

He was also a better jumper. Bill Helkie saw that as a good thing.

"Unseld jumped so high it took away from his speed," said Helkie. "It took him so long to come down."

"Unseld wasn't all that tall," recalled another player, "but God he was wide. The man had frightful shoulders."

Whether it was the exhausting travel schedule or the Christmas doldrums, the team was not ready to play. Army was down by ten within five minutes and by thirteen at the half. During one stretch Louisville would outscore Army 21–5. Army would lose the rebounding battle 47–29.

"Just got hammered," recalled Knight.

Silliman was the one player not skating, and he scored thirty of the team's points on 50 percent shooting in the 84–56 loss. The rest of the team shot 27 percent. The two other Army scorers, Helkie and Schutsky, combined for four. Murray went one for eight.

Knight would end up clearing the bench, giving Heiner another chance to run the offense.

"I ended up hittin' four shots at garbage time," said Heiner, "and I ended up second high scorer for us."

The twenty-eight-point drubbing would be the third-worst loss in Knight's six-year career at Army.

"Wes was just strong," said Silliman.

"I remember going up for a rebound against Unseld," said Billy Schutsky. "I came down, I had like half of his arm underneath my fingernails with blood and everything and the guy doesn't even look down. He didn't even know it happened. I went along and I said, 'Holy cow! This guy is like Superman.'"

"We were just flat," said Silliman.

In the head-to-head matchup, Unseld led all rebounders with eighteen. Silliman got only half that but outscored Wes thirty to twenty. Wes had seven assists. Mike, two. The battle of the centers was a wash.

When the interminable game finally ended, an unhappy Bob Knight continued laying the foundation for his temperamental stereotype.

According to a local newspaper, the "disgruntled" coach placed the locker room "off limits" and wouldn't speak to reporters for twenty minutes after the game.

That night the cadets slipped out of Louisville for their three-day Christmas vacation.

———◆———

Bob Knight called Paul Heiner back to West Point early, and Paul and his dad drove down from Schnectady the day after Christmas.

"He and [coach] Mike Schuler took me into the field house—I was the only kid on campus—and we spent about three or four hours," recalled Heiner. "He had me shooting from all these spots on the floor."

"We were lookin' for a guard that could shoot," said Knight.

In Army's first seven games, Knight had started five different guard combinations. In game four against Cornell, although there were six true guards on the team, Knight had switched forward Murray to the guard position for good. Since then he had been looking for someone to complement Murray: someone who could handle the ball, score a little bit, play defense.

While Jocko Mikula had started six of the first seven games, three opposite Murray, Knight had decided that "Jocko was slow and he wasn't a real good shooter." Knight had tried Bobby Seigle—"a talkin' machine," as trainer Jim Wallace described him—pairing him with both Mikula and Murray. Seigle was the best ball handler on the team, but he couldn't shoot and at 5′ 11″ was just too small. Two other guards had gotten a shot, but it hadn't worked out.

"Everybody played the other guard," said Knight.

Well, almost everybody. After being embarrassed at Louisville, Knight decided to start Paul Heiner for the first time. While there were, shall we say, "maturity" issues, Heiner "was a very good athlete," said Knight. "He was a hell of a jumper. Quick. And he could shoot the ball."

To no one's surprise, Heiner agreed. "I could shoot the ball," he said. "We were really struggling to get points. Silliman got points. Helkie got points. But we didn't score very much."

So Paul Heiner would closet his trademark smirk in time to start against Villanova in Knight's "dream come true" first game as a head coach at Madison Square Garden.

"When I was a kid in Ohio I used to be able to get Garden games on the radio," said Knight. "I'd lie in bed and listen to those games, and I'd tell myself I'd be there one day."

"There wasn't anything that would have surpassed the feeling of going into Madison Square Garden taking a team," said Knight. "The only thing that would have been better than that was to go to Madison Square Garden and win."

And win they did, routing the Villanova Wildcats 89–68 in Knight's first Madison Square Garden victory. While future NBA star Bill Melchionni would gain entrance to the thousand-point club with a thirty-point shooting exhibition, the graduation-depleted Wildcats proved to be a one-trick pony. Silliman scored twenty-seven and Helkie and Schutsky would get back on track with twenty-two and seventeen respectively. New starter Paul Heiner chipped in four.

"Villanova was playing that matchup zone against us," said Knight. "We handled it extremely well, obviously, to score eighty-nine points in the game."

At least nine of Helkie's twenty-two would come off of three-point plays. There was no three-point line in those days, of course, and a player made a "three-point play" by being fouled while making a basket and hitting the ensuing free throw. Helkie's trifectas were no accident.

Surrounded underneath the basket by hulking defenders, a player's natural inclination is to avoid the defense by falling away or ad-libbing some kind of squirrelly shot that has little chance of being blocked and, in most cases, an equally slim chance of going in. Knight had a better way. At Army, players trapped under the basket were taught not to avoid, but to go up through defenders. The worst thing that could happen was the bad guys would collect another foul, and the shooter would have a chance at two free throws. It was another small step in the game's evolution to a full-tilt contact sport.

Villanova had been overwhelmed by Army's "customary hustle and methodical efficiency," as Norm Miller would phrase it in the *Daily News*, "New York's Picture Newspaper." Among the pictures on the sports page that day, a shot of Army's Jack Isenhour making a lay-up. This one basket alone would better the strikingly handsome guard's 1.6 average by four-tenths of a point.

When the Villanova game ended, Knight would learn a valuable lesson from Wildcat mentor Jack Kraft, a veteran coach Knight both liked and respected.

"We're walkin' off the floor," recalled Knight, "and Jack said, 'You're just a young guy, you wanta be careful not to run the score up on people like you did on us.'"

"Well, they'd just beaten Scranton by about fifty, like the game before they played us," continued Knight. "That was kinda interesting."

Next up was Boston College, which had overwhelmed Colorado 86–64 in the first round of the tournament. There was bad blood between Army and Boston College on two accounts. First, Knight made no attempt to hide his disdain for the BC coach, later saying he "never really, y'know, cared for Cousy." Yes, that was "Houdini of the Hardwood" Bob Cousy, the legendary Boston Celtic playmaker who at the time was a role model for every guard playing the game both at home and abroad.

"My biggest thrill was getting to meet Cousy," Army player Billy Platt would say a generation later.

The second beef: in a preseason scrimmage at West Point—even without Mike Silliman, who was still recovering from his appendectomy—Army had embarrassed the Eagles.

"We just killed them. Buried them," said Knight.

Boston College had asked for it.

"See Cousy had a guy named Jack McGee who was assistant coach," said Knight. "And he called me to come down and scrimmage us because we could put 'em up in the visiting team barracks and feed 'em."

All gratis, of course. The scrimmage was planned for a Saturday in late November.

"McGee calls me like on a Wednesday and Cousy doesn't want to come down and I really got pissed off," said Knight. "I said, 'Goddamnit we have a lotta schools that'll come in here and scrimmage cause it doesn't cost you anything—we feed you, we house you, we scrimmage, it's a great thing. Now you took one of those scrimmages. Now who the hell am I gonna get now?' So I really made 'em come down which worked to our disadvantage when we played 'em in the Holiday Festival."

The scrimmage had started out as a low-key, casual affair: just two teams trying to get in some work against unfamiliar faces. Sure Cousy seemed "a little aloof," as one awestruck Army player put it, and the coaches were only speaking through intermediaries, but, hey, the scoreboard wasn't even on.

"Then all of a sudden, Cousy lets out, 'We're only eight points down,'" recalled Dick Murray. "Cousy apparently was really playin' this thing to win."

Nothing gets a competitor going like keeping score, and it was "who let the dogs out?" from there on in.

"We got really fired up as a result of that," said Murray.

Bob Cousy tells a different story. "We started scrimmaging, and within ten minutes, it was mayhem," wrote Cousy in *On the Celtic Mystique.* "I remember saying to my guys, 'Scratch this one. Just protect yourself.'"

How rough did it get? Cousy claims the coaches spent the next ninety minutes breaking up fights. The scrimmage got so hot that Knight called on an "enforcer" named Isenhour to punish a BC player Knight had decided was a cheap-shot artist. Isenhour's remedy? Another cheap shot.

"I don't know what the score would have been," said Knight, "but we had to beat them by twenty-something. And I mean we just dominated them."

By the time the forced scrimmage was over, Knight and his charges had managed to piss off Bob Cousy and the entire BC squad. They would pay for it. Fast forward to December 28 and Army's second game of the Holiday Festival.

The Army–Boston College game would be close, tied nine times, the last at 71–71 with 6:30 remaining. But after that, it was BC who would do the dominating. In the next four minutes or so, the squad would go on a 14–6 run, taking an eight-point lead and eventually winning by a score of 92–85. Eagles star John Austin, who had been held without a field goal during the first twenty-five minutes of the game, would end up scoring twelve of the Eagles last twenty-one points as BC pulled away. Silliman got twenty-nine and Murray sixteen. Helkie, on an off night, recalls getting four points and four fouls during four minutes of play. Heiner got two in his second start.

Knight blamed the loss on the scrimmage.

"Had we not scrimmaged Boston College earlier in the year," said Knight, "I don't think there's any way we could have lost."

Knight also singled out Murray for a special ass chewing.

"I was not performing as he expected me as a captain," said Murray. "I gave him some lip back. That was about the only time that I said some things back to him that I probably shouldn't have said."

Following the game, the New York image makers would make a small addition to the Bob Knight résumé.

"Bob Knight, Army's first-year head coach, was obviously upset by some of the calls," wrote the *New York Times'* Gordon S. White, Jr. of "a struggle that had players and coaches angry with officials."

Norm Miller of the *Daily News* didn't mention Knight specifically, but observed that "there were many who felt the Cadets didn't get the best of the officiating."

Seigle was one of them.

"Bobby Seigle, one of Army's little scramblers on the court, yelled at Jim Lennon, an official, and stood toe-to-toe with Lennon *a la* [baseball bad boy] Leo Durocher after one call against Army," said the *Times.*

Seigle's uncharacteristic outburst helped feed the Army stereotype. The New York press had been watching the evolution of the West Point style of basketball for two years in the NIT and now the Holiday Festival. Not that they knew what they were seeing.

The sportswriters had filled their quivers with stock words and phrases: words like "ragged" and "sloppy," "scrappy" and "stamina"; and phrases like "rough and tumble" and "hustle and determination." There were also words that applied in the negative, like "finesse" and "talent."

So the *Herald Tribune* would describe the Army-BC game as "ragged, even sloppy" as the Eagles "with infinitely more finesse, were harassed by the hustle and determination of the Cadets who neither asked for anything nor gave anything."

Meanwhile the *Daily News* described a "scrappy Army" that "hung in there on sheer determination and stamina in the final minutes before yielding to BC's talent." (Funny Army didn't "yield" to BC's "talent" while running their asses out of the gym at West Point a month before.) "There is more muscle per square foot of Army player than of any team in the country," continued the *News.* "There is also more heart."

Add to all the stock words and phrases the overarching thesis that the team had more determination than talent, and you had the makings of a stereotype that would follow Knight teams throughout his six-year run at Army.

It was all a myth, of course.

In that first year the team had three starters, Silliman, Helkie, and Schutsky, who would make one All-American team or another in their careers. And because Knight and his assistants, as Knight put it, "worked harder at recruiting than anybody ever in college basketball worked at recruiting," five of the coach's six West Point teams would have a current or future All-American on the roster. Those kinds of individual honors presumably aren't awarded for mere "determination and stamina." Perhaps there was a prejudice against Army's rugged style, a prejudice against Bobby Ball, in an era when finesse was equated with true basketball talent, and a player who played the game as hard as the rules allowed, who mixed it up, was obviously just a guy trying to stay in shape until the start of spring practice. Sportswriters of the day were attuned to finesse, a quality not found in a Bob Knight team. A player who wasn't willing to bowl over a couple of people diving for a loose ball, commit a felony box out, and offer his body up as a human sacrifice while taking a charge from a man who outweighed him by forty pounds, would simply not play. In the vernacular of Bobby Ball, "finesse" was a word reserved for sissies. While the quintessential Bob Knight player would have the *skills* of a finesse player, he had the heart of a linebacker.

That was the essence of Bobby Ball, this new way of playing the game, and the befuddled sportswriters didn't know quite what to make of it.

Chapter 20

Scramble Them Brains!

Army would take on Illinois in the consolation game of the Holiday Festival. At stake was a third-place finish. To win, Army had to stop 6′ 7″ Illinois sophomore Rich Jones, who had scored sixty-three points in the first two games of the tournament, and senior guard Don Freeman, who had scored thirty-three against Georgetown in the opening round. Silliman would guard Jones; Schrage, Freeman.

While junior Danny Schrage had started two earlier games, Knight had hesitated to go with him because Danny just couldn't score, getting only five points combined in two previous starts.

"Danny's shot—Danny was like he had boxing gloves on," said Dick Murray.

How bad a shooter was he? It was Schrage's shooting that had led to the earliest Knight "choking" incident on record. According to author Joan Mellen, Schrage had snagged a rebound during some unspecified game and then, predictably, shot and missed a wide-open jump shot from about twelve feet. Knight called a time-out and grabbed Danny by the throat.

"Someday do you want to be a general?" Knight asked.

"Yes sir," replied Schrage.

"You've got no chance of being a goddamn second lieutenant if you shoot that son of a bitch one more time," said Knight.

In the Illinois game, "a leech-like defense was Army's chief weapon" wrote the *Herald Tribune*'s Irving T. Marsh as the Illini went scoreless for the first six minutes. Army jumped out to an 8–1 lead and led the rest of the way, winning 78–69. Silliman scored twenty-six, Schutsky twenty, Helkie seventeen.

The *Tribune* described the win over "potent Illinois" as "something of a surprise." The *Daily News* called it an "upset."

While Illinois's Don Freeman would end up with thirty, Knight would still praise Schrage for holding the 6′ 3″ senior to just five baskets in the first half. Silliman had better luck on Rich Jones, who got only nine points on three-of-fourteen shooting and called it "the poorest game of my life."

"The fine job that Silliman did on Rich Jones around the basket made the big difference," said Knight following his first win over a Big Ten team.

"I was concentrating on my defense against Jones," said Silliman. "I was there to keep him off the boards."

"One of these nights we'll do better than third," said Knight. True. But not at Army. At Indiana, where Knight would win the tourney fourteen years later.

Ho hum. Oh, did I mention the chair?

"There was this guy sittin' behind the bench," said Bob Kinney, then on the West Point sports information staff. "He had obviously had too much to drink and he went—got up—to go to the men's room."

"And there was a call that didn't go our way," continued Kinney, "and Bob turned around and he was looking for something to kick. And he kicked that guy's chair. Reduced it to a pile of kindling, and the guy staggered back and looked at where he was sittin' and wondered what had happened. Then just walked away because there was no chair left to sit in. And then he—Bob—was upset, 'cause he had, uh—his wing-tip shoes, he had scraped 'em."

The only thing missing from this tale was the "Once upon a time." Not that the story wasn't true. It was just that, like a lot of "Bob Knight stories," it had long since been clothed in the raiment of mythology.

Kinney remembers the incident as happening during the Illinois game. Maybe, but that game was never in doubt, and it seems more likely that, if it happened at the Holiday Festival at all, it probably occurred during the Boston College game, where even the *Daily News* admitted the officiating sucked and Knight was described as "obviously upset" by the staid *New York Times.*

In his bio, *Knight Fall,* Phil Berger says it did happen during the BC game. Bob Cousy seconds that in *Cousy on the Celtic Mystique,* writing that Knight "kicked over the entire bench" into the laps of "all that Army brass sitting behind him." Berger claims it cost Knight a technical. Maybe so, but neither the chair kick nor a technical is mentioned in game accounts the next day in either the *New York Times,* the *Herald Tribune,* or the *Daily News.*

This story is one of two circa 1965–66 Knight chair-abuse tales going around. The other story claims the first chair thrashing came at the NIT in March when, in team manager Brian Ashbaugh's version, a ref made a bad call and Knight "kicked the chair and made toothpicks out of it." In Knight pal Rich Cardillo's telling, the chair belonged to the Garden announcer. In another account, it's timekeeper Feets Broudy's chair that was destroyed. But whether a chair was kicked at the Holiday Festival or the NIT or both, all the stories agree on one thing: Bob Knight took out his first chair at Madison Square Garden, the reigning palace of college basketball, during his rookie season as head coach.

As for Knight, he remembered nothing about a chair or chairs. Not that he didn't on occasion drop-kick one thing or another in the direction of the rafters: like a water cooler. In the days before Gatorade and individual water bottles, glass water coolers were placed down at the end of the bench along with a dispenser holding conical paper cups. And as Knight remembered the story, it was a water cooler, not a chair, that was the object of his wrath.

"I broke the water cooler, smashed the water cooler somewhere along the way," recalled Knight.

Picture a high kick, the envy of any Rockette, and a breaking wave of drinking water carrying a flotsam of white paper cups.

"I don't really think a chair had anything to do with it," said Knight, "unless I kicked a chair and it hit the water cooler."

And when did this happen?

"It was at the NIT, actually," said Knight.

The reason it's impossible to nail down the exact game when Knight misbehaved is that newspapers of the day made no mention of it. That's hard to believe today when the sports media tend to get absolutely over-wrought about any behavior they regard as "outside the game."

The criteria for what's "outside the game" and therefore unaccept-able is easy for players: it's either within the rules or it's not. For coaches, there are no clear guidelines. Yelling at officials is okay up to a point. You can even throw in a little profanity. Log that under "passion, under-standable." Ditto stomping around, flailing the air, ranting at players. But at some point a coach's antics cross over into a red zone defined by officials and sportswriters. The behavior then inspires the same kind of newspaper/talk-show outrage as Shaquille O'Neal throwing a punch or Roger Clemens sidearming a splintered bat shard in the general direc-tion of a hitter. Now that was a teachable moment.

The setting was Yankee Stadium, the second game of the 2000 World Series. Yankee pitcher Clemens was facing Mets batter Mike Piazza. The two had a history. Back in July, Clemens had beaned Piazza, knocking him unconscious, during a totally meaningless All-Star game. Now in this, their next meeting, Clemens sawed off Piazza's bat with his fourth pitch, and a big chunk of it ended up on the mound. Clemens fielded the bat remnant, slung a two-hopper across the base path in front of Piazza, and the rest is history. Oh the ink, the ink!

"Gettin' Ugly," proclaimed the *New York Post* headline.

"Unsportsmanlike conduct?" asked *Baseball Weekly*.

"A weird Tyson moment," the *Daily News* called it.

That October there was much discussion as to Clemens's intent. Was he actually trying to hit Piazza with the tossed bat shard? There had been no such discussion of the beaning incident back in July since then Clemens's intent was clear. He had hurled a fastball at Piazza's head to convince him that backing off the plate might be prudent. Hit him, don't hit him, "don't matter." Piazza ended up in the hospital with a concussion.

A caller on one of those ubiquitous sports talk shows pointed out that in baseball hitting people is "just part of the game." In fact, it's so much a part that Major League Baseball actually maintains stats on hit batters. "Hit by pitch" (HBP), they call it, and Clemens made the top twenty in 2000, hitting ten. The leader hit eighteen.

While throwing balls at batters may be acceptable, tossing bat shards ain't. And while Clemens's off-target, two-hopper posed substantially less risk than a fastball thrown at somebody's head, it was "outside the game" and woke up fans and reporters alike to the intensity of what was happening on the field.

Welcome to big-time competition.

"I'm serious about it," said Clemens.

You would think that about a man willing to scramble an opponent's brains to win a baseball game.

"Physically, I'm going to try to beat you," Clemens told reporters in a news conference before the Piazza incident at the World Series game. "Mentally, I'm going to try to beat you. Emotionally, I'm going to try to beat you."

So there's not much left when Clemens is done. Normally that kind of raw competitive fervor is masked by everyday sports parlance: a "sack," a "hard foul," a "brushback pitch." But Clemens throws a bat shard, Shaq throws a punch, Knight smashes a chair, and suddenly there's an interruption in the sports-time continuum, giving face and voice to that ugly, carnivorous, fastball-to-the-head competitiveness that is at the very heart of big-time sports. The "harnessed rage" players talk about is set free to scamper across the scowling faces of Bob Knight and Shaquille O'Neal and Roger Clemens. They are possessed, and only wins can exorcise the demons.

Oh, the horror! The horror!

Maybe that's what was in the back of Mel Nowell's mind in 1982. That was the year Nowell told *Sport* magazine that while Knight, his old Ohio State teammate, was the best coach in the country, "I would not send my son to play for him."

That sentiment had legs and eventually evolved into the now famous question: "Would you want your son to play for Bob Knight?" Opposing recruiters loved that one. But that's never been the real question for all those doting parents out there. The real question for the moms and dads of America: "Do you want your son to become the kind of kid who's willing to throw a fastball at the head of somebody else's son to win a baseball game?" If so, Bob Knight's your man. Scramble them brains! For that's what it means to play competitive sports at the major-college level, where every competitor in every sport on every court, rink, track, and playing field in America is willing to deliver their sport's equivalent of a fastball to the head. That's what being a "great competitor" is all about. Wanta play for fun? Go to the YMCA. Some people, a lot of them on campus, believe this competition thing is a problem to be solved. Others, a lot of them on basketball courts, disagree. Take Bob Knight.

"I don't think people who are great competitors have a problem," said Knight. "If somebody wants to say you have a problem because you compete too much, too hard, then I think that's a pretty good recommendation."

And when spectators see Roger Clemens throw a bat shard or Knight take on a chair, they are getting a glimpse of the intensity hiding just beneath the surface in every "great competitor." And while the resultant behavior may fall outside the rules of the game, it is dead center of the emotional context of what is actually happening on the field of play: the choreographed violence, the harnessed rage.

So next time you see Bob and Roger doing their thing, remember: it's not Clemens and Knight who are ugly. It's the competition.

Chapter 21

Long-Ball Hitter

When the Holiday Festival ended, Madison Square Garden may or may not have been down one wooden chair and up a pile of kindling, but one thing was not in doubt. Army was a disappointing 6–4, three of those losses coming with superstar Mike Silliman in the lineup. While Mike had served out his sentence for the drunken rampage, had fully recovered from his appendectomy, and was scoring twenty-six points per game, the team as a whole was not living up to its potential. The good news was Army had played only three games at home and five of the next seven would be at the Academy. The long road trip had been enough to make even the butt-ugly field house look good.

Over the next seven games the team's record would improve as it faced the soft part of the schedule. Against these mostly familiar New England teams, Army's combined record over the preceding five years had been 20–2. What's more, with end-of-semester exams coming up, the games would be spread out over thirty-four days, giving players plenty of time to rest and, oh yeah, study.

After a week off, Army "coasted to a 64–52 victory over Lehigh," reported the Associated Press. With Army leading 43–18 at the half, subs played the rest of the way. Silliman led all scorers with twenty-one. The team had a tougher time on the parquet floor at Seton Hall in South Orange, New Jersey. The game was on the line, score tied at fifty-seven with fourteen seconds left, when Knight called a time-out.

Knight then drew up an out-of-bounds play the players had never seen before. A "Fred Taylor special," he called it, after his Ohio State coach. Time-out over, Murray took the ball out of bounds at half court. The other four players lined up on the midcourt line. Mike Silliman was the third man back. Seton Hall took the bait, standing thigh to thigh with the Army squad. When Murray slapped the ball, three Army players broke left toward Seton Hall's basket. Meanwhile Silliman faked left and went right.

A real sucker play.

"It was everybody go one way and I went the other," said Silliman.

The man guarding Silliman fell for it, and Mike ended up wide open streaking toward the Army basket.

"I'm not saying I was a Bart Starr or anything," said Murray. "He was so wide open that I couldn't have missed him."

"I had about a four- or five-foot lead on this guy," said Silliman. "I caught the ball right there, right near the key or right past the key, and laid it in and we beat 'em by two."

The final score was 59–57. Mike had scored twenty, setting a new West Point career scoring record at 1,202 with more than half the regular season still ahead of him.

For Knight it was *deja vu* all over again.

"I think I made a pass very similar to that in a game where [Jerry] Lucas got a bucket to set the Big Ten scoring record," said Knight.

"We play Fordham this Saturday for our ninth win," Silliman would write home. "Practice has not been that good this week probably because most of us are getting stale and somewhat tired of it all. Final exams are causing some concern too among the boys."

Some were more concerned than others.

Academically, exactly half the team was at serious risk. The year before, all seven of these scholastically challenged "student athletes" had been ranked in the bottom 16 percent of their respective classes, and two had made the bottom one percent. For these seven, "Gloom Period" 1966 meant more than just bitter cold and gray, overcast skies.

Unlike most opponents on the January schedule, Fordham, a Jesuit school from the Bronx, posed a real threat. Army had lost two of the last three to the Rams, including a 60–53 loss the year before. But after a slow start, Silliman and Helkie would combine for forty-three in a 59–53 win. Heiner was starting to settle in at the other guard slot and was attracting some unwanted attention for his flamboyant style of play.

"Helkie wrote on the back of my sneaks, 'Hot Dog,'" said Heiner. "My left sneak had 'Hot.' My right had 'Dog.'"

Another week of exams and then a laugher against Colgate, the starters spending most of the game on the bench exhorting the subs to push the score over a hundred. They didn't quite manage. Army won 97–60 to make it five straight.

Then, at the end of January, the losses began to pile up. Not on the court, in the classroom.

"Times are bad. By the time you get this, I may be winging my way home on a beautiful DC-7," Isenhour wrote home.

It was an academic meltdown. Four players would be called off the practice floor after flunking exams, including starting guard Paul Heiner, Jocko Mikula, Towney Clarke, and Isenhour. But all was not lost. At West Point, they wouldn't just kick your ass out of there and be done with it. At West Point, they tightened the screws. Cadets who flunked the first round of exams were given a second chance, a so-called "turn-back exam," and if they failed that, a third chance, "a re-entrance exam" that offered a final opportunity to prove they were worthy.

"So now I have to study all this stuff over and take a new and better exam lasting four wonderful hours," Isenhour whined after flunking the first round of four exams in civil engineering. "I just sit here and break pencils. I am sure that I must be cracking up. That would be a blessed relief. I am so sick of all this."

With only ten players left on the squad, barely enough to scrimmage, Knight's decision in early January to combine practice with the plebes now seemed prescient. The idea was for the plebes, including a point guard named Mike Krzyzewski, to act as stand-ins for upcoming opponents. In an unintended side effect, varsity players who seldom got into games now couldn't even count on playing time in practice. After warm-ups, they would often spend the rest of practice just sitting in the bleachers.

"He started bringing those guys down and man, it's like you disappeared," recalled Billy Pratt.

That was one of the things Platt wanted to talk about when he asked for a meeting with Coach Knight. Platt, "the forgotten guard," was the only one of the six true guards on the squad who had not started even one game that season.

"I didn't feel I ever really got a chance," said Platt.

So Platt met with Knight and made his plea.

"I says, 'Coach, I just wanta play,'" recalled Platt. "I said, 'I probably love the game as much as anybody here.'"

"I've done everything you've ever asked and busted my rear and I'm not askin' to start," Platt told Knight. "I'd just like to get in occasionally."

Then Platt complained about spending most of practice sitting in the bleachers.

"It's killin' me," Platt said. "I can't take it."

Knight was not sympathetic.

"I got no encouragement from him," said Platt. "He just says, 'I'll see you tomorrow at practice or I won't see you.'"

Platt didn't show up the next day and, with that, became the first player in history to quit a Knight team.

Platt would soon go out for the track team.

"Billy, what are you doin?" Heiner asked him. "He says, 'Well at least this way I get out of it what I put into it.'"

With Platt gone and four "student-athletes" taking re-examinations, West Point now faced the risk of finishing the basketball season with only nine players. This looked like a job tailor-made for the dean of the academic board, Brigadier General John Jannarone. Known as "Long Ball Johnnie" for his baseball prowess as a cadet, Jannarone was a man who, according to his wife, was "always lookin' after the athletes."

"I knew he tried to help basketball, football, hockey—every kind of player," recalled wife Ann Jannarone.

As an example, Ann Jannarone cited her husband's interest in a "great baseball player" (who shall remain nameless) who had turned down an offer from a major league club before coming to West Point. A "terrible student," this blue-chip athlete was so far behind in chemistry his sophomore year that "he decided 'to heck with it,' he wouldn't even take the chemistry exam," said Ann Jannarone. "And then he'd get kicked out. Well, my husband called him and said, 'I never flunk out a long-ball hitter.'"

So the long-ball hitter took the chemistry exam and ended up "passing." It couldn't have hurt that General Jannarone, before his promotion to dean, had been head of the Department of Chemistry and Physics. The long-ball hitter would eventually graduate—barely, "fourth from the bottom of this class," said Ann Jannarone—before going on to a successful thirty-year career in the Army.

Of the four players at risk that January, only All-American linebacker Towney Clarke was definitely in the "long-ball hitter" category—and that for his football skills. Heiner and Mikula were on the fringe. As for Isenhour, he was well advised to keep the old slide rule limber. Would Jannarone step up?

When the re-exams were over in late January, Clarke, Mikula, and Isenhour had survived. But Clarke, who went on to get an MBA from Harvard, would quit the basketball team to devote more time to his studies. Heiner was not so lucky. In a double whammy, the politburo decided Paul was "deficient" in both English and social studies and sent him home. And just like that, Knight was back to looking for a second guard.

By the way, don't waste your tears on the "Hot Dog from Schenectady." A couple of years later Heiner would end up with a math degree from Plattsburgh State in upstate New York and would make All-Conference guard on a team where playing basketball "was a lot more fun."

What's more, the whole West Point experience had turned out to be "a home run" for Heiner. Not only had he satisfied his active-duty military obligation, effectively inoculating himself against "service" in the Vietnam War, he had built a foundation for a lucrative career.

"I had been introduced to the computer at West Point so that's the industry I got in," said Heiner. "I hit that friggin' thing on the ground floor."

Remember this was in the sixties.

After twenty years with General Electric, Heiner went out on his own and is now the CEO of his own software firm.

"So it all worked out for me," said Heiner with uncharacteristic understatement.

And as for Jannarone's involvement one way or the other? Knight still hasn't responded to that question. While the general obviously didn't help Heiner, Jocko remains convinced that he wouldn't have graduated without Jannarone's help.

"I don't know the details. I just know that if it weren't for him," said Jocko, "I would've been gone."

Mikula had reached that conclusion after being summoned to the office of his tactical officer, one of the scary guys, during his senior year.

"He says, 'You know you're gonna end up at the bottom of your class,'" recalled Jocko. "I said, 'Well, no, I'm not gonna be last in the class.'"

"So big fuckin' deal," said Jocko in so many words and then told the tac, "'I'm gonna graduate and I'm gonna be a good officer.' He says, 'The only reason you came here was to play basketball. Isn't that right?' I says, 'Yes sir.' And he leaped up from behind his desk and said, 'I'm gonna get your ass thrown out of here.'"

That was no idle threat. There were a dozen ways a determined scary guy could get a cadet tossed out. But it never happened. Jocko would graduate with the Class of 1967, and while he wasn't at the top of his class, he wasn't dead last either. All this, said Jocko, due the unseen hand of Brigadier General John R. Jannarone, the man who would never "flunk out a long-ball hitter."

—————◦•◦—————

In the Associated Press poll at the end of January 1966, Duke was ranked number one followed by Kentucky. Other ranked teams of interest included Jimmy Walker's Providence team, the winner of the Holiday Festival, at number three; Vanderbilt, which had moved up to number four; and, at number six, obscure Texas Western (later Texas El Paso), a team that would soon make history.

Chapter 22

Who's Silliman?

It was a little after four o'clock on a snowy January Wednesday, and West Point trainer Jim Wallace had to go to the hospital anyway.

"My wife had called me, my daughter had a sleigh-ride accident," said Wallace. "Went into a tree and split her lip open and all that; needed sutures."

The game had been under way for less than four minutes when Wallace rushed onto the floor, and now players from both teams were just standing around, Rutgers in red, Army in white. For the pole vaulter working out at the far end of the field house, it was hard to tell anything momentous was going on. Only a few cadets had slogged through the snow to watch the game, and bleachers that would seat around five thousand were all but empty. And without the sounds of cheering, the echoes of the bouncing ball and screeching shoes, there was little to attract the attention of the runners kicking up dust as they circled the cinder track in the cavernous building.

Empty bleachers were not unusual for these Wednesday afternoon games. At West Point, classes didn't let out until 3:15, and when a game started forty-five minutes later, there might be only a couple dozen cadets in the stands and then the rest would just, uh, dribble in, if they showed up at all. Attendance figures in the four hundreds were common. So for visiting teams like Rutgers, the atmosphere was more like a practice than a game.

"They'd come into this place and there's nobody there," said Neal Hughes.

"Track guys running around," said Jocko Mikula.

Two years before, Army had played a top-twenty Ohio University team in one of these Wednesday afternoon games.

"They were a good team," said Bobby Seigle. "They just never woke up to the fact this wasn't practice."

Seigle had a couple of friends on that team from his home state, and they questioned him after the 58–45 Army win.

"What are we doing playing at four o'clock in the afternoon?" Seigle recalled them asking.

"That's the advantage we get on you guys," Seigle replied. "You think it's nap time or something like that and we're ready to go."

Knight, in what he described as "a monumental chore," would eventually get the Wednesday afternoon games moved to Wednesday night.

But that would be years later.

Jim Wallace helped the injured player to the bench, and, as play resumed, he called in head trainer Ed Pillings for a second opinion. If there had been a crowd, the fans would have been hushed, stunned, dazed.

"I said to Ed, 'He's got a definite problem here,'" recalled Wallace. "'So we oughta get him to the doctor.'"

Pillings agreed.

Mike Silliman had been running down the floor, the trailer on a rare Army fast break.

"Nobody near him," recalled Bob Kinney.

Bill Helkie threw a pass in Mike's direction. It never got there.

"[I] planted my foot to make a turn and the part of the leg above the knee turned, but the bottom part didn't," said Silliman, "and I just felt something snap."

"I obviously came to a quick halt and tried to take a step and just knew something was wrong," continued Silliman.

"Couldn't straighten the leg nor could I put any pressure on it. Just couldn't go forward. Couldn't go."

Trainers Ed Pillings and Jim Wallace hovered over the best basketball player in West Point history. They both knew it was bad.

Pillings "looked at Mike and said, 'We gotta get him out of here,'" recalled Wallace.

"I'll call the team—one of the orthopods—and they can look at him," Wallace said and, after asking Pillings to cover for him, took Mike to the emergency room.

"The doctor looked at it and he said, 'You're gonna need an operation,'" recalled Silliman.

Silliman had torn both the cartilage and acruciate ligament in his left knee. Mike Silliman's college basketball career was over.

A couple of days later, doctors drilled a hole in Silliman's left femur, threaded the acruciate ligament through, and tied it in a knot so it wouldn't slip out. After the operation, the doctor told Silliman what he had done.

"I said, 'My goodness, that's the balance of my career,'" recalled Silliman. "'I'm not gonna play any more athletics.' And he said, 'Oh, no, you're gonna be fine. You'll be okay.'"

The doctor was right.

"I started first base, I think April 3, on the baseball team. I couldn't believe it," said Silliman.

Silliman would end his basketball career with 1,342 total points and 784 rebounds in only two and a half seasons, still good enough to rank seventh and fourth, respectively, all time. For the year he had averaged twenty-two points and eleven rebounds a game.

———————⇒•⇐———————

"Rutgers was pretty good," said Knight.

And as the game continued on that snowy Wednesday afternoon, it became clear that, without Silliman on the floor, the teams were evenly matched.

The 8–3 Scarlet Knights were led by Bobby Lloyd. Then averaging 26.6 a game, Lloyd remains the second all-time leading scorer in

Rutgers' history. Rutgers also had a fiery guard named Jim Valvano. "Mr. Defense" they called him. The team's biggest win had come against Princeton on the road, the same Princeton team that had blown out Army in the first game of the season. Of course, Army had been without Silliman in the opener. Just like they were on this day.

Army "led by as many as ten points twice in the second half," said the *New York Times,* and hung on to win 62–61. Bobby Lloyd led all scorers with thirty-three. Noonan got sixteen filling in for Silliman, and Helkie led the team with eighteen. Army was now a more than respectable 11–4, but with Mike Silliman gone nobody knew where the next win was coming from.

"My reaction to when Mike went down: there goes our season," recalled Dick Murray.

Nobody would have faulted the twenty-five-year-old Knight for having a few doubts himself. And while today Knight is just-another-day-at-the-office blasé about the loss of what he's called the best college player he ever coached, there is some evidence that, at the time, he was anything but nonchalant.

After getting the news about Silliman, Knight made his usual postgame call to then future Hall of Famer Clair Bee, the man he talked to "after every ball game, win or lose."

"I see him once a week too," Knight said at the time. "We usually manage to have lunch and talk a little more basketball."

Bee was among the first of a series of legendary coaches Knight would take on as mentors over the years. Men like St. John's Joe Lapchick and the University of California's Pete Newell.

Nearing seventy, Bee lived at nearby Cornwall on Hudson where he was director of athletics at the prep New York Military Academy. Bee followed the Army team, sometimes even slipping in to watch games without telling Knight. The coach had made his reputation a generation earlier while leading Long Island University to two undefeated seasons, two NIT titles, and one honorary Helms Foundation national championship (1939) before resigning in the early fifties after his players got caught up in the point-shaving scandals.

Today the late Bee continues to rank first among college coaches in overall winning percentage (82.6 percent) besting the likes of Adolph Rupp, John Wooden, and Dean Smith. This was the man the young Knight would turn to for advice when Mike Silliman went down.

"What am I going to do without Silliman?" Knight reportedly asked Bee.

"Who's Silliman?" Bee replied.

Bee's point, as the New York *Daily News* Mike Lupica wrote some thirty years later, was that "[t]he team that had Silliman as its star didn't exist anymore and Bee didn't want Knight to waste another minute worrying about it. The old man was telling Bob Knight to coach the team he had."

Yeah, but . . .

"I just returned from Buffalo, New York, where we played Canisius College (who?) and, believe it or not, they beat us," one player wrote home. "Two weeks ago there were fourteen members of the basketball team. We now have nine. We lost two starters among the five that are gone. One guy quit to run track. One was kicked off for failing academics. Mike Silliman tore the cartilage in his knee and won't play anymore. He was our All-American center. One fellow quit because he can't play and keep his grades up. Another guy is on the borderline. Nobody knows when or if he'll be back. Now you know why we were beaten. Times are bad for the Army team."

The final score at Canisius was 81–77 against a team Army had beaten by twenty-eight the year before. Maybe they are in denial, but nobody on the team remembered much about this game except sophomore guard Neal Hughes, and he probably would have been wiser to keep it to himself.

"The guy I was guarding scored thirty-seven," volunteered Hughes.

That turned out to be right. John Morrison made the Canisius record book with that performance, which is still tied for twentieth in the category of "single game scoring highs."

"If I'd held him to thirty, we would've probably won," added Hughes, who just wouldn't shut up.

Right again. Army wins by three if Hughes "holds" Morrison to thirty.

Hughes was also only one of two players to remember the blizzard, which turned out to be a good thing.

"There was a terrible, terrible snowstorm," recalled Hughes. "We took the bus back. It took us like forever, eight hours, to get back to West Point because all the highways were just clogged with snow."

The wide-ranging storm blanketed the whole East Coast and led to the cancellation of the Army–Bucknell game two days later. That gave Coach Knight exactly seven days to prepare for Penn State, a fourteen-point favorite. And as Al McGuire, the late Marquette coach, said of Bob Knight in the introduction to *A Season on the Brink:* "If he had a week to prepare for you, he would find a way to take away the things you did best."

"Give Bob time to prepare," continued McGuire, "and most often he would figure out a way to beat you."

Chapter 23

Roasted, Salted Pecans

It could have been a blizzard-induced snow blindness that spread to his brain following the eight-hour bus ride from Buffalo, or it could have been some manner of Gloom Period "hyster-thermia." Whatever it was, from the outside, Bob Knight's new starting lineup looked moronic. Danny Schrage, all of 6'1" of him, would take the place of the 6'6" Silliman. You remember Schrage. He was the jump-shot challenged, "defensive ace" who had last started against Illinois in the Holiday Festival. His job that night had been to shut down sharpshooter Don Freeman. Freeman ended up with thirty.

Then there was Knight's new starting guard, Jordan. Not Michael, Eddie, the other Jordan, a frail white kid who had played his high school ball at the YMCA, unable to make the team at Sidney Lanier High School—nickname "Poets"—in Montgomery, Alabama.

"Eddie was a tall string bean," said Dick Murray.

Why Eddie?

He had "played really well in the last three minutes of the Canisius game," said Knight.

Perfect.

First off, Jordan wasn't a guard, he was a forward. And not much of one.

"He got banged around a little bit," said Knight. "He wasn't effective as a rebounder, and he really wasn't a great ball handler."

Not that Jordan had handled it enough for anybody to notice. This walk-on had played in only six games all year, because at 6′3½″ and 165 pounds, "I wasn't strong enough to be inside."

"The other Jordan" was so thin that a PR guy had dubbed him "Sticks" although the team preferred "Fast Eddie," a name he'd earned not for hustling pool like the Paul Newman character in the movie *Hud*, but for out-sprinting everybody on the team.

And as for Jordan's defensive skills at his new position: "I could always be taken at any time by a real guard."

Looking at Knight's two new starters, it was hard to see how he expected to make up Silliman's twenty-two points and eleven rebounds. Schrage couldn't shoot and Jordan had twenty-five points for the year. And while Schrage was a good rebounder for a 6′1″ guy, Jordan had already proven he couldn't block out an opposing cheerleader. From the looks of this new, if not improved, starting lineup, Knight had just said "to hell with it" and was going to try a little of this and a little of that until this snake-bit, nightmare of a season was finally over.

"It was certainly a shock to me that he would start me at guard," said Jordan.

Knight asked assistant coach Mike Schuler to "show Jordan how to bring the ball up the court," a basic skill any real guard would have picked up during recess in grammar school.

"We worked every day like hell on his ball handling," said Knight.

"My technique was really just to get 'em moving one way and as soon as they start moving one way, switch over to the other way," said Jordan.

Oh Christ.

"We made a guard out of Eddie in a week," said Knight.

Sure.

A few days after "the other Jordan" was introduced to the crossover dribble, the game began at 8 P.M. on a cold West Point Saturday night. Still in contention for an at-large NCAA birth, the highly favored Penn State team was 11–3 and had made it to the NCAA tournament the year before, losing to Bill Bradley and his Final Four Princeton squad in the first round. Penn State's star was future All-American Carver Clinton, a

6′ 4″ black kid who had been forced to migrate nine hundred miles north from a place called Selma, Alabama, to play his college ball.

Army started the game with Danny Schrage jumping center while guard-of-the-moment Ed Jordan demurred, allowing Dick Murray, the other forward playing guard, the honor of bringing the ball up the floor.

"Not the strength I brought to it," admitted Jordan.

Jordan's strength, Knight figured, would be as a "rebounding guard." Usually that was an oxymoron. By training, guards didn't do a lot of rebounding. On offense, guards stayed back when the ball was shot so they could shut down any possible fast-break attempt by the other team. On defense, guards would get open on the wing and wait for one of the big guys to throw them the ball. For a true guard, this whole boxing-out, crashing-the-boards thing didn't come naturally. Then there was converted forward Eddie Jordan.

"He didn't have to block out anybody now," said Knight.

That gave Eddie a running start.

"I remember Eddie swooping down from the top of the key like a crane on a mission," recalled one player. "There would be a lot of commotion and then this skinny, curly-haired wraith would come out of the pack clutching the ball."

That would happen a game-high thirteen times in the Penn State game.

Meanwhile to chants of "Dee-fense! Dee-fense!" coming from twenty-eight-hundred screaming fans, mostly gray-clad cadets, Danny Schrage was putting the clamps on Carver Clinton.

"He held Carver Clinton of Penn State to one field goal," said Knight.

Clinton would score this first and last field goal 6:54 into the first half. But it was not just Carver Clinton who was having trouble with the Army defense.

"They were so desperate to get off shots, they were coming from near midcourt," said Bob Kinney from the West Point sports information office.

Sound like mega-hype from a PR guy? Here's the *New York Times* version: "Penn State became careless, shot from desperation distances of thirty and forty feet, missing all the time."

Forty feet. Let's see. That's about sixteen feet beyond the current NBA three-point line.

When the first twenty minutes were mercifully over, that one Carver Clinton bucket, the one that dropped through about seven minutes into the game, would be the last field goal Penn State scored in the half. The Nittany Lions had gone two for twenty-four, shooting only 8 percent, and trailed 24–7.

At the intermission, John Egli, Penn State's coach-turned-comedian, glanced up at that seven on the scoreboard and said, "It's good we made that extra point else we'd really be in trouble."

Meanwhile back on offense.

"Eddie Jordan, tall lanky kid, was in effect our point guard," said Bob Kinney.

"He had those long arms and he could stand out front on a zone and pass over the top," said Neal Hughes.

Jordan recalled hitting guys for lay-ups "three or four times in a row."

But Eddie wasn't just a passer. He could shoot well enough to keep the defense from dropping off him to clog up the passing lanes.

"I had a decent shot at the top of the key," said Jordan, "so they had to guard me."

The final score was 59–39. Army had thirty-nine rebounds, Penn State, eighteen. Billy Schutsky was the leading scorer with fifteen, two of those on technicals following a scuffle with a frustrated Carver Clinton. The second leading scorer was true guard Neal Hughes, another frail skinny guy, who poured in eleven straight points in the second half on 86-percent shooting.

"Just a tremendous game," said Bob Kinney.

Even the *New York Times* gushed, calling it "[o]ne of the most amazing basketball games of the current college season."

After a one-game letdown, Bobby Ball was back.

It had been the kind of game Bob Knight teams would become famous for over the years: the stifling defense, the intensity. So does the man himself look back and say of the Penn State rout: "Now that was a Bob Knight basketball game?"

"No. I'm not sure [stifling yawn] what all that means or entails," said Knight. "I just thought it was a game that was really based on how we planned to play the game, the planning that we put into it, and the defensive approach that we had, along with just how hard we played."

In other words, things went as planned.

And as for new starting guard Eddie Jordan, Knight's choice made him look like some kind of mad genius. A generation later, Jordan remained modest.

"There were few times when I showed any initiative. I went out there and did the things he told me to do," said Jordan. "I was basically an average player and he got everything out of me. I didn't have any great skills or anything."

Jordan was partly right. It would have been hard to find anyone on the team from one end of the bench to the other who didn't have more "talent" than Eddie Jordan, who couldn't beat him one-on-one. The big guys would out-muscle him, the little guys would out-quick him, and most could out-shoot him, out-defend him, and handle the ball better. But the game was not played one-on-one. And while Jordan may have had fewer skills, he was the better player because he was the missing ingredient, the guy who made everything work. And in a team game where the object is winning, not racking up style points, a new definition of what exactly constitutes "talent" may be long overdue.

"I've never picked this five or that five or anything, but whatever I would pick for a team, Eddie would be a part of it," said Knight thirty-four years later. "For what amounted to about a year and a half, Eddie was a helluva player. I mean a really good player."

And with that, Eddie Jordan, the perennial bench warmer, would join the ranks of superstars like Mike Silliman and Isiah Thomas.

Following the Penn State rout, Knight sent a telegram to Jordan's parents in Montgomery, "saying basically what a good job I had done," said Eddie.

That sold the Jordan elders and from then on they shipped Knight the same gift every Christmas.

"Mom would always send him roasted, salted pecans," said Jordan. "She was always a big Knight supporter. Of course, she wasn't there at practice."

Chapter 24

Bisons, Peacocks, Redmen

T he Bucknell Bisons came up from Lewisburg, Pennsylvania, on the Monday after the Penn State win to make up the snowed-out game from the week before. During warm-ups, second-year coach Don Smith stood at half court chatting it up with Knight.

"He was snickering that Penn State only scored thirty-nine points on us," said Murray.

Big mistake.

Knight took that as "a slam," said Murray, and back in the locker room, the "enraged" coach used it to fire up the team. The tactic worked.

"Army reeled off eleven straight points to take a 14–1 lead and it was over," reported the Associated Press. That one Bucknell point came 7:20 into the half, and when the game was over, no Bucknell player had scored more than two field goals. As for the final score, Bucknell ended up scoring one less point than Penn State, as Army "stampeded" the Bisons 84–38.

Four days later the Cadets "plucked" the Peacocks of St. Peters 64–58 in one of those four o'clock afternoon games. Schutsky scored a season-high twenty-eight on this team from his home state of New Jersey.

Army was now 14–5 and, with three games remaining in the regular season, still needed a couple of wins to guarantee an NIT bid. Boston

University and Navy didn't look to be much of a challenge, but the next game up, St. John's, was another story.

"I figured if we beat St. John's, we'd be in the NIT," said Knight.

St. John's was such a big game that Knight went in to see the athletic director, Colonel Ray Murphy, to ask for something that was unheard of at the time.

"We're trying to get into the NIT," Knight told Murphy, "and, uh, boy we gotta go to class Saturday morning—I don't know."

"So he set it up for us to go down to New York without going to class," continued Knight. "We would just rest all day, play the game that night."

So Murphy had crawled out on a limb for Knight and what did Knight do? He hacked that limb off right next to the trunk.

"Instead of leaving, I just took the team down to the field house," said Knight, "and we worked on preparation for the game."

Murphy found out, of course. West Point is a very small place.

"It was snowin' like hell and he came into the field house, got that big ole green Army overcoat on. 'What the hell are you doin' down here?' [asked Murphy]. I says, 'Well, I just figured if they were gonna get on your ass because we left, they could get on my ass because we prepared for the game.'"

"I said, 'Who the hell do we need to tell we're gonna do this?' and he said, 'Tell? Tell? We're not gonna tell anybody. And when they find out about it, it'll already be done.' He said, 'They can get my ass and then it'll be over with.'"

"Now that's why he was great," continued Knight. "Nobody was better than him that wanted to help you from the standpoint of winning that I've ever worked for."

How long ago was this? It was Lou Carnesecca's first year as head coach of St. John's, a program he would head off and on for twenty-four years before retiring in 1992. Carnesecca had replaced the legendary Joe Lapchick, a player for the Original Celtics, the ones from New York, back in the twenties. Coach Lapchick had gone out in style the year before, winning the 1965 NIT in his final game at St. John's. His team had beaten Army in the semis, and, as a measure of the respect Tates Locke held for the coach, win-happy Tates had told his players after the game that losing ain't so bad if you're losing to the likes of Joe Lapchick.

Knight was also a big fan. It was Lapchick who, according to John Feinstein in *A Season on the Brink,* advised Knight, "[I]f you want to be liked, don't coach."

Not that being liked was ever a Knight priority.

"I'd talk to him a lot," Knight said of Lapchick. "He always rooted like hell for us. See he had a son that was a West Point graduate."

After Lapchick died in 1970, his wife, reported Feinstein, pulled Knight aside at the funeral. "You know, you never played for Joe," she said, "but you should know you were always one of his favorite boys."

Because of the close ties between the coaches, the St. John's game always felt like a traditional rivalry. It wasn't. The schools had been playing each other regularly for only six years. But since St. John's was a fabled basketball school, beating the team from Jamaica, Queens, was a benchmark for a still-emerging Army program.

And Army was gaining. Coming into St. John's Alumni Hall that snowy February night in 1966, the Cadets had won two of the last three against the Redmen (whose nickname was changed to the "Red Storm" for obvious reasons in 1994), and the rivalry was such that the Academy had dispatched 450 cadets and a forty-five-man pep band to cheer on the squad.

Like most of the Army–St. John's games, it came down to the final minutes. While Army had led most of the way, the team was trailing 51–47 with 3:19 left. Knight called a time-out.

Years later Knight would remember little about this game except that "Murray might have missed a bunch of free throws."

Dick Murray's memory was a lot better. During the time-out, "Knight was going absolutely ballistic," he said.

The issue? While Army was outplaying—both out-shooting and out-rebounding—the Redmen, Murray couldn't buy a free throw, ending up two of seven for the night.

"He said words to the effect—in the huddle—'you lost this game for us,'" recalled Murray.

"The next minute, I scored two baskets," Murray continued. "So we tied the ball game up and then we came into the huddle and Knight was overjoyed."

This time St. John's had called the time-out. Lou Carnesecca's strategy: "freeze" the ball, pass it back and forth out front until the clock ran down and then try for a last shot. (There was no shot clock in those days.)

So St. John's froze the ball for more than two minutes and then Carnesecca called a final time-out with nineteen seconds left to set up a play for team captain, 6′ 6″ Bob McIntyre. While McIntyre, who was averaging twenty-one points, had made only three field goals up to that juncture, earlier in the year he had hit a last-second game winner against Georgetown. So St. John's hopes rested on McIntyre, and with ten seconds left, he made his move. The Army defense forced the play way outside, and it looked like the game was headed for overtime as McIntyre threw up a prayer, a fall-away jump shot from twenty-five feet.

Here's the play-by-play from *Daily News* sportswriter Red Foley.

"His shot was straight as two yards of pump water and it passed through the hoop as the final buzzer sounded," raved the colorful and politically incorrect Foley of the jumper that "sent 6,133 happy Redmen rooters to their teepees."

In a short article, Foley would variously describe the miracle shot as a "final arrow," "desperation flip," "clutch chuck," and, in an uninspired moment, "a twenty-five-foot jumper."

"If the Indians"—the ones on the TV westerns popular at the time—"used a freeze similar" to St. John's, wrote Foley, they "might just end up winning one before the final commercial."

"Played a hell of a game," Knight said of his squad a generation later, but on the night of February 12, 1966, he didn't share that sentiment with the team. Rather Knight was in the locker room "going absolutely bonkers," as Murray remembered it, or "acting like a wild Indian," as Foley might have phrased it, when Lou Carnesecca walked in. Carnesecca wanted to congratulate the Army squad for a great game. "You guys have a lot to be proud of," Murray recalled him saying.

Later Carnesecca graciously put in a good word with the press.

"This is without a doubt the toughest defensive club we have played all season," Carnesecca told the *New York Times*. "You can't count them out of the National Invitation Tournament."

After Carnesecca had left, Knight "went into one of his little tirades again," said Murray.

The point Murray was trying to make: "I saw about five different personalities—not five different—but changes in personality in about a twelve- to fifteen-minute time span."

It began with Knight's anger when Murray missed the free throws, moved to joy when Murray tied up the game, and continued through the off-and-on anger in the locker room. As team captain and designated whipping boy, Murray was at the center of all these mood swings, not only for the St. John's game, but all year long.

While Knight champions may forever argue that, as one said, "A lot of his temper is designed to send a message," that his tirades are pre-meditated attempts to, say, work the officials, the coach himself has denied there has ever been any method to his madness, literally.

"I have never consciously tried to do anything like that," said Knight.

The fact is, the man simply got pissed off, his emotions dictated by the ups and downs of the game. While there might have been some object lesson in there somewhere ("This is how much I hate losing and you should hate it just as much," or "This is what a great competitor looks like"), all that was a happy accident.

Not that this kind of rough treatment was anything new for Dick Murray. He had put up with a lot when Tates Locke was coach. (Remember Locke had knocked Murray down with a well-aimed pass to the head.) But while Murray saw both coaches as "taskmasters," there was a difference.

"Tates had the capability to come over to you, put his arm around you, and pump you back up. I never felt Knight had that capability," said Murray. "I was never inspired by Knight being a positive force."

And consequently, "I had had it by the end of my senior year in terms of wanting to play any more basketball," said Murray. And he would turn down opportunities to play during his time in the Army.

Knight's rage aside, there had been a lot to be positive about following the St. John's loss. Like the coach later said, the team had played "a hell of a game," out-shooting St. Johns 50 to 32 percent and out-rebounding the taller team twenty-two to sixteen. And Army had led by as much as seven, forcing St. John's "to rally to beat this peppery bunch of little men," as Gordon S. White, Jr. put it in the *Times*. But the team had still lost, and that gave the upcoming Boston University game a special urgency.

"We lose to BU," Knight told Helkie, "we're not going to the NIT."

"He wanted to make sure my head was in the game," said Helkie.

Happy super happy Valentine's Day to you. Unfortunately, I can't remember exactly what we did on the one Valentine's Day we were together, but I bet it was fun. I'm sure it was fun. We were a bit flippant then. Flippant. Flippant. Now we're all grown up and serious-worried about the Viet Cong who don't even have a Valentine's Day.

We had our branch selection drawing tonight. Everybody gets together and picks a branch of the Army to go into [upon graduation] by order of class rank. (Just a certain quota can go into any one branch.) I am now a proud member of the Infantry.

— player's letter to girlfriend, February 14, 1966

When the near six-hundred members of the Class of 1966 gathered in South Auditorium of Thayer Hall on that frigid Valentine's night, there were five branches to choose from, the so-called "combat arms": Infantry, Artillery, Armor, Corps of Engineers, and Signal Corps. There are a couple of footnotes. First, the only two branches where the descriptor "combat" really fit, where the word was used in the common sense, were the Infantry and Armor. In those branches a soldier's primary job was actually "to close with and destroy the enemy" instead of, say, build bridges, string telephone wire, or sit back a couple of miles and lob exploding things in the general direction of opposing foxholes. Second, cadets chose in order of class rank and, since there were quotas, the choices were limited for guys at the bottom of the pile. The reason American dams are among the safest in the world is that no dumb guy ever made it into the Corps of Engineers. Third, the Signal Corps was for wimps. Fourth, while the defining West Point ethic was built around the gung-ho, "Let-me-hear-you-say-*kill!*" Infantry, a minority would choose that branch. While the ranking cadet, Norm Fretwell, was encouraged to and did choose Infantry in 1966, only 179 (less than a third of the class) chose the so-called "Queen of Battle." (Wonder if they've changed that moniker since the "Don't ask, don't tell" thing?) Another 11 percent of the class would choose Armor. The boys in Armor and Infantry were the ones who in as little as a year would actually be, as the rhetoric went, "leading men into combat."

Some just couldn't wait. And for them there was another quota: this one for volunteers for Vietnam. With about a quarter million troops and counting then in Southeast Asia—including the Army's First Infantry Division—it was inevitable that virtually every officer not only from the Class of 1966, but then working at the Academy, would end up in Vietnam in the next few years. In recognition of that, desk plaques and signs had popped up in the bowels of Thayer Hall. There in the windowless offices of mostly junior officers who had yet to witness their first "sucking chest wound" was seen the pithy slogan "Fighting's Our Business and Business Is Good." To help "grow" this business, ninety-eight volunteers from the Class of 1966 were allowed to step forward. Their Vietnam tours would begin about six months after graduation. The Army didn't want to send the raw second lieutenants straight into combat, having learned from the heavy losses suffered by the Class of 1950 in the Korean War. Yet before the Vietnam debacle was over, thirty boys from the Class of 1966 would die, and more than a hundred others would be wounded, resulting in the highest casualty rate of any West Point class—a rate which, percentage-wise, would exceed even the Korean War losses of the Class of 1950.

Business was good indeed.

———•◦•———

The Saturday following Valentine's Day, Army went on the road to face Boston University. Because of the gym, playing BU at home had the feel of one of those Wednesday afternoon games at West Point.

"Played in that little ole gym up there. Kinda like a high school gym," recalled Knight.

"It was really hard to get motivated," said Helkie.

Although Helkie got only ten points, the team summoned enough motivation to win 54–47.

A week later, Navy came to town.

"We just thrashed them," recalled Knight.

The final score was 70–56, but it was a lot uglier than that.

"Let me tell you exactly how badly we beat them. We had 'em down seventy to forty-four, and we didn't score again," recalled Knight. "They scored the last twelve points of the game."

Knight's first Army-Navy game was the last for Navy Coach Ben Carnevale. The fifty-year-old Carnevale had resigned to take a job as athletic director at New York University, his alma mater. Carnevale would end his Navy career with a lifetime record of thirteen wins and seven losses against Army. Knight's career record against Navy? Six wins, no losses, with an average victory margin of almost seventeen points.

Two days after Knight's first Navy win, Army received its third straight bid to the NIT and the coach kicked Mike Noonan off the team.

Chapter 25

I'll Take Manhattan

T he National Invitation Tournament (NIT) was created in 1938 by Edward "Ned" Irish, a natty, thirty-three-year-old sportswriter turned entrepreneur. By then, the so-called "Boy Promoter" had been staging basketball "spectacles" at Madison Square Garden for seven years and was well on his way to making the Hall of Fame for "the development of college basketball as a major spectator sport."

The inaugural NIT would follow a formula Irish had perfected over the years. He would pit the best in the East versus the best of the rest in hopes of crowning a mythical national champion in what he took to calling the "Rose Bowl of College Basketball." That first year the East's NYU, LIU (Long Island University), Bradley, and Temple, the eventual winner, would match up against Oklahoma A&M and Colorado.

The NIT was a turnstile-spinning hit from the start. It would go on to become the nation's premiere showcase for college basketball from the late thirties until the emergence of the NCAA tournament in the mid-fifties. But even after it was eclipsed by the NCAA, the NIT retained a measure of prestige simply because it was one of only two "games" in town.

Consider 1966.

"At that time, there were only twenty-two teams in the NCAA and fourteen in the NIT," recalled former West Point PR guy Bob Kinney. "At the end of the year, there were only thirty-six teams still playing basketball."

That's compared to the sixty-four teams in the NCAA alone today. So anybody still playing in March in those days was part of an elite few.

In 1966 the NIT still followed the original Ned Irish formula, and the East lineup that year would include, along with Army, Temple and Villanova, both from Philadelphia; Boston College; and the usual contingent of New York teams: Manhattan, NYU, and St. John's. The best of the rest included three major-conference runners-up; Brigham Young, San Francisco, and Wichita, plus DePaul, Louisville, Penn State, and Virginia Tech.

Army would face Manhattan at 7 P.M. on Saturday, March 12, in the opening round with or without Mike Noonan.

Mike Noonan wasn't any big star or anything, but the $6\frac{1}{2}'$ sophomore center had played in eight of Army's last nine games, averaging seven points and seven rebounds. He was also the tallest guy left on the ten-man squad and, in an NIT bracket that included teams like San Francisco with a 6′8″ center and Brigham Young with three guys around 6′11″, Noonan might have come in handy. So what did he do to deserve getting booted off the team?

"I'm shooting free throws before practice," said Noonan, "and I didn't run after the ball and Knight saw me and threw me off the team for bad attitude, lackadaisical effort, or whatever."

And with that, Noonan became the first man Knight ever tossed.

"I was crushed," said Noonan.

Noonan sought the counsel of team captain Dick Murray.

"You're gonna have to apologize to Coach and ask to be brought back on the team," Noonan recalled Murray advising him.

"And, of course, me being Mike Noonan, as stubborn as a mule from Missouri, which I'm [originally] from, I said 'Man, why? I didn't know I did anything wrong.' And he said, 'Doesn't matter. You gotta tell the coach whatever you were doing, it wasn't appropriate.'"

Flash forward to the NBA play-offs sometime in the late nineties. It was the closing seconds of a crucial game. John Stockton of the Utah Jazz came up with a rebound, looked down court, and sailed a perfect pass to the streaking Karl Malone, who laid the ball in to seal the win. At the postgame news conference, a reporter asked Stockton what he was thinking when he threw "the pass." Stockton returned a blank stare. That's because Stockton wasn't thinking anything. He was reacting.

"Don't think," Pete Newell always told his players. "When you think, you weaken the team."

This from a coach Bob Knight has described as "simply the best there ever was."

If Stockton had taken even a half second to think "Is Malone open?" the play would have been over. By the time a player gets to the floor, the "thinking" is already done. Now there is just conditioned reflex.

"There's nothing between you and the pure playing," as Woody Allen once said of the clarinet. "There's nothing cerebral in it at all."

Which brings us back to Noonan. Whenever a player is on the court, he is developing conditioned reflexes. So whether the player is tossing in jump shots on a backyard goal, playing a three-on-three pickup game, or shooting foul shots before practice, he is developing habits good or bad, seeing and reacting to situations that will come up in games. That means a serious competitor can never play for fun, can never go half speed, can never saunter after a rebound even before practice because he is developing bad habits that will come back around and bite him on the ass in a game. That's why Bob Knight kicked Noonan off the team.

Being a nineteen-year-old kid, Noonan didn't understand any of that, but he apologized anyway. So Knight took him back, and the team set about the task of taking first-round NIT foe Manhattan College seriously. It shouldn't have been hard. A traditional rival, Manhattan had won six of the last ten including a twenty-five-point blowout only three years before. But players have short memories and, in the two previous meetings, Army had run the Jaspers out of the gym, winning by an average of twenty-one points. So this year at least, Manhattan would get no respect. There were grounds.

First thing: In eight previous NIT appearances dating back to 1943, the Jaspers (named after Brother Jasper, a former AD credited with inventing the seventh-inning stretch) had been eliminated in the first round six times.

Second thing: Manhattan College wasn't even in Manhattan. It was in the Bronx, up around Broadway and West 240th Street and had been since the early twenties.

Final thing: While the team representing the small, three-thousand-plus, all-boys Catholic school had come out on top in the Metropolitan Conference, their overall record was 13–8. In short, Manhattan really wasn't very good. But their fans didn't know that.

A raucous mob showed up, many wearing green and white toboggans, while a thousand cadets in stylish (at least in the eighteenth century) gray filed into the other side of the arena. The cadets were primed.

"The team's efforts are enhanced when there is lots of shouting for them in the stands," Knight had told *Slum and Gravy* (it's not worth explaining), the cadet sports magazine.

"Manhattan has a tough team," continued Knight, talkin' the talk. "I know they are capable of beating us. But I also know we can beat them. It can go either way. It depends on the effort put into it."

Slum and Gravy had gone on to provide cadets new to Madison Square Garden with a list of "dos and don'ts"

At the top of the list: "Take along some cough drops. The cigarette smoke and the 'hollering' in the stands tend to make for sore throats."

Okay, have it your way. *Slum and Gravy* is a West Point fight song dating from the twenties, its tune stolen from an operetta titled *The Vangabond King*. The lyrics are original to West Point, author unknown. Here's a sampling:

> Sons of slum and gravy,
> will you let the Navy,
> take from us a victory?

Now the term "slum" is slang for a canned meat the Army served to soldiers in World War I and perhaps earlier, and "sons of slum and gravy" an apparent reference to soldiers in that so-called "Great War."

I told you so.

<hr/>

The *Daily News* would call the Army-Manhattan game a "travesty."

"The boys seemed infinitely more interested in belting each other around than in trying to make a basket," wrote the *Herald Tribune*'s Irving T. Marsh.

That was the second half. The first half was presentable, if sloppy, and Army led by 39–37 at the intermission, Helkie scoring nineteen. In the second go-around, Army would gradually build up a lead and with 6:30 left on the clock would lead by eleven. The game was all but over. Against a disciplined, ball-control team like Army, an eleven-point lead was insurmountable if the Cadets hit their free throws. And since the team was shooting about 70 percent for the year, there was no reason to believe they wouldn't.

But during those last six and a half minutes, Army would score only eight of a possible thirty-two points from the line. The Jaspers would take advantage, cutting Army's lead to three with about two minutes remaining. Manhattan then went into their "hack-a-cadet" defense. Things got hot.

"Manhattan tried to mix it up with the well-conditioned West Point muscle and got the worst of it," reported the *Daily News.*

Sixty fouls would be called (the NCAA average for that year was around thirty-eight per game), and six players would foul out, four from Manhattan and two from Army. Referees would have to step in twice to head off potential fights. Intense, physical, the game was Bobby Ball in the raw. The only difference was that on this night the officials were actually calling all the fouls.

As *People* magazine reported years later: "The only reason more violations are not called against Knight's players is that all five of them are constantly committing fouls, thus inducing a state of such apoplexy among referees that they cannot blow their whistles."

Toward the end of the game, the Jaspers fans began tossing drinks on the court, "presumably soft," said the *Times*. (Could have been either, given the New York drinking age of eighteen at the time.) Officials would stop play twice to mop up the court, and two Manhattan drink-tossers would be thrown out of the arena.

Army would regain its foul-shooting touch during the last few minutes and end up winning 71–66. Norm Miller of the *Daily News* called it "a rough-house game that at times resembled the Battle of the Bulge." Helkie scored twenty-seven, a season high.

One down, three to go.

Earlier that day at the Loew's Midtown Motor Inn, Dick Murray had been watching NIT rivals Penn State and San Francisco go at it on television. (Academy budgeteers made sure Tates Locke's flirtation with the Waldorf Astoria was a one-night stand.)

"I remember Frank McGuire being the television commentator at the time," recalled Murray. McGuire was a nomadic coach who had squired winning programs at St. John's, North Carolina, and South Carolina, his current school. And according to McGuire's expert opinion, "San Francisco will destroy the winner of Manhattan and Army."

It was enough to make Murray lose faith in sportscasters, even a future Hall of Fame coach like McGuire.

"What it showed me at the time," recalled Murray, "is that many of these sports commentators don't know their butts—they really don't realize what's going on."

San Francisco would beat Penn State by twelve that afternoon and would face Army three days later at 7 P.M. on Tuesday, March 15, in the first game of a Madison Square Garden doubleheader.

That afternoon, before the game, an Army player holed up in his room at that same Loew's Midtown Motor Inn would write a letter home.

"We play San Francisco tonight," he wrote, "and we are supposed to get stomped. I have a feeling we might surprise somebody."

Chapter 26

The National Implausible Tournament

If you believe team lore, 6′1″ Danny Schrage got the opening tip against 6′8″ Edwin Mueller, who would make the NBA All-Rookie team the next year. If you believe Bob Knight, "Eddie Jordan stole the ball the very first play. He came up from behind the guy and just took it away." And if you believe the Associated Press, Bill Helkie was "a coach's dream come true" when Army took on San Francisco on that March night in Madison Square Garden.

Bill Helkie hit his first six shots, mostly from what's now three-point range. He then missed one and hit five more in a row. Army led 27–15.

"From the first seconds, the Cadets were in control," reported the *Daily News*.

On hand for the doubleheader, a Tuesday-night crowd of 14,132, including five hundred cadets chanting "Dee-fense! Dee-fense!" and Wilt Chamberlain, who was in town to pick up the NBA player-of-the-year award from the Metropolitan Basketball Writers Association.

San Francisco would soon become "frantic." Not only could they not stop Helkie, they couldn't seem to score themselves.

"The Army defense threw the Dons completely off their game," said the *New York Post*.

"They had us forcing our shots. We lost our poise out there," said Dons Coach Pete Peletta.

Knight told the *Post* he had called on an unnamed "friend in California" to help with his defensive scheme.

"This friend of mine, a former coach, told me over the phone about San Francisco's style," said Knight.

The defensive game plan called for Bill Helkie to guard Dons center Edwin Mueller, who had lit it up for thirty-one against Penn State in the opening round.

"If he dunks," Knight warned Helkie, "you better go through the basket with the ball."

Billy Schutsky and Eddie Jordan would "sag" off their men to help on Mueller.

"That made it a gamble leaving Russ Gamina open," said Knight.

A similar ploy had cost Army the Vanderbilt game back in December when Vandy's "Russ Gamina," Jerry Southwood, scored twenty-three points. But this time, "[T]he boys did a great job helping each other out," said Knight. "San Francisco couldn't get the ball to Mueller much and their outside shooting was off."

San Francisco's outside shooting was more than just "off." It was "off the charts." Danny Schrage shut down the Dons' leading outside scorer, 6′6″ Joe Ellis. He got zero points in the first half. Guards Russ Gamina and Larry Blum were little better. The two would hit only five of twenty-five attempts—20 percent for the game.

"So our gamble was successful," said Knight.

While Mueller would shoot well, hitting half his attempts, he could get off only a dozen shots.

At halftime Army led 39–24 behind Helkie's twenty-five. Athletic Director Ray Murphy rushed into the locker room. "I've never seen basketball played this well," he said, according to Knight's autobiography.

"Be quiet!" responded Knight, not wanting to jinx it, then "stepped in the shower room and threw up."

In the second half, the lead would get as high as twenty-four before Army went into a stall with ten minutes left. San Francisco was forced to foul. But unlike in the opening round, when the Cadets' lousy foul shooting let Manhattan back in the game, Army shot 74 percent and the lead was never less than fourteen. The team ended up winning 80–63.

"Cadets Clobber Dons," read one headline; "Army Raises Helkie With the Dons," read another.

Norm Miller in the *Daily News* called it "the biggest upset of the 1966 NIT," while Irving T. Marsh at the *Herald Tribune* called it "Army's finest hour."

Still another sportswriter suggested a new name for the 1966 tourney, "The National Implausible Tournament," after witnessing what he called "one of the biggest surprises in NIT history."

"We just stunk the joint out," said San Francisco trainer Joe Romo.

"I never saw a team play a better game than we played that day," said Knight a generation later of this triumph for Bobby Ball, adding, "We played as well as a team could conceivably play."

The team played so well that one reporter got a little giddy and suggested that Army might even be a better team without Mike Silliman, who had watched the game from the bench.

"Not even close!" Knight would say.

"They looked like they felt all they had to do was show up to beat us," Dick Murray said.

San Francisco coach Pete Peletta denied it. "We had respect for Army. We weren't overconfident," he insisted.

No one, not even Murray, suggested that Army was simply better. There had to be some other explanation and, of course, the sportswriters already had one in the can.

It was "hustle and muscle," "discipline," and "gameness" that made it possible for the "superlatively conditioned" if "out-manned" and "lightly regarded quintet" to beat the "overconfident" San Francisco team.

"Lightly regarded" by whom? Other sportswriters?

There was some progress. While that old standby "scrappy" was still being used to describe the team, this time there was no mention of Army's lack of talent and finesse. Maybe that had something to do with the team's 69-percent shooting, best ever in the Garden, and the twenty-one assists, seven from Billy Schutsky alone.

While reporter Norm Miller from the *Daily News* was savvy enough to notice "Army's beautifully-disciplined, pattern-style offense, playing for only the best shots" and that "the Cadets also boxed out well" (when's the last time you saw that mentioned in a game account?), he didn't say anything about the sagging defense that was a key to the win, an oversight shared by the *Times* and *Tribune*. Only the *New York Post* remarked on the defensive scheme that "shackled" Mueller and dared the guards to shoot outside.

In retrospect, historians should be happy the reporters stayed awake. It would have been easy for the sports scribes to put in a little siesta time after Helkie spoon-fed them their lead with his thirty-four points, a career high, and fifteen-of-twenty, 75-percent shooting. When it was over, Murray was calling Helkie "the best shooter in the East." As for Helkie, the gunner who still brags he had the fewest turnovers in West Point history because he refused to pass the ball, he was matter of fact.

"I've always been a good shooter," he said. "I never was tall or exceptionally strong, so I had to learn how to shoot in order to play."

And who was Knight's mysterious, turncoat friend from California, the one who gave him the goods on San Francisco? Was the mole Pete Newell, who had once coached at San Francisco? "Probably," said Knight, many years later although he had no specific memory. Probably not. According to the Newell biography, the two didn't meet until 1969.

After the game, Knight would go out of his way to mention another coaching mentor. He interrupted the crowd of reporters huddled around Helkie in the locker room to give special credit to Clair Bee for his "overall advice" during the season.

"I want to mention Bee to you fellows because the public may have forgotten him and what a great coach he is," said Knight.

The biggest win of twenty-five-year-old Knight's short career and he was dishing out credit to the seventy-year-old Clair Bee, who hadn't coached a game in over ten years. That was simply nice and demonstrated the kind of generosity, the willingness to share the credit, that would become a Knight trademark over the years.

The San Francisco win would put Army, the "scrappy," "disciplined," "game," "superlatively conditioned," and "lightly regarded" squad, in the semifinals of the NIT for a third straight year. They would be facing the top seed, a sure-to-not-be-overconfident Brigham Young.

Chapter 27

An Evening with Bob

The pressure on the players was mounting. There was the game, of course. Aside from Vanderbilt, nineteenth-ranked Brigham Young would be the best team Army faced all year. Then there were the academics, ready to resurface after lying dormant since January. "I have been missing so much class, I'll never catch up," one player complained. All that plus the endless quest. Everybody was "trying to get laid," as one player indelicately phrased it, "and of course, you never got laid. Very frustrating."

How pathetic was it? Forget "getting laid." That winter the love-hungry cadets had started lining up to get their teeth cleaned after word got around that the hygienist at the West Point hospital would press a breast against your ear while trying to scrape that last little bit of tartar off a back molar. Really.

So anytime a player set foot outside the gray stone fortress of West Point, he saw it as his mission to establish a bridgehead with that other gender since the opportunities were rare and, as one put it the day before the Brigham Young game, "It may be the last time I get out until graduation [in June]."

There were a few guys with steady girlfriends, maybe a high school flame who was content with seeing her beau six weeks a year. But most were caught up in the ongoing search for love or "something like it" in the towns, villages, and backseats of America.

One player had dated a Miss Teenage America. Another a former bunny from the New York Playboy Club. "Stewardesses" were considered a catch. During his sophomore year, Mike Silliman had been "going steady" with two girls at the same time until they caught him at it. But that doesn't mean anybody was, well, you know. This was before free love and women's liberation and Madonna. Although the pill was around, had been since 1960, it was redundant, what with the ubiquitous panty girdle and the prevailing moral code, which dictated that a girl without birth control, to borrow a phrase, was like "a fish without a bicycle." To put it crudely, few players were gettin' any on a regular basis.

Here's a case study in why.

New York City. March 1966. Millions of women to choose from. The exotic species can be found everywhere from the golden lobby of the Plaza Hotel in midtown to the jazz clubs in Greenwich Village. But our composite hero, role model "Bond, James Bond," a boy who, if lucky, could count the number of women he'd slept with on one finger, chose to take up the hunt in the corridors of the Loew's Midtown Motor Inn on Eighth Avenue between 48th and 49th Streets.

In those days "getting lucky" was no empty phrase. Without at least the promise of a relationship, a nice, middle-class boy had a better chance of doing the fox-trot with a frock-wearing J. Edgar Hoover at the Roseland Ballroom than getting the average Manhattan girl in the sack. Even sweet talk and liquor didn't help, because by the standards of the day, a girl who even indulged in "heavy petting" was considered a "slut." (Before Madonna, that was considered a bad thing.)

One older member of the Class of 1966 realized what he *wasn't* up against and had on occasion hired an "escort." He had become the talk of the class the previous fall when his date for one of the Academy's fru-fru formal balls had been a hard-looking "professional" woman of about thirty-five who stood out amongst the vestal virgins.

So anyway, our hero was stalking the halls of Loew's Midtown Motor Inn. All was not lost. There were girls there. Choices. So what does the gray-clad Romeo do? He cozies up to a flock of BYU cheerleaders. Mormons. The anti-sex.

Wholesome as an unshucked ear of corn, these were some serious white girls. They looked like those otherworldly creatures in the classic Breck shampoo ads with their perfectly coifed hair and flawless pink skin. What our hero didn't know was that when it came to Mormon girls, the chances of any actual "shucking" going on rivaled that of getting the wife of a Southern Baptist preacher to engage in water sports in her hubby's baptismal on Easter Sunday. But cloaked in ignorance, our hero trudged on, at one point even begging one vision of a cheerleader to allow him to sleep on the floor at the foot of her bed. Amazingly, she laughed that one off, but when he tempted her with a glass of caffeine-laced iced tea, she sent him packing.

So our hero would spend another night alone at Loew's. But just as there would be no shame in a possible loss to favored BYU, there was little shame in this, still another rejection, since the degree of difficulty had been so high.

The two teams couldn't have been more different. Brigham Young played a racehorse, run-and-gun style of basketball. For the season, BYU had averaged ninety-two points per game, while Army had scored only sixty-nine and held opponents to sixty-two. (The team would end the year eighth in the nation in total defense.) During the year, BYU had been ranked as high as sixth in the AP poll and was an eight-point favorite against an Army team that had been the underdog against every decent team it had faced all season.

"They had two guards, a guy named Dick Nemelka who was an All-American and then they had a guy named Jeff Congdon who ultimately led the ABA in assists," recalled Dick Murray. "They had a guy named Kramer and they had two really tall guys, like seven feet that played a double post down low."

Murray was off a little on this one. The "really tall guys" weren't seven footers. They were "only" 6′11″ and there weren't two of them, there were three: Jim Eakins, Craig Raymond, and Orville Fisher.

Nemelka and Congdon, both around six feet, averaged fifteen a game, but the 6′4″, two-hundred-pound Steve Kramer was the team's leading scorer, averaging eighteen.

It started out like the Penn State Game. BYU didn't score its first basket until seven and a half minutes in, and Army led 14–2. But the Cougars didn't panic and by halftime the Army lead was only seven. Schrage had held leading scorer Kramer to three points.

"We had those guys. We had 'em," said Dick Murray.

Not quite. The five Army starters had played all but forty-five seconds of the San Francisco game two nights before, and Knight had worried before the game that they might tire against BYU.

Tired or not, the Cougars caught up with Army about midway through the second half, tying the game at forty-one. There would be five more ties, then with a little over two minutes left, Army leading 58–56, it happened.

"Dick Nemelka drove into a mass of Army defenders," reported the *Daily News.*

Bill Helkie ended up on his butt in the middle of the lane, and the referees were faced with a decision.

"It was one of those borderline calls," said the *News.*

Block or charge? That was the question. Was Helkie moving laterally, or had he established position? Did Nemelka barrel headlong into Helkie's chest?

Out front, Lou Eisenstein, the official closest to the play, raised his arm to signal a charge. Underneath, official Bud Fidgeon rushed forward to call a block.

The decision was critical. Helkie and Nemelka both had four fouls, and the man on the losing end of this one would sit down. Plus if Army got the call, the team would go up by four with 2:17 to go, assuming 84-percent foul shooter Helkie would make them both. Even if BYU scored again, Army would get the ball back with under two minutes left, and these masters of ball control would "freeze" it, sink their foul shots, and walk away with a "major upset." But if BYU got the call, anything could happen.

"Eisenstein had his arm back, his whistle ready, to make a charging call against Nemelka," Knight told the *New York Times*.

"But Eisenstein never blew his whistle," the newspaper reported. Instead the veteran official let Fidgeon, who Knight claimed was "screened out of view by three players," make the call.

Fidgeon called the block, Helkie sat down, and Nemelka hit both free throws to tie the game.

"It was a rotten call," Knight told the *Herald Tribune*.

"That was a real deciding point," said Dick Murray.

"That's one of the two or three biggest calls that I've ever had made in a game," Knight would say a generation later. (And it could have been the call that led to Knight totaling a chair or a water cooler or both. Nobody remembers.)

As Knight continued to rage on the sidelines, a BYU sub named Jim Jimas "made a slick steal" from Murray and laid it in. Less than a minute after that, Jimas would take a feed for another lay-up and Army never recovered. BYU won 66–60.

"That was the worst fuckin' call," recalled Tates Locke. "I was at the game. Myself, Fred Taylor, and a bunch of guys."

They had driven up from College Park, Maryland, where the NCAA tournament was being played that year.

"We were up in the y'know scout boxes up on the second tier at Madison Square Garden," recalled Locke. "I almost fell out because I was so mad."

Knight was mad too.

"He followed the official—it was an older official—Eisenstein might have been his name," recalled Bob Kinney, the West Point sports PR guy. "He followed him back behind the stands and really let him have it."

Eisenstein escaped to the officials' locker room and Knight faced the press. A "boiling mad" Knight was "fighting hard to keep control of himself" but, in the end, "tossed a tantrum," according to the newspapers. By various accounts Knight cursed, punched a locker, kicked a door, and slapped a wall as he "teed off on the officials, especially Eisenstein."

"One call cost us the game," Knight said.

Knight had picked the wrong guy to bad-mouth. One of the most respected officials of his era, the fifty-three-year-old Eisenstein had played college ball at NYU, was a founder and one-time president of the Collegiate Basketball Officials Association, and was the only official to ever referee the finals of the NBA, NCAA, and NIT in the same year. A mainstay at Madison Square Garden, Eisenstein would oversee twenty NIT finals before his retirement in 1976.

"Never," the twenty-five-year-old Knight told the *New York Times,* "have I ever said anything about officiating. But that was a gutless call tonight. Gutless."

This wasn't the first time Knight had called Eisenstein "gutless." He had said it to his face during the game.

"I'll show you how much guts I have," Eisenstein replied. "I'll throw you out of the building."

Didn't happen, and if there was a technical called, the newspapers didn't mention it.

"I just bit my lip and didn't answer him," said Eisenstein's running mate, Bud Fidgeon. "We're supposed to be quiet and cool out there."

Keeping quiet and cool would be even tougher after the game, according to Tates Locke. Following the bitter loss, Locke and former St. John's coach Joe Lapchick would end up outside the Army locker room trying to calm Knight.

"There's Coach Lapchick and me trying to restrain Bobby back in the locker room. He wanted to kill Lou," said Locke. "We had everything under control and he bolted from us. Those little narrow halls in the old Garden? He went down that hall so damn fast. Criminey! He was in that [officials'] locker room like a cat."

It was not unfamiliar territory. This was Knight's second trip on record to an officials' locker room. The first had gotten him booted out of the Washington State game the year before.

"Eisenstein looked like a deer in the headlights, just hit right in the eyes. Oh shit! Those were the good days. Those were fun days," continued Locke. "[Knight] grabbed him. He was tryin' to grab him, but Eisenstein was so fat he couldn't lift him off the floor."

"And every other word was—I dunno—it was ugly," said Tates. "We finally got him out in the hall."

Now there's a classic "Bob Knight story." Bad call; uncontrollable anger; not only berating, but grabbing an official. That's the Bob Knight of legend: the bullying Neanderthal, the xenophobic competitor we know and love. But was that how it really went down?

Toward the end of the news conference, according to newspaper accounts, Knight, his "narrow eyes red," his skinny, dark blue tie jerked open to his breast bone, calmed down a bit and "smoothed his crew cut" as he continued talking to reporters.

"Maybe I'm saying things I shouldn't," he told the *New York Post*. "I hope you fellows understand why I'm this way, but I can't justify protecting the officials. I hope you won't make this sound too bad in the papers."

It was only then, according to the *Post*, that Knight made his way to the officials' locker room. Not to raise hell, but to apologize.

"Knight came in here to tell us he was sorry that he had popped off," official Lou Eisenstein told the *Post*. "He said he had been upset because his kids had tried so hard all year and had lost his head talking to the writers after the game."

According to Eisenstein, Knight told the refs, "You two are great. You can work Army games anytime."

Whatever happened between Knight and Eisenstein, the fun-filled "evening with Bob" did not end in the officials' locker room. There was still time for another "Bob Knight story," and this one's not in dispute. Not much anyway. It happened after Knight and his entourage returned to the Loew's Midtown Motor Inn.

"I was in Bob's hotel room when the phone rang and it was Colonel Murphy, the athletic director," said Bob Kinney.

An argument began.

Knight pal Rich Cardillo said Knight got upset because the "higher-ups" were challenging "his honest appraisal of a poor call."

"There was a lot of shouting," said Head Trainer Ed Pillings.

"I remember being there with Ed," said Kinney, "and we're looking at each other with kind of surprised looks on our faces."

"Colonel Ray Murphy. He called up and he was pissed off at Knight," said Pillings. "And Knight just ripped him up. Knight started cryin' and he [Knight] called him a son of a bitch. Murphy backed off. Murphy was gonna fire him."

When asked if he was sure Murphy said he was going to fire him, Pillings himself backed off. "I dunno what happened," he said.

Whether or not Murphy made the threat, the argument was so heated that Kinney had no doubt the rookie coach was history. After all, here was Knight, a twenty-five-year-old kid, only four months away from being a Private First Class whose typical responsibilities included peeling potatoes on KP, raising hell with a bird colonel whose typical responsibilities included commanding a regiment of two or three thousand men in combat.

"I learned a few new words that night," said Kinney. "I also thought we would be making an announcement the next day that we had a new basketball coach."

"Oh, seriously?" a reporter asked.

"Oh he, Bob, really ripped into the colonel."

In the heat of the moment, Knight himself at least considered leaving.

"I think I'll just leave this place," Knight told Cardillo. "I'll do something else."

Somewhere in here, Pillings pulled Kinney aside and said, "Hell, I'm not gonna worry about this goddamn thing. I'm going down and get a beer. And he said, 'I'm coming with you.' And we went down and had a beer and laughed it off."

Later, Cardillo and Knight would hit the newsstands. "I think we bought every paper in New York," said Cardillo. "He was interested in seeing the reaction of the press."

By modern, *Sports Illustrated* standards, it was nothing. "Army Coach: A Knight Errant," read the *New York Post* headline. "Foul Call Key to Army Defeat," said the *Tribune*. "Army Is Stunned By Referees Call," said the *Times*.

Former athletic director Ray Murphy remembers little of this.

"I was at that game and I was of the opinion that Eisenstein," said Murphy, "he just didn't have the courage of his convictions."

As for the Knight ass chewing, Murphy at first denied it ever happened, then wasn't so sure.

"I would never do that to Bob. I don't think I would anyhow," Murphy said. "It's now how many years later? It's thirty years later."

Still somebody called Knight, and three witnesses say it was Murphy.

Like Murphy, Knight's postgame memory is dim at best. He does remember Locke and company trying to keep him from going into the officials' locker room. He doesn't remember whether they were successful or not. When asked if he confronted Eisenstein, he said, "I don't think so. Y'know, I don't remember." He also didn't recall any phone conversation with Murphy.

"He might have called, told me to be quiet," said Knight. "I think he told me, just to, to be quiet, and I'm sure he would have done that."

But of all the "Bob Knight stories" from that first year, this one is the most credible, owing not only to the number but the attitude of the witnesses. Two, Cardillo and Kinney, remain big Knight fans. Cardillo considers Knight his best friend, and Kinney, who is "absolutely positive" it was Murphy on the phone, says Knight "was great to work with." Even Head Trainer Pillings, who was wary of Knight at the time, can ultimately be put in the "fan" column.

"A lot of people thought he was a SOB. Yeah, because he was so mean and ornery," said Pillings. "I treated him like a little baby fox. It was tricky, but we got along great. I never had any difficulty with him at all."

So you had a young, rookie coach blowing up in the face of his boss, a forty-seven-year-old athletic director. It was like a cocksure plebe taking on a scary guy, say Brigadier General Richard G. Stilwell. In military circles, that's just not done. This was not Shady Elm U, motto "Truth, Beauty, Goodness"; this was "Duty, Honor, Country" West Point, where there was a standard operating procedure for dealing with insubordinate little snits: something involving Leavenworth and "hard labor." But all that could wait. Plenty of time to deal with Knight's indiscretions when the season ended. Now the goal was to just get through the NIT consolation game with Villanova without any more incidents, at least in public.

Murphy spoke to then major Cardillo, who was one of Knight's official military handlers.

"If his personality was going to be the focus, that would not be good," Cardillo recalled Murphy telling him before the game. "The focus should be on the team."

Before the noon tip-off on Saturday, Murphy came down to the court to make sure Cardillo got the message.

"I want you to be sure you keep that guy on the bench today," Murphy told Cardillo, worried that "the newspaper guys were after him."

There was little reason to worry. Army had beaten the same Villanova team by twenty-one in the opening round of the Holiday Festival back in December. All they had to do, it seemed, was just show up to take home third place in the tournament.

The rebounders showed. Army won that contest 52–34. So did the free-throw shooters. Army hit twice as many as the Wildcats. As for the outside shooters, the guys arcing those long-range jump shots over Villanova's "sturdy two-three zone?" They shot just 36 percent.

As a coach once put it: "We have a great bunch of outside shooters. Unfortunately all our games are played indoors."

Meanwhile Villanova, led by tournament MVP Bill Melchionni with twenty-nine, hit more than half their shots. The decisive moment came when Army "ran out of gas" with eleven minutes to go and the Wildcats went on a 14–1 run. The lead was then seventeen, and the game was over.

Even though Lou Eisenstein was again officiating, Knight behaved himself, leading the *Herald Tribune* to report there were "no recriminations regarding the officiating" during the game. Afterward, Knight once more made his way to the officials' locker room and apologized to Eisenstein a second time.

"I'm sorry it was you, because you know how I feel about you as a referee and a person," Knight said, according to Eisenstein's account in the *New York Post*.

BYU would win the final, beating NYU by thirteen.

Meanwhile, about two hundred miles south, obscure Texas Western would face fabled Kentucky in the finals of the NCAA tournament in College Park, Maryland. Western Coach Don Haskins would use only seven players in the game, all black, against an all-white—as in "we surrender"—Kentucky team. Western won 72–65, and recruiting in the land of the magnolias would never be the same.

"Around the South everything changed for black players," sportswriter Dan Wetzel observed many years later in *Basketball Times*.

In the spring of 1966, winning had accomplished what conscience could not.

Chapter 28

What West Point Is All About

To most athletic directors it would have seemed like a gift from God. Bobby Knight had a job offer. Following just a decent 18–8 season, the University of Florida was asking Knight to export Bobby Ball to Gainesville. Colonel Ray Murphy had a chance to unload the temperamental Knight without a whisper of controversy. He could rid himself of an immature lout who was guilty not only of embarrassing image-conscious West Point, but of "acts of gross insubordination" that would have gotten any military man court-martialed. Hell, to make it look good, Murphy could even throw Knight a farewell party before going about the business of finding a coach more attuned to the sensitivities of an institution whose very bedrock was discipline.

But if Murphy had ever wanted to fire Knight, he was over it by the time the coach accepted the Florida offer. "It was obvious to me he was a tremendous coach and he was getting the most out of his players," said Murphy.

So Murphy tried to talk Knight into staying.

"You're not ready to leave," Murphy told the young coach. "If you go out there, you're gonna get clobbered."

"I used to try to impress on him that he had to stay until he made his mark," said Murphy.

But according to Knight, it was something ex-coach Fred Taylor said that finally convinced him to stay.

"I just want you to think about the fact that they gave you a chance and nobody else was going to," Taylor advised the rookie coach.

So Knight thought about it and changed his mind. When he showed up at Murphy's office to tell him the news, the colonel was sitting at his desk working, writing something.

"Colonel, I've decided to stay," Knight recalled saying.

Murphy just kept writing, didn't even look up.

"I knew you would," Murphy said.

"I thought he had great potential," Murphy recalled, "and at West Point, particularly with the New York press and all the other exposure he had there, that was the place for him to become a real well-known coach."

That's the same New York press that would soon label Knight "Bobby T," as in "technical." Wasn't his behavior an issue?

"We had several discussions about the conduct on the bench," said Murphy. "And he had a few flare-ups there. Nothing I thought we couldn't resolve."

And with that, the official acquiescence, the last piece of the Bob Knight jigsaw puzzle fell into place. Now the soon to be infamous temper, the acting out, and the defiance were codified as, if not acceptable, at least tolerable behavior. So at West Point, for God's sake, the model of decorum, a pattern was established that would be refined over the years, but at its heart would never really change.

And what exactly other than coaching "potential" was West Point getting out of this burgeoning PR nightmare?

"He had the Corps of Cadets behind him," said Murphy. "It was obvious the way the Corps responded to that team and in many respects carried the team by their enthusiasm and spirit."

So suddenly what the cadets thought mattered? Save it for the press kit. Something much more fundamental had to be going on. Here's a theory.

If ever anyone personified General Douglas MacArthur's adage, "There is no substitute for victory," it was Bob Knight. Even his players were astonished at how much he wanted to win, his bitterness in defeat.

"At West Point I made up my mind to win—gotta win," Knight told *Sports Illustrated*'s Frank Deford in 1981. "Winning was the hub of everything I was doing."

And at an institution dedicated to training leaders in the art of war, the ultimate competition, winning matters. It matters a lot. So while to outsiders Knight might have seem crazed, almost insane, to the insiders in charge of the Academy, he was a role model.

In 1966 West Point was being run by the World War II generation, veterans like Colonel Ray Murphy and Brigadier General John Jannarone. This was the generation that demanded "unconditional surrender" in Europe and the Far East. The generation who firebombed Dresden. The generation that dropped two atomic bombs on Japan. All in the name of winning. Jannarone himself had worked on the development of "the bomb" as had one just-departed West Point superintendent. To the men of this generation, Knight's win-at-any-cost attitude was not necessarily a bad thing.

"Those guys were really good for me, because I think they understood," said Knight. "I mean those guys really understood what I was trying to do."

To them, Bobby Ball and Bob Knight, the skinny guy with a black crew cut raging on the sidelines of a college basketball game, were what "the will to win" looked like in the flesh.

"I wanted our basketball team to be able to play anywhere in America," said Knight, "and whoever came to the game would walk away saying, 'Man, if that's what West Point is all about, we are really in good hands as far as our military is concerned.'"

"If that's an example of the kind of competitor—the kind of fighter—that West Point produces," as Knight would put it in his autobiography, "our country is in great shape."

And after watching Army play, said Knight, "I think you go away, if you know anything about basketball, and you say, 'Whew, I've never seen anybody play as hard as those guys play.' And then I think that conveys what West Point is all about to me."

The mullahs of West Point apparently shared that sentiment. So they kept him on. And while they might sometimes cringe at Knight's antics, they saw that whenever Bob Knight fielded a team, he showcased those "what-West-Point-is-all-about" values to the world. They were not the values of Harvard or Williams College or even Indiana University. They were the values of a warrior class willing to incinerate tens of thousands of people at Dresden, Hiroshima, and Nagasaki, driven by, as MacArthur said, "the sure knowledge that in war there is no substitute for victory; that if you lose, the nation will be destroyed." Values that dictated that the nation's warriors do whatever is necessary to win. Those were the values of West Point and the values of Bob Knight, then and now.

"I have interesting heroes," Knight told *Playboy* in 2001. Among them: "Harry Truman, who had the courage to drop the atomic bomb and live with the consequences. Probably the most devastating decision ever made in world history."

"How many millions of lives did Harry Truman save?" Knight had asked in another *Playboy* interview, this one in 1984. "Truman may be the greatest American who ever lived."

Knight is still fond of saying he's "never gotten over West Point." When asked to elaborate, he'll give a listener the old "levels of discipline" spiel with that patented forearm choreography or say beginning at West Point he's always "pushed and pushed and pushed" to get the most out of the players he had, the hand he was dealt. But there's much more to the West Point influence than that. Not that anybody will ever get it out of Knight. He simply doesn't think that way.

When asked point blank how West Point as an institution influenced him as a coach, Knight bitched about how he couldn't get permission to take the team to some off-campus steak house on the other side of the Hudson. Whatever.

Even if he couldn't articulate them, the Academy's influences could be seen in the "what-West-Point-is-all-about" values Knight wanted his teams to display on the basketball floor. That was West Point incarnate out there: the toughness, the smart play, the relentless determination.

"We just never quit," said Knight.

And even today, when watching a Bob Knight team play, spectators in the know can see the ghostly presence of West Point and the Corps of Cadets. They can see Beast Barracks and Recondo and scary guys and four-part civil-engineering exams and, on occasion, a demonstration of just how much crap one kid is expected to take and still soldier on. All in the name of winning, of course. For as long as you stay within the rules, at West Point and on a Bob Knight team, winning *is* the only thing. And what does Coach Knight say to those who dispute that, who worry today there is "too much emphasis on winning?"

"Nothing."

After a long pause while he flips through the sports page, his tortoiseshell reading glasses perched at the end of his nose, Knight picks up on the thought.

"Why say anything to those people? They don't understand. How can you overemphasize winning, for Christ's sake?"

He looks up from the sports page.

"I mean I'm goddamned glad they overemphasized winning in World War II," he says, fighting a grin. "Jesus!" he grunts, turning back to his paper.

Profane, dismissive, the answer is vintage Knight. Just the kind of response sure to rankle a philosophy professor turned university president named Myles Brand.

Part IV

FIRED!

Chapter 29

An Absolute Moron

Bloomington, Indiana. Monday, September 11, 2000. I check into the Hampton Inn around 8 P.M., swing by McDonald's, and head straight for Assembly Hall to see what's going on. Bob Knight has been fired—"the guy in the red sweater got the pink slip," as CNN's Andy Katz put it.

It had happened during a phone call that began at 7:30 A.M. Sunday morning. Knight, who was in Canada on a fishing trip, had called Indiana University President Myles Brand to check in. This in the wake of charges that the coach had manhandled student Kent Harvey four days before. During that early morning call, Brand would ask the coach to resign. When Knight refused, Brand fired him. The university president would make the firing public at a televised news conference in Indianapolis that afternoon.

That's when I start packing my bag, not sure whether I'm drawn to Bloomington to help out, report, or merely sneak sidelong glances at the crumpled body under the sheet. I just know I have to come, and so on the second Monday in September, I make the six-hour drive from Nashville to Bloomington and find myself in jeans and a faded blue T-shirt in the parking lot outside the south entrance to Assembly Hall, eating a Big Mac and fries off the trunk of my car, feeling like a reporter again.

Others have given in to a similar impulse. To my left are a dozen television remote trucks. This multimillion-dollar aggregation of hardware has been dispatched from Indianapolis, Louisville, CNN, ESPN, Chicago. All the trucks face away from the building, tentacle-like cables trailing out the back to a grassy plot between the parking lot and the entrance. There are a couple of lonely camera tripods squatting on the grass, a few pairs of lights. This is the spot where television reporters will strike a pose for stand-ups and live shots with the gray concrete expanse of Assembly Hall looming in the background. The trucks are idling, and there's the smell of diesel in the air.

It's that balanced moment between daylight and dusk, and while the sun is still above the horizon, there's a near-full moon visible, a few wispy clouds. A slight gust of wind scatters what's left of my French fries on the ground. I clean them up and then take a stroll down satellite row.

All the trucks are white except for WLKY-Louisville's solid blue, and all have brightly colored logos and slogans plastered on the sides and back. Red, white, and blue are popular for obvious reasons. There's WHAS-TV with "Coverage you can count on" and WAVE-TV "Where news comes first." The top edges of the trucks are festooned with little running lights, and the bold colors, the sparkling lights, the hum of the engines—all create the promise of something splendid, festive, like a carnival midway an hour before the gates open. But now there is just waiting and the occasional solitary soul meandering the seventy-five yards back and forth to Assembly Hall.

I flag down a fellow reporter. Is Knight inside? Is he coming out to "tell his side of the story" like he promised last night? The reporter is not sure. So we wait.

I look around for evidence of the riot the night before. On Sunday, more than two thousand students had marched from here to the center of campus and back again to protest Knight's firing. The only sign of anything out of the ordinary is a cotton sweater draped over the sign reading "South Entrance, Assembly Hall." The Indiana-red pullover with white accents at the collar, cuff, and shoulder is covered with black scribbles. The most prominent: "Without Coach Knight this is just a shirt."

I reestablish my vigil, leaning on the trunk of the car. A fancy pickup rumbles up beside me, all electric blue and chrome. Inside, two men in their twenties are looking for action. The driver is wearing a T-shirt celebrating NASCAR, maybe a particular driver. There are so many logos juxtaposed side to side, top to bottom, I can't sort it out. He drops an elbow out the window and asks me what's going on. "Just waiting," I tell him. When he finds out I'm a reporter, he makes some gentle probes to find where I fall on the Knight issue. I'm vague, but still pass the test.

The driver tells me he didn't actually attend Indiana University or anything, but he's a Knight fan. When not cruising the Assembly Hall parking lot, he drives a Wonder Bread truck. His route includes nearby Nashville, Indiana, hometown of Kent Harvey, the boy whose run-in with Knight brought all these satellite trucks to Bloomington.

"If I see the kid, I'll run over him," says the driver.

Now there's a headline: "Knight Accuser Flattened by Wonder Bread Truck." How perfectly American is that?

I take the driver's threat to be metaphorical, but in time Kent Harvey—in fact all three of the Harvey triplets: Kent, Kevin, and Kyle—will get run over, but not by a bread truck.

I gaze at the entrance of Assembly Hall where Knight met Harvey in the, uh, "fateful encounter." It had happened five days before, at about 2 P.M. on Thursday afternoon. Freshman Kent Harvey, a boyhood alum of Knight's basketball school, in only his tenth day as an Indiana student, was leaving the building after picking up football tickets. He chose a set of double doors on the left. But one of the doors was stuck, wouldn't open, and so there was barely enough room for two people to go through at the same time. Knight opens the working door, and both he and Kent Harvey turn sideways, sliding through. Harvey spots the coach and says either "What's up, Knight!" (Harvey's version) or "Hi, Knight!" (Knight's version). Then the fifty-nine-year-old Knight grabs the nineteen-year-old Harvey by the crook of his right arm and pulls him aside for a lecture on how to address his elders. None of this is in dispute. The dispute is over the character of the encounter. Knight and his key witness, assistant coach Mike Davis, say it was a mild rebuke: stern, but not angry.

"He never said a curse word, and he never raised his voice," said Davis.

The Kent triplets and two of their friends say the run-in was angry, and brother Kevin Harvey and another witness say it was profane.

Knight says he was never angry and in a "conversational tone" simply told Harvey: "Son, my name isn't 'Knight' to you. It's 'Coach Knight' or it's 'Mr. Knight.' I don't call people by their last names and neither should you."

Kent Harvey tells a different story. "It was pretty wild. He kinda got in my face," he told CNN. "He wasn't yelling at me. But he wasn't happy at all. He was very upset."

Kent would later show reporters marks on his arm, left by Knight, he said. As for the cursing, Kent doesn't remember that. It's brother Kevin who claims Knight said, "Show me some fucking respect. I'm older than you."

Coach Mike Davis called that a "flat-out lie."

How long did all this last? Thirty seconds to two minutes say the Harveys. A few seconds says Knight.

As one CNN reporter commented: "We all wish we were there to see who's embellishing on the story."

Maybe nobody.

Some of the differences can be explained as varying perceptions. For mere mortals, being in the presence of a superstar kicks everything into another emotional gear. As for Knight, since his normal intensity level approaches that of a five-car pileup at Bristol Motor Speedway, to him this brief moment of social intercourse may have seemed no different than a number of other "interactions" during a given week.

What seems to skew the argument in Harvey's favor are the "red marks" and "broken skin" on his forearm.

While Knight may not have been angry this time, he was in a similar situation years earlier. That's according to John Feinstein, author of *A Season on the Brink*. While working on that book, Feinstein claims he was trailing along behind Knight one morning, and someone asked him what he was doing that day. Feinstein jokingly said something like, "Oh,

I'm going to do what I do every day. I'm going to follow Knight around." Knight heard him and went postal. "Don't you ever call me that!" he shouted. "Who do you think you are?"

It would be hard to fault Feinstein if he had replied, "Who do you think *you* are?"

How reliable is this story? Hard to tell since Knight and Feinstein are now sworn enemies.

After the run-in with Knight, the Harvey triplets left Assembly Hall and called their stepfather, Mark Shaw, around 2:30. Angered, Shaw called Christopher Simpson, the Indiana University vice president for public affairs and government relations—the PR guy.

"Are you ready to test zero tolerance?" asked Shaw, according to Simpson. "Well, you better be, because Bob Knight just accosted my stepson."

Shaw demanded an apology. Somebody notified the media. IU says it was Shaw. Shaw says it was IU. The story picked up steam, and at 11 A.M. the next morning, Simpson issued a statement saying that a "serious allegation has been raised" and that the university was launching an investigation.

By the time Harvey went to the IU police station to file a formal complaint around 4:00 that Friday afternoon, he was greeted by three dozen reporters and a platoon of television remote trucks. The feeding frenzy was on.

Inside, Harvey told his story, showed campus police the marks on his arm. Pictures were taken. The cops weren't convinced and would later discount the injury, saying they "could not verify that marks found on the student's arm were caused by Knight." True enough. And I imagine that police often cannot "verify" that marks found on a battered woman's face were caused by her husband. So they just have to take the victim's word for it. Here the police don't do that. So we are asked to believe that the marks Kent Harvey says Knight left on his arm got there some other way, and the boy is lying about it.

That's a stretch. The only thing that gives this theory any credence is the looming presence of the triplets' stepfather, Mark Shaw, an attorney, author, and former Bloomington talk-show host with an ax to grind. Shaw was an outspoken critic of Knight. "Probably the most vitriolic," said Knight.

Later, in a fit of pique, Knight would offer *Playboy* a more colorful characterization.

"The fucking stepfather was a fucking goddamned asshole from the word goddamn go!" Knight told interviewer Lawrence Grobel. "He fucking lied and he lied and he lied!"

Why would he lie? Because the coach rejected a series of five book proposals from Shaw. So was Shaw out to get Knight? Shaw claims all he ever asked for was an apology, not Knight's head. Then what about his "test of zero tolerance" remark reported by Simpson? Perhaps that was merely rhetorical. But if all he wanted was an apology, why go to the cops? Why talk to (some would say "court") every news outlet on the planet? As a talk-show veteran, Shaw had enough media savvy to know where that would end up. Perhaps Shaw was out to get Knight only until he realized the whole thing was backfiring on him, until he saw stepson Kent burned in effigy, saw the "Wanted Dead" posters with his stepson's picture, read the death threats.

On that same Friday afternoon, after Harvey went to the IU police, Knight, accompanied by Mike Davis, called the press together at Assembly Hall to tell his side of the story. He started out by saying he's forever teaching kids to show respect for older people. For example, he forces them to say "thank you" when he gives them an autograph.

As the news conference continued, Knight told a less than warm and fuzzy story about how a former coach had put a ten- or eleven-year-old Knight in his place, in church no less, after a young Bobby called the coach by his nickname, "Chub," as in "chubby." He went on to say he had never addressed his college coach, Fred Taylor, by his first name.

"I've called him 'Coach' or 'Coach Taylor' from the time I was seventeen years old to today. That's forty-three years."

Knight has always had an affinity for older people. Maybe that's because he was surrounded by them growing up as an only child in Orrville, Ohio. His parents had married in their thirties, and in 1953, the year Knight turned thirteen, his dad, Pat, was fifty-six and his mom,

Hazel, fifty. And since both parents worked, Pat for the railroad, Hazel as a third grade teacher, young Bobby spent most of his time with his maternal grandmother, Sarah Montgomery, who lived with the family.

"A classy lady—the love of Bobby's life," a neighbor said.

"I think he was closer to his grandmother than he ever was to me or his father," Hazel Knight would tell *Sports Illustrated* in 1981.

Later Knight would parlay his affinity for older people into a lifetime of teaching youngsters "the proper form of introducing themselves to their elders," as writer Joan Mellen put it.

As the news conference continued, Knight gave his version of what happened with Kent Harvey and summed it up with this all-inclusive statement:

> That is what happened and that's entirely what happened and any deviation from that is absolutely inaccurate. Completely inaccurate.

Then, in case somebody didn't get it, he characterized the Harveys' version as absurd.

"I would have to be an absolute moron, an absolute moron, with the things that have been laid down on me to grab a kid in public and curse at a kid in public."

But he did "grab a kid in public." No question about that. And that is, as the zero-tolerance policy phrased it, "inappropriate physical contact" by anybody's definition.

And from Kent Harvey's perspective? "It was like somebody grabbing me because they were pissed off."

As for the cursing: Here's a man whose everyday vocabulary includes a whole lot of profanity. He once said, "In my language 'son of a bitch' is a pronoun," and he has even called his beloved grandson "sumbitch" in print. A guy who swears that routinely might not even notice when he uses the "f-word." But since Kent Harvey himself doesn't remember it, my inclination is to rely on assistant coach Mike Davis, who says Knight never cursed. As for brother Kevin's version, I'm guessing the intensity and heat of the exchange made it seem as if the coach used profanity whether he did or not, and let's just leave it at that.

"He scared the hell out of me, basically," said Kent Harvey.

Of course, that could be said of anybody in the same room with Knight at a given moment. The rub is the "red marks," the "broken skin" on Kent Harvey's arm. If Knight is responsible for those marks, that's inexcusable and an indicator of misplaced intensity. Knight doesn't know how hard he grabbed the boy? He's wound a bit tight?

Stepdad Mark Shaw would say Knight was lucky Kent "didn't beat the absolute shit out of him." Lucky he didn't try, I'd guess. Knight is, as he might put it, "a really big sumbitch."

At 10:30 Friday night, after Kent Harvey took his case to the cops and after Knight's Assembly Hall news conference, Myles Brand would call Knight at home to "discuss the allegations." During that conversation, Brand learned that Knight was planning to leave for a Canadian fishing trip the next morning. Brand asked the coach to stay in town. By Brand's account, Knight "adamantly refused" in a move the president would later characterize as "gross insubordination." It was the proverbial last straw.

On Saturday, Brand would spend most of the day lining up support from the IU board of trustees in preparation for the fateful phone call on Sunday morning. On Sunday afternoon, he would announce his decision to fire Knight, and shortly thereafter students would begin their march on Brand's on-campus residence.

———◆◆◆———

My vigil continues at Assembly Hall. A slight boy in a red T-shirt walks up and bums a cigarette. There's a white "IDS" stenciled on his right breast, the logo for the *Indiana Daily Student,* the student newspaper. Turns out he's the editor. The kid clumsily lights up, takes a few shallow puffs, and it's obvious he hasn't mastered the choreography of smoking. He needs something for his nerves, he says, since he's about to get interviewed by CNN. Live, he thinks. Soon a pair of lights blink on in the grassy area, the reporter waves, and the student editor wanders over to get a little face time on national TV.

My spirits aren't high. Six months ago, I'd planned a lighthearted little romp down memory lane, but this story has made a sharp turn into something else. What started out as a remembrance of a basketball team and the debut of a young coach madly in love with basketball is slipping away. This story has all the charm of a salmonella outbreak at a meat packing plant. The little go-around with Kent Harvey has nothing to do with basketball, and, worse yet, it's wreaking havoc with my thesis that Knight is basketball incarnate, that the game and its underlying ferocity explain everything.

Kent Harvey was not going to win or lose Coach Knight any basketball games. What's more, the boy was not attacking Knight's family or country, challenging his religion, politics, or even his manhood. He was being slightly ill-mannered, and while most adults would be mildly annoyed by some pip-squeak nineteen-year-old calling them by their last name, few make a career out of scolding other people's disrespectful children. That's a life's work. One that Coach Knight has apparently taken on.

More than a decade ago, in *Bob Knight: His Own Man,* author Joan Mellen wrote of Knight's "impulse always to teach someone a lesson . . . strangers no less than players," and told this story. One day as Knight eased his car onto Kirkwood Avenue just outside the IU campus, he inadvertently cut off an approaching student on a bicycle. Not realizing it was the coach, the kid let loose with a Knight-worthy string of obscenities. The coach stopped the car and hopped out to teach the cyclist some manners.

"Coach, I had no idea it was you," the student said.

"What difference does it make?" replied Knight. "I'm not an asshole." And so, apparently, he didn't want to be treated like one.

In the midst of this altercation, a photographer from the student newspaper materialized. When he attempted to take a picture, "Knight just picked him up and set him into the hedges," reports Mellen. (Isn't "set" an interesting choice of a verbs? Knight biographer Phil Berger opted for "shoved.") Knight's passenger, the dean of the IU law school, would later apologize to the photographer "on Knight's behalf."

So we have a traffic violation that inspires an angry outburst, a confrontation with a student, and an assault and battery on a photographer. In some quarters that incident alone would qualify as a job-threatening, "lengthy pattern of inappropriate behavior" as Indiana University President Myles Brand had phrased it back in May. Throw in a hell of a witness—the dean, no less, of the law school—and you have a lot to work with.

But to get back to the point: what's this kind of behavior got to do with winning basketball games?

With only a few exceptions, the Bob Knight low-light reel, from manhandling an LSU fan to throwing the chair to clutching Neil Reed by the throat—"the litany" as Mellen characterized it—features incidents directly related to basketball. In the heat of the moment, Knight's behavior—sometimes justifiable, sometimes not, often an overreaction—is directly related to playing and winning the game. That behavior, if not always forgivable, is at least understandable. But this thing with Harvey, this schoolmarmish, even prissy insistence on meaningless decorum makes no sense whatsoever. None.

"I do think Kent was out of line calling him by his last name," said Kent's brother Kevin, "but a simple 'I'm "Coach" to you' would have been enough. He didn't have to grab him and get in his face."

Exactly. Or as Knight put it: "I would have to be an absolute moron, an absolute moron, with the things that have been laid down on me to grab a kid in public and curse at a kid in public."

Well, yeah.

Chapter 30

A Five-Fish Riot

Tuesday morning, September 12, 2000. A cloudy, gloomy day in the seventies. The satellite village at Assembly Hall has shrunk to only five trucks: four originals plus a new rental unit out of St. Louis. "Broadcast Biscuit," the outfit is called, and the logo stenciled on the beige exterior features a nicely browned biscuit sporting fluffy, baby chick wings, soaring above a red-and-white-checkered tablecloth. A banner across the bottom guarantees "the ultimate in video vittles." But with only a handful of the original dozen trucks still on hand, it looks like there's not much of an appetite for vittles today. At least not here. I wonder if I'm missing something.

On the morning news, I heard that Steve Alford, star of Indiana's 1987 NCAA championship team and now head coach at Iowa, is having a news conference at eleven o'clock. Rumors have been flying that Alford will be replacing Knight. But that gabfest is happening four hundred miles away in Iowa City. Maybe there's something going on with the players. The rebellion that started on Sunday has escalated, with three players threatening to quit and three or four others leaning in that direction if the university doesn't name one of the two assistant coaches, Mike Davis or John Treloar, head coach. There's word Knight is going to do an interview on ESPN, but that's not until 6 P.M.

I decide to go to the source and head inside Assembly Hall to the basketball office. Amazingly, there's no security, no receptionist, no nothing, and I walk in unchallenged. Inside, straight ahead, there's a boy behind one desk, and to my left I see Knight's secretary, Mary Ann Davis, behind another. Both are on the phone. Knight's office looks the same as four months before: a landfill for IU memorabilia. A dozen or so empty cardboard boxes are scattered about at random as if someone had it in their mind to start packing the various debris, then said, "To hell with it."

An attractive middle-aged couple stick their heads in the door, nod at the boy.

"This is for Coach," the woman says, handing a small package to the kid, like she was dropping off a casserole following a death in the family. The kid thanks them and they back out, all but genuflecting.

Mary Ann hangs up the phone.

"How are things going?" I ask.

Mary Ann is an attractive, single woman, I'm guessing in her late thirties or early forties, since she has two sons in school at IU. She's wearing a long-sleeved white knit shirt with horizontal blue stripes and jeans. Normally personable, if guarded, today she's in no mood.

"About as could be expected," she mutters.

I had called before I left Nashville to let her and Coach Knight know I was coming, would be staying at the Hampton Inn, and would be available to help any way I could. If I got lucky I might follow Knight around, get some behind-the-scenes stuff, perhaps an interview. Dream on. It's obvious nobody was eagerly anticipating my arrival.

The kid takes another call as I ask Mary Ann if Coach will be coming in today. She's not sure. The kid interrupts to ask Mary Ann if Knight will be doing the ESPN interview from his house. She doesn't know. She goes back to puttering around like I'm not there.

"Just wanted to let you know I'm in town," I said, retreating toward the door. "Tell Coach I said 'hello' if you talk to him."

"Oh, I'll talk to him," said Mary Ann, bending over a filing cabinet, her back to me.

I'll be checking my phone messages periodically, but I have the sense that nobody is going to be asking me for any "help." As for the cold shoulder: that's not bad news. Now I can report on that crumpled body under the sheet without feeling the insider's guilt about violating somebody's trust.

I head back to the Hampton Inn to catch the news. Steve Alford is staying at Iowa.

"I wish them the best in their search," he said. "But I don't want that search to include me."

Meanwhile the generally reliable Associated Press is reporting Assistant Coach Mike Davis will be named "interim" head coach at Indiana. A news conference announcing the Davis appointment will be held at Assembly Hall at 4 P.M. My schedule set for the rest of the day—the Davis news conference at 4:00 and the Knight ESPN interview at 6:00—I decide to take a look around campus.

I enter off Kirkwood Avenue through the university's Sample Gates, two faux-gothic limestone portals flanked by low walls and skinny, square towers with more gothic flourishes on top. Whimsical, purely decorative, it's easy to imagine Robert Goulet strutting through these gates and bursting into "Camelot."

Just inside on the right is a cobblestone path disappearing into an inviting wooded park, but I veer left up a slight rise on a broad sidewalk swarming with students, passing limestone buildings. A good first impression: pretty buildings, pretty girls, pretty boys. Everyone seems to have backpacks. It must be ultra-casual day: shorts, cargo pants, and T-shirts for the boys; short shorts with halter tops and clunky shoes for the girls. By comparison, my khakis and polo shirt look almost stuffy. A few adults hurry by wearing solemn, professorial faces.

I'm in search of Bryan House, a rallying point for the rioters on Sunday night. The ruckus began after Indiana University President Myles Brand announced the firing of the man he had described as "a terrific university citizen" only six months before. The mob, which had grown from sixty kids listening to the Brand news conference on a

Toyota Corolla radio outside Assembly Hall in midafternoon to several thousand by midnight, had made two round trips between the arena and Bryan House, President Brand's on-campus residence.

I soon give up on my campus map and flag down a pair of boys who give me directions sprinkled with "yes sirs" and "no sirs." Thanks to Knight, this may be the only campus in America where a fifty-something, silver-haired white guy gets any respect.

I stroll past the chemistry building, cross a little creek, start up a rise and see the back of what looks like a residence. I ask a couple of kids if it's Bryan House. "Yeah," one says. "Did you come to set it on fire?"

The brick house sits atop a "grassy knoll" (coincidence? I don't think so), and the broad lawn brings to mind tea parties, croquet, women strolling in hoop skirts beneath ruffled parasols that protect delicate, peaches-and-cream complexions. Around front, the unassuming, almost shy entrance makes the rambling, seven-thousand-square-foot house look small. The dark brick is set off by white trim, squat white columns, white shutters, everything in perfect order. Quite a contrast to Bob Knight's on-campus hangout.

Assembly Hall opened in 1971, Knight's first year, and is an example of what might be called "arena modern" architecture. In this version, massive, swooping expanses of gray concrete are interrupted by recti- linear towers and what look like flying buttresses to create the impres- sion of a tethered spacecraft poised for takeoff. Even now, thirty years later, Assembly Hall harkens to the future while Bryan House, only a short walk away, is a reminder of a more genteel past. Built in the early twenties during the reign of its namesake, IU President William Lowe Bryan, a philosopher like Brand, the house is all cozy symmetry, flat planes, right angles. It's a house where Woodrow Wilson would have felt comfortable. Or Truman Capote.

At the peak of the Sunday riot, the more than two thousand protest- ers were attended by 205 cops, two fire trucks, four ambulances, and several police dogs. The rioters knocked down a couple of lampposts, slashed tires, snapped off rearview mirrors, broke windshields, and scrawled a little graffiti here and there. Before the night ended there would be eight arrests for things like vandalism, disorderly conduct, assault. A month later, various sources put damage estimates at around twenty thousand dollars, most of that inflicted on Showalter Fountain in the heart of the campus.

That happened on the second trip to Bryan House. At around 7:30 P.M., after students chanting "Hey hey, ho ho, Myles Brand has got to go!" burned the IU president in effigy, the "two dozen state troopers" surrounding Bryan House decided the protesters were posing a real threat to the president's residence (Brand and wife Peg Zeglin weren't home), and they "pushed" the students back toward Showalter Fountain. Bad move. The fountain has been a traditional object of student abuse.

It's a tempting target.

The centerpiece of the large fountain is a two-ton bronze sculpture celebrating the birth of the Venus. This reclining figure of the goddess is surrounded by five dolphin-like leaping fish with water spurting out of their mouths.

"These fish have been targets for merrymakers over the years," said Kathy Foster, curator of nineteenth- and twentieth-century art at IU.

The maintenance guys confirmed that.

"We've repaired the fountain so many times, it's second nature," said the assistant physical plant manager. "Fish get yanked out so many times, just not all at once."

The night of the riot several hundred students ended up standing in the fountain. Driven into a frenzy by drenched coeds who, according to *Salon,* responded positively to calls of "Tits for Knight!" and "Boobs for Bobby!", the boys, like their predecessors, had their way with the fish. Usually students abuse only one or two fish, but this time they went all the way, damaging all five and removing four from the fountain to the chant of "Fish! Fish! Fish!" Three of the 350-pound fish were recovered nearby while the fourth was "hoisted up by protesters and carried to Assembly Hall," according to the student newspaper, where it was "dropped at the feet of the Indiana State Police."

Nice touch.

The last five-fish riot had occurred after Indiana won the NCAA basketball championship in 1987. This time damage to the fountain alone was estimated at fourteen thousand dollars.

From the fountain the mob headed toward Kirkwood Avenue and the off-campus business district. But police weren't about to let students do damage to the bars and pizza joints on Kirkwood.

"This is not going anywhere," said one cop.

About fifty cops in riot gear stood shoulder-to-shoulder and turned the mob north toward Assembly Hall.

This was around nine o'clock. On the way back to Assembly Hall—chanting "Fuck Myles Brand!", "Go to hell, Harvey!", and "Die, Harvey, Die!", according to *Salon*—the protesters swung by the football stadium to tear down the south goalposts. At 10 P.M., under a full moon, police had some success in dispersing the crowd in front of the arena, but by midnight the mob had regrouped and was back to full strength. Things were getting tense when Bob Knight came out at 12:30 and "quelled the riot."

"I'm gonna tell you my side of this thing," Knight told the kids through a bullhorn borrowed from the cops, promising to get together with students in the next few days to tell his side of the story.

"I think you'll be interested in hearing it," Knight said. "Now let's give these guys [the cops] a break so they can go home to their families."

With that, the riot was over.

Now, only two days later, Bryan House seems no worse for the wear. The only hint anything ever happened is a police car out front. I don't even see the trampled flowers and broken tree limbs reported in the student newspaper. As I retreat off the grassy knoll, I'm in sympathy with IU marketing czar Christopher Simpson, who had quarreled with the media's characterization of the protest as "a student riot." But, then again, such misinterpretations are possible when reporters run across baton-wielding police "in riot gear, complete with shields and helmets."

Chapter 31

Looking Forward
to Going Forward

It's nearly 4 P.M. and the satellite village at Assembly Hall has reformed, and then some. There are now eighteen trucks versus a dozen the night before. I follow the cables snaking their way across the parking lot, over the grassy plot, through the side doors, and onto the basketball floor, talking my way into the Mike Davis news conference. Not hard in laid-back Bloomington.

A podium sprouting scads of microphones has been set up at the edge of the center jump circle facing the sidelines. This half of the basketball floor is protected by overlapping gray runners about four feet wide. Reporters mill around amid several dozen white plastic chairs that have been lined up in rows facing the podium. There are a couple rows of empty red chairs over to the right. I count two dozen television cameras and more than a hundred reporters, photographers, and hangers on. I prop my tape recorder up against one of the thigh-high, black speakers and move back behind the row of TV photographers.

At 4:05 a herd of players, managers, whatever—I count twenty-two kids—shuffle in, heads down, sullen teenage body language grunting "death in the family." I spot a distraught looking Dane Fife, the kid who's been telling anyone that would listen he's going to quit the team. Looks like he changed his mind.

Fife's ensemble matches his mood. The outfit looks like it was plucked out of the bargain bin at a local thrift store. He's wearing tan cargo pants about four inches too long, a warm-up jacket the color of cigarette ashes zipped to the chin, running shoes, and a shapeless, cotton baseball cap. As for the rest of the players, three of the black kids are wearing respectable-looking sweaters and pants, but the others are done up in a motley array of T-shirts, shorts, jeans. There's one guy in the group wearing a tie: Mike Davis, the coach elect. The group settles into the two rows of red chairs on the right. There are cameo appearances by a PR guy and some vice president before Athletic Director Clarence Doninger comes to the lectern to "make a very important announcement."

Like the players, the sixty-something Doninger is in casual mode, wearing a white polo shirt with red horizontal stripes and gray pants that match his comb-over. Doninger tries to establish a light tone, saying he "would have worn a coat and tie" if he'd known there was going to be a news conference. (If the athletic director didn't know, who did?) There's no reaction. Then, although he's an attorney himself, Doninger makes a lame crack about lawyers. Again, nobody laughs. Finally, Doninger gets "on message" and makes the first of two likely scripted talking points: folks at Indiana University are positive.

"I've tried to be positive during those times [the past year] and I'm *definitely* positive today," says Doninger.

Then comes the big announcement.

"The new interim head coach at Indiana University is Mike Davis. The interim associate head coach is John Treloar."

And with that, Mike Davis becomes the successor to a legend and the first African American to coach a major sport at Indiana University. Still no reaction. Tough crowd.

Doninger moves on to likely scripted talking point number two: Everybody—the administration, coaches, and especially the players—is "going forward."

"We're pleased that they're willing to go forward with us and looking forward to going forward with us in this great program that we have."

Then Doninger introduces Davis, and the funereal silence is finally broken by scattered applause.

A scowling Davis comes forward to the lectern, and the team lines up two deep behind him. About 6′4″ and still in good shape, Davis looks like a basketball player and dresses like a banker. He's wearing a conservative gray suit with a subtle stripe which will be invisible in newspaper pictures, a pale blue shirt with a white collar, a gray-and-red tie, and black shoes.

Davis is stern, earnest, uncomfortable in the limelight, and, perhaps anticipating an avalanche of criticism that will never really come, he launches the first volley of what sounds like a defense for replacing a man he will characterize as "a good friend."

"The first thing I'd like to say is there's no way I could turn this job down because of the players and their parents," says Davis.

"Watching television every day, listening to them talk, the way they came to the front for me to be a head coach," continues Davis, "it really touched me."

So Davis claims his main reason for taking the job is the support demonstrated by the players.

Hmmm. Not a good start. Davis's opening lines are not only border-line defensive, they're disingenuous. For starters, forget the players. Truth is, there's "no way" the soon-to-be-forty Mike Davis would turn down *any* head coaching job at this point in his career. Second, this is not just any job, it's Indiana, baby, one of the nine or ten best basketball programs in America. And as Davis will say only minutes later, "For Mike Davis to be head coach at Indiana is a miracle."

Davis grew up poor in Fayette, Alabama, a flyspeck of a community forever in the shadow of Tuscaloosa, a metropolis of eighty-three thousand best known for its football team and an adjunct called the University of Alabama. The Davis family lived in a house so small—about five hundred square feet, Mike guesses—it didn't even have a kitchen, just a table and stove where mother Vandella's budget called for spaghetti three nights a week. The house was so small that when Davis was lucky enough to get a ride home after practice, he'd have the coaches drop him off at his grand-father's more respectable house nearby. But there was plenty of room in the yard for the dirt court and basketball goal where Mike learned to compete, playing against older brother Van. Mike was the youngest of four kids, and he and Van lived with their mother while his oldest brother, Bill, lived with his maternal grandfather, a minister, and sister Janice with an aunt. Mike's estranged father died in Denver following open heart surgery when Davis was twelve.

Growing up, Mike played football, baseball, and basketball and earned pocket money mowing grass, picking blueberries, hauling hay. Meanwhile mother Vandella worked as a secretary at the black high school where her brother was the principal and at the phone company where she was the first black employee. Vandella struggled to keep her kids in school and in church, and Mike Davis remains a devout Baptist.

As a high school senior, Mike was named Alabama's "Mr. Basket-ball" and a *Parade* All-American. That earned him a scholarship to the University of Alabama, and Davis still says the move from tiny Fayette to Tuscaloosa was the biggest day of his life. At Alabama, Davis lettered all four years and became known for his defensive skills against players like Michael Jordan and Charles Barkley.

"If they scored," Davis said, "whew, it was like they were taking the life out of me."

What Mike lacked in talent he made up for in effort, and he would earn the Alabama "Mr. Hustle" award all four years and be named to the SEC all-defensive team. After graduation Davis would play and coach pro ball for several years before moving into college coaching. Knight had hired him three years before.

Back at the news conference, Davis continues with his prepared statement, telling reporters a fable to illustrate how he feels about getting the job.

One night a man on horseback rides into a pitch-black forest and comes upon a stream, says Davis. Here a "voice" orders him to scoop up some rocks from the streambed and put them in a sack.

"In the morning," the voice tells him, "you'll be both happy and sad."

The man scoops up the rocks and continues on his journey. When daylight comes, the man opens the sack and sees the rocks are gold. He's happy because he has some gold, sad because he didn't get more.

Davis feels the same way, he says, both happy and sad. Happy to be the new coach, but sad "because of the way it happened."

Davis keeps talking, something about Indiana basketball being "bigger than any of us," but I'm still back there with the man on horseback. While I understand why Davis and the man would both feel "happy and sad," I'm trying to decipher the deeper, presumably hidden, meaning. Does Davis see this interim coaching gig as half a bag of gold and feel like he would have gotten all the gold, the whole job, if he'd only been equipped with some kind of metaphysical flashlight to illuminate the streambed of opportunity? Then I remember. This is sports. It doesn't have to make sense.

"I'm sad because I know what the Knight family is going through," continues Davis.

Meanwhile Mike's wife, Tamilya, running late, is listening to the news conference on the car radio, at first with her fingers crossed, then relieved as she tells fifteen-year-old Mike Jr., "Your dad sounds good on radio."

Five hundred miles south in Alabama, Mike's mother, Vandella Davis, and family friend Josephine Kennedy are watching the news conference on television. At first they are "afraid to breathe." But after Mike makes it through the first couple of minutes without incident, the two settle in to listen to what Mike is saying instead of worrying about how he's saying it.

There was reason to worry.

Throughout his youth, even at the University of Alabama, Davis had struggled with a "crippling speech impediment." But today, while no one would ever mistake him for Martin Luther King, there is "[n]o stuttering. No half sentences," as Josephine Kennedy put it.

"It was beautiful," said Vandella. "I was very proud and happy."

A retired school teacher, Josephine Kennedy had worked with Davis as a child—a child who stuttered so badly he had to complete oral assignments in private sessions with a teacher; a child who switched from quarterback to running back in football so he wouldn't "have to worry about saying anything."

"People don't know," Mike Davis later said, "but I'm struggling for every word I say."

There's no evidence of that today as Davis talks to the reporters, even though he'll claim he hadn't slept the night before worrying about a possible news conference.

"I talked to every player here," continues Davis. "They're on board with us."

Actually the players were "on board" even before Davis had figured out what he wanted to do. On Sunday, during a meeting with Myles Brand, before the news conference announcing Knight had been fired, and before Knight had returned to campus from the fishing trip in Quebec, the players were already threatening to quit if both Davis and Treloar were not kept on.

A day later that demand would turn into an ultimatum.

"We've spoken to Coach Knight," Dane Fife told ESPN, "and he agrees that we would still play here under Coach Treloar and Mike Davis if they were retained."

Reporter Jeremy Schaap: "And if they are not?"

"Indiana won't have a team next year."

On Monday afternoon a group of at least six players delivered that ultimatum in person to Athletic Director Clarence Doninger.

In the beginning, Davis was noncommittal.

"A lot of guys would just jump on it, right now, y'know," Davis told ESPN. "I'm gonna discuss this with Coach Knight. Whatever Coach Knight tells me to do. Y'know. What Coach says and what the players say."

But later that same day, Davis himself was delivering an ultimatum, saying the only way he would stay at Indiana was as head coach.

"If I came back as an assistant, I would feel like that's a disrespect to me as a coach," Davis told reporters.

How real were the threats by Davis and the players? Very real, thanks to Bob Knight.

Knight offered to pay both Davis and Treloar their full salaries for the year out of his own pocket if they chose not to return to Indiana. That's a cash outlay in the neighborhood of two hundred thousand dollars. What's more, he promised to take them along to his next coaching job. As for the players, Knight played Jiminy Cricket to their Pinocchio and told them to "let their conscience be their guide" and that he'd help, whatever they decided to do.

"He said he'd help us get into another school if we wanted to leave," said one player.

And there were some offers coming in, according to Dana Caldwell of *The News Sentinel* in Fort Wayne. One player was claiming that "representatives from Georgia Tech, Cincinnati, Iowa State, and other teams" had been calling since the story broke. And immediately following the news conference announcing the firing, Caldwell reported hearing this exchange between players Jeffrey Newton and Jared Jeffries.

"Where you going?" Jeffries asked Newton.

"Don't know yet. Maybe Cincinnati," replied Newton.

After Dane Fife told Knight he was leaving, the coach reportedly shopped him around to at least one other school. So the ultimatums delivered by both the players and Davis were made more credible because one Bob Knight was willing to back them up. Athletic Director Clarence Doninger really had no choice.

Faced with the prospect of losing two assistant coaches and as many as seven players, Doninger caved, offering a co-coaching job to Davis and Treloar. Treloar demurred, saying it was old pal Davis's turn.

"They wanted us to be co-head coaches," says Davis. "And Coach Treloar stepped up and said that he wanted me to have this job, because I had worked so hard to become a head coach."

Treloar and Davis have a long history. Treloar, who is white, says he considers Davis a "kid brother." He first coached Davis at Alabama, where he was an assistant. Then Davis both played for and coached with

Treloar in the Continental Basketball Association. In all, the two spent six years together before coming to Indiana in 1997.

Back at the news conference, Davis is taking questions. I see a teenage black boy and a black woman carrying a toddler walk across the upper level of the "end zone" seats behind the basket to Davis's left. Facing front, Davis can't see them, but it turns out to be his wife, Tamilya, and sons, twenty-two-month-old Antoine and fifteen-year-old Mike Jr. Davis had apologized for his wife earlier, saying she might not be able to leave her classroom at Perry Meridian High School.

Tamilya and the kids finally make it down to the floor and settle into the red seats vacated by the players. A beautiful woman, Tamilya is Davis's second wife. Mike Jr. is one of two children from Davis's first marriage. The second child, Nicole, was killed in a car accident in 1990. Davis also has a grown daughter, Lateesha, the result of a high school romance, who now lives in Atlanta.

Reporters are asking if Davis has talked to Knight.

"We talked yesterday and the day before," replied Davis, "and, uh, he supported me staying here. And he asked me the first night he came back on Sunday, 'Did I want to stay?' And I'm here."

That sounds like a Knight endorsement, and *SportsCenter*, the Associated Press, and a slew of newspapers including *USA Today* would report that Knight signed off on Davis taking the job. That wasn't the case.

Earlier in the news conference, as part of his opening remarks, Davis shared an anecdote making it clear that all was not well with Knight.

"I had a friend last year who died from cancer," Davis told reporters. "And when it got to the end, he called me a couple of times and I didn't talk to him, because it was so difficult for me to talk to him."

Difficult for Davis?

Following that astonishing admission, Davis revealed he had not actually talked to Knight after he was offered the job.

"I called Coach Knight a couple of times and I left messages for him, but I'm really happy that he didn't answer the phone because it would have been difficult for me to talk to him."

Difficult for Davis?

Six weeks later, Knight still had not responded to those messages, and Pat Knight was declaring that Davis and Treloar "stabbed my father and me in the back."

The problem? "I've got some bad personal feelings about Mike that he didn't take the job in the right way," said Pat.

According to insiders, Davis and Treloar asked Knight for help getting NBA jobs and then cut a deal with IU officials behind his back.

"[I]nstead of driving ten minutes to tell [Knight] face to face," said Pat, "he leaves a message and we haven't spoken since."

As for Coach Knight, Davis and Treloar have slipped into the coach's "those people" category. Not for what they did to him, but for what they did to Pat. According to Knight, Pat was instrumental in helping both men get jobs at Indiana. (Pat had been an assistant to Treloar at the Connecticut Pride of the Continental Basketball Association.) But after Davis and Treloar took over at Indiana, they never once contacted Pat. That's not the way Bob would have handled it.

"I think I would have said, you know, 'Is there anything we can do for you?'" said Knight on *Larry King Live* in March 2001. "'Can we help you? I mean, you know, I have a chance here because you helped me get it and I really appreciate that.' Pat has had no contact with those people at all."

To be fair, aside from the pure awkwardness of it all, how could Davis and Treloar have helped? Pat had told anyone who would listen that he didn't want to coach at IU. On Monday, *before* Davis took the job, Pat told an Indianapolis TV station, "If my dad goes, I do. I'd rather go pick tomatoes for a living."

Later Pat told the *Indianapolis Star,* "Heck, I got fired along with my dad. That's the way I see it."

And when asked directly if he would stay on as an assistant, Pat told the Associated Press, "No. I'm going with my dad. I stand by him."

So really Pat had no interest in staying at Indiana. His loyalty was to his father. Secondly, if your dad is Bob Knight, it's unlikely you need any help getting a coaching job from a couple of then basketball footnotes like Mike Davis and John Treloar. And, sure enough, only nineteen days later, the University of Akron coach, a Knight pal, announced Pat would be his new assistant.

But whatever the facts, one thing is not in dispute: Knight did feel betrayed. At the least, some kind of gesture on the part of Davis and Treloar was expected, some homage to loyalty, and it never came.

In October, Davis would tell the *Indianapolis Star* that he didn't believe loyalty to Knight entered into the equation. He said his loyalty was to the players and IU.

As for loyalty to Knight: "I was loyal to him when he was here," said Davis. "Now I'm remaining loyal to Indiana University."

Actually Davis wasn't loyal to anybody. He broke ranks with the university and the players when he issued his ultimatum: make me head coach or I walk. He broke ranks with Knight when he took the job without his approval.

"To be loyal means that you 'stand by' the object of loyalty," writes Pauline Kaurin, a philosopher at Pacific Lutheran University. What's more, if you're loyal, continues Kaurin, "you consider claims of obligation related to that object of loyalty to outweigh other claims—whether your own or from other sources."

Clearly, the reason Davis stayed had nothing to do with loyalty. It had to do with ambition.

"I stayed because it was an opportunity for me as a head coach," said Davis.

Now we're getting somewhere. Ambition trumped loyalty. And why not? Sure Davis should have dropped by Knight's house and taken his medicine, maybe suffered through a tantrum, but turn down the Indiana job because of some squabble between Myles Brand and Bob Knight, a couple of honky senior citizens? Get real.

In the end Davis takes the advice of his fifteen-year-old son. "Y'know, Daddy, you gotta take this job." Why? Again: It's Indiana, baby! So Davis takes over as head coach at Indiana University in a move akin to marrying your best friend's ex-wife six months after the divorce. Nothing illegal about it. Nothing really immoral. Who can fault true love? Sure there are rouge-cheeked loyalty issues popping up like ex-girlfriends at a high school reunion, and while the whole thing is—as the folks in Mike's hometown of Fayette, Alabama, might say—"a tiny bit tacky," America is just going to have to get over it. The only thing surprising here is that John Treloar handed the job over. Now that's loyalty—or something.

—————◆——————

Fifteen minutes after the news conference is over, the white chairs in front of the podium are empty, the reporters and photographers having spilled out onto the court, traipsing on the unprotected side of the floor. They coagulate around the newsmakers, lights glaring, cameras rolling, hanging on these boys' every word. Dane Fife, the leader of the player rebellion, is getting the most attention as the group surrounding him soon swells to eighteen. Kirk Haston, another team spokesman, towers above six more. I walk around, overhearing snatches of interviews.

"Did any thoughts of leaving cross your mind?" a reporter asks.

"There's only one Coach Knight," a player says.

Are the reporters expecting wisdom? Insight? If so, they should check out the group of four players on the other side of the court who have resumed their usual teenage grab-assing. For a second, the curtain drops and you can see how very, very young they are.

Outside, the adults have set up seven cameras on the grassy plot between Assembly Hall and the parking lot, reporters doing live shots and stand-ups, corkscrew wires trailing out their ears as they tell the world what all the tall teenagers in Bloomington have to say. A gum-smacking, sandy-haired Indianapolis sports anchor, in wire-rimmed glasses, black suit, and a gray T-shirt waits for his cue; a woman with a short, geometric haircut, wearing a black blazer, jeans—which won't show on camera—and black high-heel boots yammers at the lens; a black man sporting the then stylish Regis Philbin look, with matching fabric in shirt and tie, waits just outside the glare of two floodlights.

I imagine Knight brooding somewhere, feeling betrayed. Suddenly he's out of the loop. People are sneakin' and hidin', running around behind his back making deals, saying one thing, doing another, no longer worried about what he might do. After thirty years, he's power-less, fired. The locomotive of defiance he set in motion at West Point more than a generation ago has finally derailed. And while he will con-tinue using IU stationery months after his dismissal, continue referring to Indiana as "we," and continue to answer to the title "coach," techni-cally he's not a coach at all. He's in limbo, *persona non grata,* a man without a country, a coach without a team.

Chapter 32

Uh Huh. Right.

I head back to the Hampton Inn, check my messages. No blinking red light, no word from Knight. I'm the jilted suitor? Nah. I'm the guy who called following a so-so first date because I said I would. He calls me back? That's cool. He doesn't? I just keep on doing what I'm doing. Whatever that is.

I duck out the back door and cross the parking lot to Denny's. I have just enough time to grab a quick supper before the Knight interview on ESPN. The place is empty except for a couple of cowboys in a back booth. I know they're cowboys because they're wearing ten-gallon hats.

There are two girls out front. Both about eighteen. Both clad in make-do waitress uniforms: black pants, white blouses, black shoes. That's where the quest for corporate conformity ends. The girl at the cash register has shaved her noggin except for two little top knots, dyed dusty pink, where her antennae should have been. A gaggle of silver bracelets race up one arm, and a matching necklace holds an amoeba-shaped pendant the size of a half dollar that dangles at the base of her throat. She's wearing clunky black shoes, and her cargo pants—so tight they're a health hazard—are showing off what is and should be a great source of personal, state, and national pride.

I flee to a back booth in the smoking section where the second girl slides a menu under my nose. Compared to her cohort, this particular woman-child looks almost conservative. Her black pants are a size or so above what's required to prove she's anatomically correct, and the half-inch-long buzz cut, in what could possibly be a natural color, looks almost luxurious.

I order coffee, then glance at the Technicolor menu although there's never any doubt about what I'm having: the legendary Grand Slam Breakfast. My first. Somehow I've made it to middle age without ever having this cholesterol *piece de resistance:* a combo of two eggs, two pieces of bacon, two sausage links, and two pancakes. I'm loading up for the long night ahead. For now there's more than just Knight's ESPN interview to look forward to.

At the Davis news conference, everybody was given a handout announcing that Christopher Simpson, the Indiana University PR flack, would be providing a "media opportunity" at Assembly Hall following the interview. The "media alert" cautioned that "This is not a news conference, only a media opportunity." I'm not sure of the distinction, but I *am* sure it means more spin, more likely-scripted talking points. Everybody on message.

This is Simpson's third gig as a university PR man. He had been director of marketing and promotion at the University of South Carolina before first hooking up with Myles Brand at the University of Oregon. His résumé also includes stops at the conservative *Washington Times* in D.C. and as press secretary for Strom Thurmond, the ultraconservative South Carolina senator said to have been present at the birth of fire. While Simpson's current title is vice president for public affairs and government relations, he describes himself as "the quintessential, behind the scenes, number two person." Knight will call him a spin doctor.

Back in May, under the headline "Foxy Flack Screws Scribes," CBS News correspondent Eric Engberg proclaimed Simpson the winner of the "Reality Check Award for Bamboozlement, Shameless Flackery, and Concealment of the Facts." Ironically, "spin king" Simpson was accorded the honor for his efforts in reconstructing Knight's image following the May 15 zero-tolerance news conference. Engberg lauded Simpson for limiting Knight's media access to "the most friendly forums possible": specifically, seven hand-picked print reporters and a pair of ESPN interviewers that included Knight's longtime friend Digger Phelps. Engberg called it a "slam dunk for Indiana University flackmeister Christopher Simpson."

This was not the first time Simpson and Knight teamed up. A year or so before, Knight had donated one hundred thousand dollars to help Simpson get something called "StoneSong" [sic] off the ground. Originally built around an outdoor production by the "world-famous" Indiana University opera, StoneSong director Tom White described the free festival as "an opportunity to expose people to types of music they might not have heard otherwise."

"This event has 'legacy' written all over it," said Knight, "and I'm happy to be a part of it from the very beginning."

By the time the festival rolled around in July 1999, the "world-famous" opera production had been axed, the "free" tickets were five bucks each, and the headliner was "cowboy folk artist" Ramblin' Jack Elliot. Only fifty-five hundred people showed up for the three-day event (organizers were hoping for ten thousand), and in October the festival "rolled over and died," as one Bloomington *Herald-Times* columnist so indelicately phrased it, its only "legacy" a spat over fund-raising between competing arts organizations.

I sip my coffee as a wizened woman in her late sixties slips out of the Denny's kitchen and lights up. She takes a drag, stares out the window at the traffic on North Walnut Street. She looks tough, down to earth, no nonsense. I figure this is a woman who knows her way around the hard side of life, knows sometimes things can get a little rough. This is a Knight person.

I put on my most charming smile. "So what do you think about this mess with Coach Knight?" I ask.

She sizes me up with a sidelong glance. "Good coach, bad person," she says, unsmiling, and turns back to the window.

Ouch.

Knight is a populist, and this woman should be part of his core constituency. If he's lost her, I figure, he's lost Bloomington, lost Indiana. And the next day an Indianapolis TV station will report a poll showing six out of ten Hoosiers think the university was right to fire Knight. That loss of community support was reflected in Myles Brand's informal and, some say, "illegal" survey of the Indiana University board of trustees on the Saturday prior to the firing. The Knight ouster reportedly got seven of nine votes.

The Grand Slam breakfast doesn't disappoint although I do feel a bit sluggish as I settle in at the Hampton Inn for the ESPN "*SportsCenter* special" live from Bloomington, Knight's "first TV interview since the firing."

Knight had arrived for the interview at the Four Winds Resort and Marina on Lake Monroe south of Bloomington at 5:30 P.M. in "a four-car caravan," Knight riding in a black Toyota sedan, Isiah Thomas in a silver Mercedes. Head down, Knight ignored the small group of reporters and spectators as he walked inside.

I aim the tape recorder at the TV speaker, start it rolling, and sit back, all but rubbing my palms together, ready for some of that famous Knight honesty we hear so much about: that willingness to call a dickhead a "dickhead." There are plenty of potential candidates: Myles Brand, Christopher Simpson, Clarence Doninger, the trustees, maybe even Mike Davis.

In his autobiography, Knight would describe "the people who ultimately dismissed me" as "deceitful and duplicitous" (that's "backstabbing liars" for those not toting a dictionary), but that night my anticipation was fueled by the harsh comments coming out of the tearful team meeting on Sunday night. Just after he returned from his Canadian fishing trip, Knight had called the team together to tell "his side of the story," and I guessed the players were parroting Knight when one said, "Myles Brand is a coward, C-O-W-A-R-D," and another: "This whole school is screwed up, basically. We were lied to, we were deceived, and now it's over, all because people wanted Coach out."

Then there was Knight's son, Pat, on Myles Brand. "He lied. He lied," said Pat, referring to the charges against his father. "He fabricated a bunch of 'em, spinning it to his advantage. And I swear to that."

Tonight's ESPN interviewer is Jeremy Schaap, son of Knight friend Dick Schaap, the highly respected ABC sports reporter. The two men face each other in a pool of light, limbo lighting it's called, sitting in director's chairs in front of a TV monitor.

After a short introduction, Schaap jumps right in. "Did you ever think you'd be fired?" he asks.

The thirty-one-year-old Schaap is dressed in a dark suit, light blue shirt, and matching tie, his dark curly hair framing a kind face. Knight's got on his usual khakis, but, in lieu of his traditional red shirt with IU insignia, he's wearing a green polo, a subtle "up yours" to the university, like a priest showing up for mass in a yarmulke.

Knight takes four minutes to answer the first question, saying he always thought he'd retire at Indiana, and in response to a second question, spends another couple of minutes saying "no," he's not feeling "embarrassed," he's feeling "proud" because of what was accomplished at IU during his tenure. Speaking of spin. In the midst of all this, Knight delivers a few wimpy riffs on his nemesis, Myles Brand.

"We have a different philosophy. We have a different approach to things," says Knight.

Myles Brand would probably second that since he is, by trade, a philosophy professor. His specialty is something called "action theory." Under that rubric, philosophers ponder questions like, "What is left over if I subtract the fact that my arm goes up from the fact that I raise my arm?"

Subtract an act from an intent.

Okay, moving along.

Knight will keep circling back around to the "different philosophies" theme throughout the interview whether remarking on how his approach differed from Brand's ("I'm not right for every administration") or was similar to those of previous presidents ("They understood some things I was trying to do").

After a while, it appears Knight is trying to sell viewers on the lofty notion that his firing had nothing to do with grabbing boys, but instead stemmed from some manner of high-minded debate between two worthy adversaries, one from Mars, the other from Orrville.

Actually Brand grew up in Brooklyn. Born on May 17, 1942, he graduated from Rensselaer Polytechnic Institute in Troy, New York, in 1964, a year after Knight left Cuyahoga Falls to become an assistant coach at West Point. Brand would get his Ph.D. in philosophy from the University of Rochester in 1967 (because he wanted to "confront the big questions"), marry, and father a son, Joshua, before embarking on a lifelong career in ivory towers all across the country. Early stops included the University of Pittsburgh and the University of Illinois-Chicago, where Brand was first named chair of a philosophy department. While in Chicago, Brand would end his first marriage, divorcing in 1976, the same year Knight would win his first national championship. Two years later Brand would wed one of his students, Peg Zeglin. These days, that's the kind of relationship that attracts unwanted attention from people like Ms. Zeglin, who describes herself as a "feminist" and whose title includes the words "gender" and "professor." But Ms. Zeglin assures us that she got no special favors because of her status.

Here's Peg: "Presently, there is controversy over persons of 'unequal power' developing relationships at a university. Things were different twenty years ago."

Uh huh. Right.

From Chicago, Brand would move on to the University of Arizona, where he added "dean" to his string of titles. While at Arizona, his book, *Intending and Acting: Toward a Naturalized Action Theory*, was published by the MIT Press. That was in 1984, the same year the Knight-coached Olympic team won the gold medal in Los Angeles. Over the years Brand had been gradually working his way out of the classroom and into the "front office" and in 1986 ended up as provost and vice president of academic affairs at Ohio State University, the same year John Feinstein's *A Season on the Brink* was published, solidifying Knight's image as basketball's premier bad boy.

In 1987 Knight would win his third and last NCAA championship at Indiana on a last-second shot by Keith Smart. A year later, still at Ohio State, Brand's past caught up with him when some smart-aleckly kids on the staff of *Engineer*, the Rensselaer student newspaper, reprinted a column student-editor Brand had written twenty-five years before. In the 1963 editorial, Brand argued that the Rensselaer administration "should not allow our traditionally male institute to adopt a policy of co-education" because the "major distractions" created by the presence of young females might lead to "mind-wandering during lectures."

In his "How embarrassing!" 1988 retraction, Brand, by then a reigning provost at Ohio State where the young females were, alas, not distracting, predictably called for the end of sexism in the classroom and the galaxy.

Leaving Ohio State, Brand would reach the top of his profession, taking over as president at the University of Oregon in 1989. Five years later, he would leave Oregon, becoming the sixteenth president of *Indianensis Universitatis*, as the university seal puts it, and the fifth school president to face the challenge of corralling Bob Knight.

As the ESPN interview with Schaap continues, Knight doesn't have much bad to say about Brand, whatever their "philosophical differences." He's being "nicey-nice," interviewing for his next job, doing "an audition for any would-be athletic directors and presidents," as Bill Benner of the *Indianapolis Star* would put it, and there's no hint of the *coup d'etat* that shattered his world only two days before. No hint his "fucking heart was ripped out," as Knight would later tell *Playboy*.

"My mistake was kind of overstaying the situation," says Knight, uh, philosophically.

I am about to slip into a Grand Slam–induced coma when Schaap wades in with his first meaty question.

"What did zero tolerance mean to you?" asks Schaap.

"Nobody ever really explained that to me, Jeremy."

The definition of zero tolerance had been at issue since a couple of weeks before when Knight announced he would not be teaching his usual "Methods in Coaching" class because of his fear that some incident might trigger a sanction.

"I asked the vice president of the university [for a definition] as recently as last Thursday," says Knight, minutely detailing his ongoing search for the precise meaning of zero tolerance. Nobody, it seems, could figure it out.

In the news conference announcing Knight's firing, Brand had met that charge head on. The university "had made clear what is acceptable behavior for Coach Knight" back in May, claimed Brand, and to prove it, he read an excerpt from the prepared statement from the earlier news conference. Included in the reading were the two, and only two, actionable clauses of the zero-tolerance policy.

(1) Any verifable, inappropriate physical contact discovered in the future with players, members of the university community, or others in connection with his employment at IU will be cause for immediate termination.

(2) Public presentations and other occasions during which Coach Knight is a representative of Indiana University will be conducted with appropriate decorum and civility.

When he finished reading, Brand declared: "In recent days it's been reported that our zero-tolerance guidelines are unclear or ill-formed. Nothing could be further from the truth."

Actually, with all due respect, Brand's choice of adjectives, "unclear and ill-formed," pretty much sums it up.

Let's start with "unclear." The list of people who characterized the zero-tolerance policy as unclear (or some variation) include John Walda, the president of the Indiana University board of trustees, PR man Christopher Simpson, and Myles Brand himself.

Knight was not even the first to point out that the policy was unclear. That honor fell to trustee John Walda, who when pressed at the May 15 news conference, told reporters: "The evaluation of acts in the future is more of an art than a science. The standard that I will apply and the trustees will apply, we will not tolerate any conduct on the part of our basketball coach which is an embarrassment to Indiana University."

At the same news conference, Brand announced the appointment of a committee to establish a code of conduct for the entire athletic department. That committee, said Brand, would ultimately decide "what's inappropriate conduct whether verbal, physical or both. And, yes, there will be some judgment calls. This is not an algorithm, a science of how to do this. Judgment will be necessary."

As for more specific, perhaps "clearer" guidelines, those would have to wait until the "commission" finished drafting the Knight-inspired code.

"We will set down very clear guidelines," said Brand on May 15— as in, they hadn't set down "clear" guidelines yet. And in case anyone thinks Brand's off-the-cuff remark was not reflective of the policy, in a news release ten days later, he is quoted as saying, "It is essential that we work together to develop firm, clear guidelines that spell out what is acceptable."

If the "clear" guidelines were yet to be developed as Brand said, then can we infer that the existing guidelines were "unclear"?

Finally, only five days before Knight was fired, Brand's right-hand man, university spokesman Christopher Simpson, told the *Indianapolis Star:* "I think it's premature to characterize the [zero-tolerance] policy as nebulous because it's not complete."

Can we agree that a policy that's "not complete" is by definition "nebulous"? Okay, moving along.

So despite Brand's protestations, he, John Walda, and Christopher Simpson had all joined Bob Knight in professing that the zero-tolerance policy was unclear, a work in progress.

As Walda and Brand said, implementing a zero-tolerance policy is an art, not a science. As for any precise definition of the type of behavior that might violate the policy, they seemed to be relying on the approach taken by Supreme Court Justice Potter Stewart who, when pushed to define obscenity, said, "I know it when I see it."

Let's not waste any more time on this. The zero-tolerance policy was a bit of a muddle. One letter writer to the Bloomington *Herald-Times* compared it to "double-secret probation." But was the policy "ill formed"? Sure. And Brand and company were likely the first to realize it.

That will become obvious as Jeremy Schaap starts working his way through an abridged list of so-called "zero-tolerance violations," the alleged "troubling pattern of inappropriate behavior" that supposedly triggered Knight's firing.

"We want to play some of [Brand's] comments for you," Schaap says, and rolls a tape from the "firing" news conference.

"There was a continued unwillingness by Coach Knight to work within the normal chain of command in the IU athletics department," says Brand.

"There was nothing that came up from May 15 to the present where I needed to interact with the athletic director in any way," replied Knight.

Uh huh. Right.

Later Knight would tell reporters that he was "the athletic director for basketball" and there was "never a need for me to act through the athletic director. Never. I schedule. I hire. Everything that needs to be done with basketball, I do."

Brand would dispute that, but according to Knight's written contract, the coach had "approval of all matters associated with Men's Varsity Basketball at Indiana University." So technically, it appears Knight was right. There was no reason to contact Doninger. What's missing here is the blood feud going on between the coach and the athletic director.

The two had been butting heads for years, their feud culminating in an ugly incident following Indiana's February 19 loss to Ohio State the previous season. After the game, Doninger showed up outside the locker room and, according to Knight's account, said, "Boy, that was a tough game." Knight says he responded: "How the hell would you know?" and asked Doninger to leave. Doninger refused and things escalated from there until team doctor Brad Bomba stepped in to end the "verbal confrontation."

"They started jawing and I just got up, got in front of Bob, walked him back three or four feet and said, 'Let's cool it,'" Bomba told the Bloomington *Herald-Times*.

So just as he did during his first year at West Point, Knight takes on an athletic director. Back then he "ripped him up" and "called him a son of a bitch," according to one witness. And just like at West Point, he got away with it. But unlike at West Point, here he makes no attempt to kiss and make up. And so seven months after the Ohio State incident, Knight was still hunkering down over at Assembly Hall, refusing to mend fences with Doninger.

Schaap rolls another video clip. This time Brand is accusing Knight of "verbally abusing a high-ranking, female university official."

Christopher Simpson had told CNN-SI that university attorney Dorothy Fratwell claimed Knight was "rude" and "profane" during a run-in described as "initially unnerving, later intimidating, and then borderline threatening."

Brand called it an "angry outburst."

"Is that true?" Schaap asks Knight.

The coach launches into a long, rambling response, and after several minutes, when there's no sign he's getting any closer to an answer, Schaap jumps in.

"Did you scream at her, Bob?"

"Would you let me finish?"

"The gist of this is did you treat her in a manner that you—"

"I'm trying to explain that, if you'll just give me a chance."

Schaap gives up. "Go at it," he says.

Knight goes on to admit he had a "negative attitude toward the entire administration" at the time of the run-in with Fratwell and, after once again being prompted by Schaap, says all he did was ask her to leave his office.

"I did not scream at her," says Knight. "I did not yell at her."

"Did you swear?"

"I did not use profanity."

Knight claims to have witnesses.

Schaap moves on to the Miss Manners episode with Kent Harvey, but Knight quickly brushes that aside to address Brand's charge that he refused to speak at "previously scheduled Varsity Club events in Indianapolis, Bloomington, and Chicago."

"There were no previously scheduled Varsity Club outings," Knight tells Schaap.

And while he had traditionally spoken in these cities, this year, due to the zero-tolerance policy, he was limiting his public appearances to the four required by his contract. To put this in perspective, Knight normally made at least twenty speeches a year. He was cutting back on the advice of his lawyer, he said.

Uh huh. Right.

"He told me I just could not afford to expose myself," says Knight.

Well, we wouldn't want that.

The university was forewarned. Way back in May, in his first interview after the announcement of the zero-tolerance policy, Knight told reporters the policy "will inhibit me from doing some pretty worthwhile things, like going to a fund-raiser, like speaking to a group." Knight also wasn't sure if he would speak to the press after games. "That has to be decided," he said.

But you have to wonder. If Coach Knight couldn't control himself at Varsity Club outings, what chance did he have of getting through an emotionally charged basketball season?

More lawyerly advice led to Knight bowing out of the "Methods in Coaching" class he had taught for twenty-nine years.

"If you're a student and you don't like something I've said to you, you get a C and you thought you should have gotten an A," Knight says to Schaap, "Is that a violation of zero tolerance?"

Nah. But we get the point.

Bob Knight had found a way to make the zero-tolerance policy his own, a way to seize the policy and wield it like a broad ax, delivering a couple of licks upside the head of Indiana University. Disregard the coy explanations. Coach Knight knew damn well he would create an uproar by canceling the class and an even greater uproar by not making his traditional appearances at Varsity Club gatherings in little alumni way stations like Chicago, Indianapolis, and Bloomington, cities that are home to the largest and most rabid congregations of Indiana fans. Think it is an accident those particular Varsity Clubs didn't make the cut? Knight was going out of his way to snub alumni, hiding behind the zero-tolerance policy.

Yet however hostile and ill-mannered, this arms-length dissing of alumni is not covered by the zero-tolerance guidelines. Neither is stonewalling the athletic director or "verbally abusing" a university lawyer. In fact, a close look at all of the incidents constituting the "very troubling pattern of inappropriate behavior" reveals that six of the seven incidents don't fall under the guidelines Brand laid down on May 15. (Other non-qualifiers left off Schaap's list include bad-mouthing trustees; Knight's refusal to cancel his Canadian fishing trip in an act of "gross insubordination," another carryover from West Point; and being generally uncooperative.)

While Brand tried to downplay it, the "I'd-have-to-be-an-absolute-moron" Harvey episode is the only incident on the list that violates the zero-tolerance policy. This is the only instance in which there is "inappropriate physical contact," the only instance in which there is a public breach of "appropriate decorum and civility" (to hear the Harveys tell it), and the only instance that caused the university any embarrassment whatever, thanks to the media coverage. None of the other episodes made it on ESPN until the university made them public. (Perhaps the definition of zero tolerance should have been "anything that makes *SportsCenter*.") While Knight did have a history of embarrassing employers (a history that began during his first year at West Point), from May 15 when the zero-tolerance policy was implemented until he was fired on September 10, only the Harvey incident met even that criteria.

Someone inside the university apparently noticed this disconnect since, after reading each charge, Brand repeated the same refrain: "This violates the letter and the spirit of the guidelines set down on May 15."

The spirit certainly. The letter? Nah. That's nothing but spin.

Wily old Coach Knight had found ways to misbehave outside the zero-tolerance guidelines. The university had set up the policy to respond to public displays of temper, not private acts of defiance. It must have been frustrating. Brand felt like he had the goods on Knight, but Knight's transgressions simply weren't covered under the guidelines. To use Brand's adjective, the policy, it seems, was "ill-formed": too vague to explain satisfactorily, but not vague enough to cover Knight's maddening insolence.

In a last-ditch attempt to prove Knight understood zero tolerance, IU would re-release Knight's written statement from May in which he said that he had "absolutely no problem with guidelines." Notice the Knight statement didn't say "*the* guidelines," and later he would claim he meant guidelines in general, not the particular ones laid down by Brand.

Uh huh. Right.

This Clintonesque parsing of words was final proof that the outbreak of disingenuousness had spread to the coaching ranks in Bloomington.

In the end, the zero-tolerance policy was unworkable because it was both unclear and ill-formed. In hindsight, it might have been wiser for the university to adopt a simpler, more elegant approach, to go with one simple time-honored guideline that's been around so long, it's universally understood, especially in the macho world of Bob Knight. Just tell the man: "Don't be an asshole" and let it go at that. All seven of Brand's charges would fit under that all-inclusive criterion, from the refusal to work with Doninger to the boy-handling of Kent Harvey. For those taking notes, the lesson here is that vague and all-inclusive is better than vague and finessable.

While Brand's charges might not have fit the guidelines, he still had plenty of good reasons to fire Knight, and the "it-takes-a-village-to-raise-a-child" episode with Kent Harvey was the least of it. Any university employee who time and again goes out of his way to thumb his nose at the president of the university, the trustees, and the alumni is begging to be fired. Brand's characterization of Knight as "defiant and hostile" seems about right. Even Knight admits to having a bad attitude. And since Knight's contract said that he could be fired with no cause whatsoever—"If the University at any time desires, Coach shall cease to serve as Head Basketball Coach"—the mystery is why Brand felt the need to pound the charges into the zero-tolerance mold. Probably some political thing. Some effort to shape public opinion. That and the arrogant—and accurate—assumption that everything would go by so fast nobody would really notice.

As for Knight, months later he told *Playboy* all the maneuvering was unnecessary.

"There's so much bullshit and so much deceit involved," said Knight. "All these people had to do was come to me and say, 'You don't fit in with what we want our basketball coach to be. You're no longer what we think is needed here.' All I'd have said is, 'That's fine. Let's settle up.'"

If it were all that simple, why didn't Knight just resign when Brand gave him the opportunity? Why force Brand to fire him? Is it possible he and Brand were involved in an old fashioned, "Did! Did not! Did too!" pissing contest?

Chapter 33

Talking Points

The ESPN interview continues as Schaap moves on to Knight's legacy. He leans forward for emphasis, grasping his legal pad with both hands.

"How important is it to you," he asks, "to be the winningest college basketball coach of all time?"

"Totally unimportant!" says Knight.

To prove it, he starts telling a story about how son Pat, while cleaning out his dad's locker, found the game balls marking Knight's six and seven hundredth wins buried under some old shirts. But before he gets very far into it, Knight delivers an aside characterizing Pat as "the real victim in this whole thing."

"But Coach—" Schaap says, trying to wedge in a question not scribbled on his legal pad.

"Let me finish, Jeremy," says Knight, a threat in his voice.

"But Coach—"

"He's the victim in this."

"Yeah, but—"

"Pat is the victim in this. Now—"

"He's the victim, but if you had abided by the rules, would he have been the victim? Would he still have his job?"

In other words, if Pat's the victim, aren't you the perpetrator?

"I don't think I had any chance to abide by the rules," says Knight, matter-of-factly, but the fuse is lit.

Knight smolders a bit, starts up about Pat again, then stops in mid-sentence and criticizes Schaap for interrupting him.

"You've got a real faculty for doing that," says Knight.

There's some merit to the charge. There have been nine interruptions to this point. Schaap chuckles, says "thank you," but Knight won't let it go.

"I don't think it's anything—"

"I'm sorry."

"—to be proud of myself," says Knight, now openly miffed.

"Bob, you came here to do an interview. I'm asking you questions."

"Well, then let me finish the answers. Is that okay, Jeremy?" says Knight, badgering, voice steeped in sarcasm. "Is that fair enough? Have I interrupted your questions yet?"

"Yes," replies Schaap, nodding.

"No, I haven't," insists Knight.

Schaap shows both palms in a sheepish "whatever" gesture.

"You've interrupted my answers with your questions and then I've tried to get back. So let me finish this."

"Continue," says Schaap.

Knight's tone has softened and he seems to be back on message, out of danger. What follows is a four-second pause, silence, dead air, an eternity on television, as Knight massages his chin with thumb and forefinger, chews on air. Then it comes.

"You've got a long way to go to be as good as your dad," says Knight, wearing a half grimace, half sneer. "You better keep that in mind."

There's a collective nationwide groan from friends and foes alike. Same old Knight. I'm stunned. Isn't Dick Schaap supposed to be Knight's friend? Hasn't Knight known Jeremy since he was a kid? While Schaap has been aggressive, that's part of the job; he's not one of these pit bull reporters. He knows when enough is enough. Knight has overreacted. Again.

Don't be an asshole.

Knight continues as if nothing happened.

"Pat came in the house and he said, 'Dad, let me tell you what I found in the bottom of your locker.'"

"Kind of a cheap shot," said Schaap following the interview. "But it's not a big deal. That's who he is. That's the way he responds to a line of questioning he doesn't like."

For sure.

Several months later, while doing an interview with *Playboy*'s Lawrence Grobel, Knight would really lose it—twice. The first blowup came in a car somewhere between Bloomington and Akron when Grobel asked about the Kent Harvey incident. Knight banged the steering wheel, reported Grobel, shouted, "Jesus Christ! This is bullshit! I'm not here for a fucking inquisition."

"You haven't brought up one fucking positive thing I've said or done since we've been talking," Knight continued.

It got worse. Later, when the fearless Grobel brought up the infamous 1985 chair toss, Knight got physical, going so far as to grab Grobel by both wrists.

"I want those goddamn tapes!" Knight cried.

He didn't get them, of course, and amazingly, before the interview ended, Knight and Grobel were back on good terms. Still it was one of the worst Knight outbursts on record. All because Grobel pursued a "line of questioning he didn't like."

As Jeremy Schaap's ESPN interview continues, Knight will keep coming back to the "philosophical differences" theme: "a group of people that didn't particularly get along with a guy and a guy that really couldn't fit in with the group of people."

Before the night is done, Knight will get all his talking points in: the pre-interview for his next job—"I'm an unemployed teacher, right now, and I'm looking for a place to teach"; the claims he's gotten along well with thirty-eight of the forty-three people he's worked for.

"That's a pretty good percentage," Knight says.

(More than 88 percent, to be exact.)

Knight's last athletic director at West Point is not included in that group of benevolent administrators. Just before he left the Academy,

Knight says he went in and told the guy, a general no less: "I know that to become a general officer requires Congressional approval. And I can't imagine we have so many Congressmen that would be dumb enough to make you a general on the basis of what I've seen."

And when the time came for Knight's West Point going-away party, this general wasn't invited.

Burn them bridges.

So how'd the Schaap interview go? Great for ESPN. Two million plus viewers tuned in, substantially more than double the usual number in that time slot. In Indianapolis the interview was the highest-rated television show all day, even besting the quiz sensation *Who Wants to Be a Millionaire.* As for Knight, he refused to shake hands with Schaap after the interview, later calling him a "little squirrel."

To get the university's take, I make the short drive to Assembly Hall, a big yellow sun in my rearview mirror. Soon PR man Christopher Simpson and Trustee Stephen Backer appear for the "media opportunity."

The news crews swarm: a dozen or so reporters and photographers surrounding Simpson, a smaller group concentrating on Backer. I raise my tape recorder at arms length over the top of the crowd and point it in Simpson's direction. Simpson is looking very corporate in his dark suit, white shirt, and tie. From my angle I can see he has a nose made for straight-on shots.

Simpson is all hearts and flowers, a sure sign the Knight interview has done no significant damage to the university. Even better, in upbraiding Schaap, Knight has just demonstrated the kind of boorish behavior the university has been talking about for three days, the kind of crap he's been allowed to get away with since his earliest days at West Point. So Simpson can afford to be generous and he is. He doesn't even respond to Knight's charges that he is, in effect, a liar. Later Simpson would brag about his ability to "control the message and flow of information" during the Knight flap.

"I see nothing productive at this juncture to get into a 'he said, she said,'" remarked Simpson.

Translation? I'm not giving this story "legs," not providing any reason for reporters to get another round of responses from Knight that will keep this story at the top of newscasts for another day. Smart. You call Knight "a liar," he calls you "a double-dog liar," and it can go on and on. Reporters love that.

Simpson goes so far as to become a Knight cheerleader. The ESPN interview, said Simpson, reminded him of "a side of Bob Knight we haven't talked about in seventy-two hours," the positive side of a man "with extraordinarily high graduation rates" who won NCAA championships, ran a clean program, and "spent an enormous amount of time doing philanthropic good."

Say what?

Simpson hoped out loud that "in the upcoming days the balance will return to the story."

I'm stunned.

The man who Knight claims "yelled longest and loudest" for him to be fired, the man who had provided reporters with all the nitty gritty details of Knight's alleged "troubling pattern of inappropriate behavior" is now criticizing the media for reporting what *he* told them. Now that's some gall. I mean you have to admire the sheer audacity. The man's got the balls of a rogue elephant.

"Much of the nation doesn't get to see the positive side of Bob Knight," trumpets Simpson. "There is a tremendously warm, caring, compassionate side, and that's been lost in the past few days, and I'm sorry that there was not more of an opportunity for the interviewer to revisit some of his successes."

Dazed, I wander away from the pack of reporters surrounding Simpson and meander over to a second pack kibitzing with Stephen Backer, one of eight white men and six lawyers, all IU law school graduates, then on the nine-member board of trustees. The only female or minority presence is Cora Breckenridge, an African-American speech pathologist from Elkhart. So much for "diversity." As I walk up, Backer, nattily dressed in a light-colored suit, is responding to a question about Knight's firing.

"Public opinion had nothing to do with it," says Backer.

At a state university? Controlled by elected officials? Governed by a board of trustees dominated by the six appointed by the governor, including Backer? Public opinion had everything to do with it. And in a democracy, what exactly is wrong with that?

Has everybody gone crazy in Bloomington? Dizzied by the spin coming from all sides, I retreat to the Hampton Inn and a couple of fingers of Johnny Walker Red. I scribble in my notebook.

"Simpson. A suited stiff.... He's so 'not Knight.'"

"What's true doesn't matter," I write. "The question is 'What will play?' How to 'manage' this information."

"Knight didn't burn the bridge in front of him. He didn't call a dickhead a 'dickhead.'"

Smart.

"So Chris the flack says, 'Let's talk about the positive.' Hello! *You* fired him. The media didn't fire him."

I have entered a world of dueling talking points, a contest to win the hearts and minds of a particular constituency: the Indiana public in the case of IU, and potential employers, athletic directors, and university presidents in the case of Knight. Here the game is to "control the message," as Simpson puts it. So Knight and Simpson alike are selecting the facts that fit their message, downplaying the facts that don't, and the goal is not getting to the truth of the matter. The goal is advancing your cause. "What do you really think?" is a question that remains unanswered.

When asked, Bob Knight will tell you first he's honest. But here honesty is giving way to something even more important in the Bob Knight–West Point hierarchy of values: winning. The "honest, straight-speaking" Knight is being overwhelmed by Knight "the great competitor." He's parsing words, lawyering every answer, in hopes of winning the debate. It won't be the last time.

Here's how Knight would try to explain away the Neil Reed "choking" incident on a couple of episodes of *Larry King Live*.

"There's probably never been a player," Knight told Larry King in late September of 2000, "that has played for me that I haven't taken and moved here or moved there."

Then, during a second appearance on *Larry King Live* in March of 2001, Knight tells King he doesn't remember what went on with Reed, but denies he has ever choked anybody. And after looking at the fuzzy tape, Knight says he's not sure he even grabbed Reed by the throat.

"You can't tell where my hand is right now," Knight told King. "You can look at that and my hand is somewhere in the upper part of the body."

Well, based on Bob Knight's past history, it's hard to imagine him not knowing precisely where his hand is. For starters, here's how Knight described his throat-grabbing "motivational" technique to a gathering of Indiana businessmen in 1992.

"You take the bottom two fingers, ring finger and little finger of the stronger hand, and you place it in the neck of the garment being worn by the person you want to motivate," Knight said as the audience yukked it up. "With the middle finger and the index finger of that same hand, you grab the Adam's apple and with the thumb, with a little practice, you can control the answers you're going to get from this person."

There's more. While it didn't come out in the seven-week Indiana University investigation concluded in May, there were enough Neil-Reed-style "choking episodes" alone, six in all, to constitute a "lengthy pattern of troubling behavior." These date back to Knight's earliest days as a head coach.

Knight himself has admitted to, even bragged about, grabbing West Point cadet Danny Schrage "by the throat" back in the sixties.

"I can remember my fingers slipping off his Adam's apple or I would have killed him," Knight gleefully told Joan Mellen in *Bob Knight: His Own Man.*

In the same era, Bob Cousy reportedly saw Knight "with a hand against a player's throat as he backed the cadet against the arena corridor."

Then, in 1976, according to the *New York Times,* Knight "choked and punched" IU assistant sports information director Kit Klingelhofer during a run-in Knight has described as "all my fault."

Louis "Buddy" Bonnecaze, Jr., the LSU fan who ended up on his butt outside a hotel bar in 1991 after calling Knight an "asshole," told Rich Wolfe in *Knightmares/Oh, What a Knight!* that the coach "grabbed me by the throat and he shoved me backward and he squeezed my neck as hard as he could."

"I had some contusions around my neck," continued Bonnecaze.

Finally, there is Chris Foster, the Bloomington guitar maker, who accused Knight of making racist remarks (the coach vehemently denied it) at an Elletsville, Indiana, restaurant in 1999.

"He whirled around and grabbed me by the throat," Foster told Wolfe. "Left marks on my neck."

So Knight has a history of clutching other people's Adam's apples. It's apparently a signature move. Not only that, in the past at least, he seemed almost proud of it, part of his image as a tough guy. So Knight's reputation for honesty is put in jeopardy when he claims to not know what he's seeing on the Reed tape. Same goes for his rationale for coach-player contact.

"There's a lot of demonstration that has to be done," Knight told King in September 2000.

"I think in coaching you're going to have to go out and you're going to show kids things," Knight continued.

Okay, let's see if I've got this right. In the middle of some routine practice, Coach Knight grabs a player by the throat and then drags his ass over to where he's supposed to set that back pick in the motion offense.

Oh, please.

To pretend what went on with Neil Reed is the same as run-of-the-mill contact between coach and player is, in a word, "bullshit." In the case of Reed and the other two players, there wasn't any "demonstrating" going on. Knight was steamed and he grabbed the players to shake them up, send a message. Why not just say that? Because that's tantamount to admitting abuse. So Reed wins. Knight loses. And that just won't do. For in Bob Knight's world, winning matters; it matters a lot.

Chapter 34

It's Only Sports

When I wake up on Wednesday morning, it is fall. Crisp, clear, there's no trace of the gauzy summer air, the shimmery suspension of dust and pollen from the day before. It's been four days since Knight's midcareer correction, twelve hours since the Schaap ESPN interview, and an hour since the start of Mike Davis's first practice—make that "voluntary workout"—as head coach of Indiana University. A new day has dawned whether or not anybody is "looking forward to going forward."

I collect my complimentary coffee in the Hampton lobby, wrestle a stack of newspapers out of the clanking racks out front, and retreat to the "smoking lounge" on the back stoop of the building. I sit on the chilly concrete steps overlooking the Denny's parking lot, light up, sip, and shake the newspapers open.

"Undaunted Knight: 'I'm looking for a place to teach,'" reads the front page headline in the hometown *Herald-Times*. "Knight to get $1.3 million in deferred compensation." Actually it'll end up being more than four million once the interest is added up. Firing coaches can be an expensive proposition.

Sixty miles north, editors of the *Indianapolis Star* take a "he said, she said" approach. "Knight fires back" says the headline, "Ex-coach says IU didn't tell the truth."

The headlines surprise me. I expected something about Knight trying to bully Schaap. To me, that brief encounter best demonstrated what Brand was trying to get at with his lengthy list of charges: the day in, day out necessity to keep your hands away from the cage. Seems West Point's "little baby fox" had developed into a full grown, snarling predator.

I dig deeper. Despite the headlines, both papers soon get to one of Knight's likely scripted talking points.

"We have a different philosophy, we have a different approach to things," reads the *Herald-Times*, quoting Knight.

I'm reminded of past newsroom battles about what to call opposing sides in the abortion debate. Naming the battle can go a long way toward winning it. Literally, who's not both "pro choice" *and* "pro life?" So if Knight can make the issue "philosophical differences" and not a "troubling pattern of inappropriate behavior," he has a better chance with all those potential bosses out there: the university presidents and athletic directors.

The steps too cold, the temptation too much, I amble down to Denny's, not sure if the lure is the convenience, the Grand Slam Breakfast, or the chance for a second look at those dusty pink antennas.

She's not there, of course, works the night shift, and I settle into a lonely booth attended by an unremarkable waitress. Ignoring the pleadings of my inner nutritionist, I order my second Grand Slam Breakfast in less than twenty-four hours.

More coffee. Another cigarette.

Oddly, Myles Brand and Bob Knight seem to share philosophies—on paper at least. "Our commitment to excellence is at the heart of all we do," reads Brand's official IU biography. "[G]ood enough will never be *good enough*. . . . [We] encourage our students and faculty to be the very best that they can be."

Excellence, it appears, is an end in itself.

Knight's version is a little more blunt. "I just say, hey, kid, goddamnit, be the best player you can be."

But there are differences. For starters, Brand's quiver of motivational arrows doesn't include things like profane tirades and thrusts to the jugular. There are limits in the pursuit of excellence. Second, in the eyes of Brand and most everybody else, if it involves sports, a "commitment to excellence" is of a lower order since sports is one of the "ancillary activities." A university employee, say a Nobel prize–winning scientist, might get away with losing his cool on the way to finding a cure for cancer, but not to win a basketball game. Was Jonas Salk civil? Does it matter? Are some things more important than being nice? Sure, but as a mere coach you are expected to rein in your, uh, enthusiasm. It's only sports, after all. Just a game.

"Sports (especially the spectator kind) is not a very serious human pursuit," wrote hotshot novelist Richard Ford in, of all places, the introduction to *The Best American Sports Writing 1999*. Sports has, Ford continued, "almost no innate importance whatsoever, except what observers and participants decide to dream up for them."

The implication being that the rest of us, like story-writer Ford, are involved in higher pursuits. But, other than raising kids, few of us are doing any work that matters much: finding that cure for cancer, ending world hunger, writing *Hamlet*. As one cynic put it, most of us are destined "to do the pointless for the ignorant." Surely it's not all that bad, but our work, as Ford says of sports, generally does lack a "moral necessity, some 'I can do no other quality' of human motive."

The Grand Slam Breakfast is even better the second go-around. The thin, dry, crispy-edged pancakes of the night before, scions of watery batter, have given way to siblings of the traditional fluffy variety, and the bacon and sausage are fresh off the griddle. I add too much butter, too much syrup, living large in Bloomington.

The essential pointlessness of sports is not lost on Bob Knight. Back in 1984, an interviewer asked him what does it matter in the grand scheme of things whether twelve kids at Indiana play well.

"It *doesn't* matter," responded Knight. "It doesn't matter at all, except I'm in charge of those twelve guys and it matters a hell of a lot to me."

"So, damn it, we're going to play it as well as we can play it," continued Knight.

Knight has the *Washington Post*'s Tony Kornheiser convinced. "If I had to select one coach to coach one game for my life," wrote Kornheiser, "it would be Bobby Knight unhesitatingly."

But sports matter even when nobody's life is on the line. Remember Brand's philosophy? "Our commitment to excellence is at the heart of all we do"; "Good enough will never be *good enough.*" Well, athletics, rightly or wrongly, have become a showcase for a university's wares, an opportunity to "walk the talk."

In this context, success has little to do with the experiences of the individual athlete. Even if every athlete claimed the playing field was "the best class I had while I was in school," as Knight once put it, there are simply too few of them to matter. What matters is showing the public what Indiana University means by a commitment to excellence. And when critics grumble there is too much emphasis on winning, that's like saying there is too much emphasis on being the best.

Would they prefer losing? Yes, in moderation, says one anonymous Division 1A university president, cited in *The Game of Life* by James L. Shulman and William G. Bowen. He advised peers to hope "for some winning [football] seasons in the range of 7–4, 8–3," warning that "a season or two of 11–0 or 10–1 records and high national rankings will change the culture of your institution."

What message does this push for mediocrity send? We'll make a half-assed effort at this athletics thing, while we wait for something important to come along because trying too hard would be unseemly. We'll really try when we're doing something that really, really matters, like finding a cure for AIDS. But for all the other stuff (translation: "life"), we have permission to be slackers. Generations of mothers were right. "If something is worth doing, it's worth doing well" and, as Knight might add, doing it well all the time. Remember when he booted Mike Noonan off the team for not hustling after a rebound *before* practice?

And as for winning, it's just a stand-in for excellence.

"Do you crave victory?" *Playboy* asked Knight in 1984.

"No, what I have is a great desire for excellence and it doesn't include victory," replied Knight. "Winning is the by-product of playing well."

Some university presidents sitting atop elite programs act as though developing a world-class basketball team is easy. It's not. It's unique. And for most, it's the one thing their school can do better than Harvard.

Instead of grumbling, they should embrace a winning program as a case study in how to achieve excellence. The hard work. The dedication. The obsession. Perhaps even the emotional commitment that leads to occasional outbursts by coaches who eat, drink, and sleep their work. Such a case study provides "models not simply for the university community, but for others throughout society," observed former University of Michigan President James J. Duderstadt, "a remarkable model of life. And those factors that lead to a program's long term success are also the factors that prepare young men and women for life itself."

Amen.

I'm starting on my third cup of coffee by the time I get to the stories about Mike Davis. His appointment gets second billing in both the newspapers. "Davis named interim IU coach" says the front page *Herald-Times* headline, accompanied by a color photo of a smiling Mike, wife Tamilya, and twenty-two-month-old Antoine.

"Interim coach known as hard-working competitor," says the *Indianapolis Star*.

The quelled player rebellion tops sports pages in both papers. "Davis promotion brings calm after the storm," says the *Herald-Times*. "Hoosiers show their unity," says the *Indianapolis Star* over a six-column-wide color photo of the team standing behind Davis during the news conference. The caption: "Standing behind their man: Indiana University basketball players show their support for interim coach Mike Davis."

Both papers include a rags-to-riches, poor-boy-made-good Davis bio and a great AP photo of the coach getting a group hug from four players, 6′ 11″ freshman Jared Jeffries laying his head on Davis's shoulder. "Tough times" says the *Indy Star* cutline. "Davis pauses to share a warm moment," says the *Herald-Times*.

One player is reported as telling Davis, "I wuv you."

Six months later, Davis will end up "wuving" the team too, when a Cinderella Indiana squad becomes the runner-up in the NCAA tournament.

While it's mentioned, neither paper makes a big deal of Davis being the first African American to coach a major sport at IU. Perhaps black "firsts" are no longer news. Even the election of Selma's first black mayor the day before is relegated to the inside pages, although, astonishingly, the loser in the election is seventy-year-old Joe Smitherman, the sitting mayor on Bloody Sunday thirty-five years before.

The *Herald-Times* devotes one sentence to the Selma story in an election roundup, the *Indy Star* three paragraphs.

Nobody reports on the rift between Knight and Davis.

I shove aside my empty plate, drain the last of my coffee, gaze out at the intersection of North Walnut and whatever, where the traffic is picking up. In twenty-four hours, I'll be taking a left and heading on out, trying to remember the directions for the short cut Knight told me about three months ago.

I weave the newspapers back together and stack them neatly, saving them for future reference. The local coverage of the Knight flap is, if not exhaustive, certainly exhausting, and I'm ready for a nap. I scribble a "to do" list in my spiral notebook: Find Dunn Meadow, where Knight is to deliver his farewell address to students tonight. Go shopping for some kind of jacket to ward off the fall chill. Catch the local midday news on TV. Exercise for the first time in five days. In other words, pretty much kill time until Knight's six o'clock speech.

A couple of hours later, I'm trapped on a treadmill at the Hampton Inn "fitness center" as some TV reporter pummels me with a sordid tale about some boy who was kidnapped, raped, and killed. The story over, I return to my senses, beating my "Difficult-for-Davis?" self up for being so squeamish. "You think it's hard to hear the story," I tell myself. "Try living it."

Back in my room, I check the phone. Still no call from Knight. I switch on the noon news where, in Indianapolis, WISH-TV reporter "Pam," a pretty brunette in her late thirties, has been assigned the Bob Knight story.

"Well, Eric and Patty," she tells the midday co-anchors, "people are talking about the interview and Bob Knight's version of what led up to his firing."

Uh oh.

The story, if you'd call it that, consists of three stale sound bites from Knight and three bites from man-on-the-street interviews, the lowest form of news. There's no voice-over.

"My mistake," says Knight. "I think I was just, kinda, overstaying the situation. The situation changed, people changed, and we have a different philosophy, we have a different approach to things."

Black man: "He's not an easy guy to work with."

This story won't be making it onto Pam's résumé tape. I figure she or maybe some intern spent about thirty minutes putting this turkey together. Maybe Pam had a doctor's appointment. Maybe she's tired. Being WISH-TV's "daybreak anchor," where she shares airtime with a beagle named Barney who once had his own show, "Barney's Bad Movies," Pam's probably been up since about 4 A.M. So what if this Knight thing will end up being named the biggest story of the year in Indiana, right ahead of the "massive White River fish kill"?

Now about that dog Barney. I would give Pam a hard time, except someone might remember my campaign for a newsroom dog back in my TV news days. Following in the tradition of J. Fred Muggs, the chimp on NBC's *Today* show in the fifties, I figured if we took care of the real news up front, we could get away with a ratings booster like raising a puppy on air. I'm sure this played no part in the station's decision to downsize my ass six months later.

Pam's "story" continues. Knight calls Simpson a liar. A black woman says Knight is "setting a bad example." Knight tells Schaap he "has a long way to go." A white kid says, "Jeremy was doing the best he could to interview him, but Bob just got out of character like he always does."

Got out of character? See what I mean about those man-on-the-street interviews?

Listening to this, I'm beginning to rethink the wisdom of Christopher Simpson's strategy. Knight is getting his "I'm just a misunderstood teacher" shtick out there (which, to be fair, dates back several decades) and owing to Simpson's hands-off approach, there's no counterargument to cast doubt.

I'm even starting to believe the Knight bit myself. Right. Like I believe Christopher Simpson is sincerely concerned that the "nation is unaware" of the "tremendously warm, caring, and compassionate side" of Bob Knight.

"There you go," Pam says, popping back up on camera for the wrap-up. "Coach Knight said that he is open to coaching again somewhere else. Well, tonight you'll hear what people around town are saying about that."

Great. More man-on-the-street interviews.

Time for the cross talk. "Noon anchor" Patty, who sidelines as an "entertainment reporter," gets it going.

"I tell you, good or bad, he does not back down, does he?" remarks Patty, a forty-something blonde whose official station bio mentions her four cats, "furry friends" Tuffy, Mimi, Fifi, and Miss Kitty.

"No," replies Pam, whose official station bio mentions her dog, Boo.

"He stands, stands his ground," continues Patty. "Okay, thank you, Pam, thanks very much."

Of all the on-air people at WISH-TV, Pam and Patty are the only two who mention pets in their official bios and the only two who mention either pets or children by name (Pam also has four stepchildren). And here these two women are paired up on the Bob Knight story. What could it all mean? I'm betting dog Boo is a carryover from Pam's single days, was part of her life before the marriage to the guy with four kids. Have Boo and Barney, the TV dog, met? Is Boo jealous of Barney? And Patty's cat names: Don't they sound more like French poodles? Tuffy, Mimi, Fifi. Miss Kitty is an aberration, maybe the oldest. Tuffy, I'm thinking, is the only male. But then "Tuffy" is not really gender specific. All of which proves that just the tiniest little bit of thinking about TV news anchors can actually destroy brain cells.

I check my watch. Five hours 'til showtime.

Chapter 35

Dunn Deal

I get to Dunn Meadow for Knight's farewell speech around 5 P.M., an hour early, and there are already a couple hundred kids milling around. Lots of tank tops, sandals, the occasional tie-dye. The sun, filtered by a picket line of trees, etches bright, elongated streaks across the grass.

Back of me, the long side of the meadow runs along Seventh Street where seventeen satellite trucks, including Broadcast Biscuit, are parked end to end in a reconstituted Satellite Row. Four others are scattered along Indiana Avenue to my right. At the corner of Seventh and Indiana, a flock of frat boys is nesting in an aerie on the roof of the Sigma Chi house, waving a sheet inscribed "• X Salutes the General," blaring music creating a party atmosphere. A cheer goes up when the pizza arrives.

From Seventh Street, the meadow slopes gently south, forming a natural amphitheater. At the bottom of the slope, early-bird squatters are staking out the best vantage points in front of the speakers' platform, a rectangular slab of concrete rigged with lectern, microphone, and giant speakers. Over to the left, two sorority girls sit behind a card table peddling T-shirts that read "Coach Knight is Indiana."

A flock of officious kids clad in bright red T-shirts scurry around. Focused, purposeful, in charge, they are staffers from the *Indiana Daily Student* newspaper. When the university refused to make arrangements for the speech, Knight asked the editors of the paper for assistance, and they agreed after the coach promised to do "everything in his power to keep the crowd civil."

Dunn Meadow has been a traditional site for concerts, protests, and political rallies over the years and, since 1963, has been an officially designated area for "open speech and debate." That meant "no one could stop [Knight's speech] from happening," said IDS editor Peter Gelling. No one was *helping* it happen either. Gelling would later complain that the university left the students on their own with "no crowd control, nobody to handle the media."

"The IU Police Department, among others, had been instructed not to help by, what they called, their 'employers,'" Gelling wrote.

So the IDS staffers are making do and their inexperience shows. They did set up "risers" for the TV cameras, but the raised platforms are big enough to accommodate only thirteen of the thirty-one TV photographers on hand. The rest have been exiled to the newspaper ghetto over to the right where I'm hanging out. The area is prescribed by a knee-high pennant line, alternating green, red, yellow, and blue plastic flags strung between orange traffic cones. The idea is to cordon off the press well back of the speakers' platform "so they won't block the view of students or upset Knight." To the media, this is no big deal. (That's why God made zoom lenses.) The only concern is that the exiled, riser-less photographers won't be able to see over the crowd. But the photographers have adjusted by cranking tripods up to six or seven feet and standing on camera cases, plastic milk crates, whatever, their heads tracing a ragged line above the crowd.

I stake out a claim behind a photographer perched on a mini-stepladder, sighting down his lens to the podium. Soon the line between the press and the crowd is completely obliterated, kids high-stepping back and forth over the pennant line, and there is one solid mass of people stretching from the speakers' platform all the way to Seventh Street and halfway down the block. Crowd estimates will run as high as eight thousand. I end up shoulder-to-shoulder with a couple of girls on my left and a curly-haired, forty-something guy from the *Atlanta Journal Constitution* on my right. One of the girls is a stunning, freckled-faced redhead, and as I mourn the fact that I'm old enough to be her grandfather, there's a stir in the crowd.

I look up and I can just see the top of Knight's silver head bobbing above the crowd as he strolls onto Dunn Meadow surrounded by a cadre of kids in red IDS T-shirts. The applause starts, turns into a roar, and then chants of "Bob-*bee!* Bob-*bee!*" sweep across the meadow. The barrel of the camera slowly pans, following Knight as, over to the left, a girl claws her way onto the shoulders of her boyfriend to get a better view. Knight breaks through the crowd onto the speakers' platform, and now I can see second-wife Karen at his side, fighting off tears. (Knight divorced first wife Nancy in the mid-eighties, remarried in 1988.) The coach is wearing a blue plaid polo shirt, beltless denim pants with a pot-belly-accommodating elastic waistband, and boat shoes. Karen's in a beige blouse and pants. Nobody's wearing Indiana red.

There's no introduction and as Knight starts talking, the crowd hushes instantly, roars stifled in midbreath. After making a pitch for an upcoming cancer benefit, Knight leans over and clumsily kisses Karen. The crowd squeals approval and Karen slowly steps up to the microphone, sniffling, dabbing her eyes, holding her glasses in one hand and a tissue in the other.

"I hope what he just did won't be termed 'inappropriate physical contact,'" she says, echoing the language of the zero-tolerance policy.

The crowd chuckles, cheers, as I stifle a groan. The kiss, the punch line—it's a set piece. Staged. Fully scripted. Lame. A real Christopher Simpson moment.

My reaction makes me feel like a turncoat, and I worry that if Knight spots me commingling with the press, he might recognize me for what I am: a media fellow traveler. But he's so far away, I'd have to be on fire, a pillar of flame, before he could pick me out of this mob and perhaps not even then, given his lifetime habit of looking over the heads of audiences to avoid stage fright. I glance his way and sure enough, he's gazing at a point somewhere above Seventh Street.

In his farewell speech, Knight has little to say about Brand and company, but he does manage to get in one final jab.

"These people in the administration are really good at one thing and that's putting a spin on things," says Knight, interrupted by applause, "putting a spin on everything possible—anything possible to work to their advantage with no attention being paid to the truth."

"Nobody is better at the spin technique than right here," Knight continues. "Charlie McCarthy and Edgar Bergen are the very best there are at it."

"Who's that?" the redhead next to me asks her friend.

"Edgar Bergen was a ventriloquist," says the reporter from the *Atlanta Journal Constitution,* jumping in to bridge the generation gap. "Charlie McCarthy was his dummy."

The redhead laughs nervously, still looking puzzled.

"Candice Bergen's father," explains the reporter.

"Okay. I guess so," she replies.

Not only is the girl too young to remember Edgar Bergen, she's too young to remember his daughter Candice, even though the ten-year run of *Murphy Brown* ended only two years before.

So which was which? Who was McCarthy and who was Bergen? Turned out Brand was the dummy and Simpson the ventriloquist.

Simpson, the spin doctor, is the brains behind this outfit? That's the Knight theory. But you don't have to be a marketing whiz to know that Bob Knight was wreaking havoc with the administration's preferred image of Indiana University. And in the end, maybe that's what this whole thing is all about.

Indiana University is the home of a world-class music school, the Kinsey Institute, and an art museum designed by renowned architect I. M. Pei (see Pyramide du Louvre, Rock and Roll Hall of Fame, Javits Convention Center). But to the public, particularly at the national level, IU is a basketball school.

"For them, the most visible and vital role played by institutions such as IU is as a sponsor of athletic teams," Brand would tell the National Press Club in January.

And the marquee athletes and coaches, a tiny percentage of the university community, get about 98 percent of the media attention. In the case of Bob Knight, crank it up a notch. The coach is not merely famous, he's a Hall of Famer who has a chance of becoming the winningest coach in history. Literally, a household name. To much of the world, Bob Knight *is* Indiana University. But this "pompous, middle-aged white man with an anger control problem," to paraphrase one letter writer to *USA Today*, is not the Indiana of Myles Brand and the current Indiana board of trustees. Rather I suspect they would choose a symbol more like Brand himself: scholarly, politically correct, and unfailingly civil. And from the beginning of the flap back in March, the overarching issue was never really Knight's behavior, but the image Knight was projecting as "a representative of Indiana University."

That's reflected in the comments coming out of the May 15 zero-tolerance news conference.

"Our goal is to protect and enhance the image of Indiana University," said John Walda, the president of the Indiana board of trustees, as Brand called on Knight to "represent Indiana University with honor and dignity."

The aim was to avoid the kind of bad press that had followed Knight since year one of his coaching career at West Point.

"If there is any case in which Indiana University is embarrassed, as it has been in the past, we will act immediately," said Brand.

In the past, generations of Indiana students, alumni, presidents, trustees, and, most importantly, the public all went along. "Bob Knight might be an asshole," they seemed to say, "but he's our asshole." But Knight is right: things changed. Brand and this group of trustees were different. The power brokers no longer wanted the cantankerous coach as a representative of the university, as a symbol of IU, and, for the first time, they had the Indiana public behind them.

In the wake of the Knight firing, an IU faculty contingent penned a letter to the local newspaper saying, "Indiana University is about education. It is not about basketball." Maybe. But ultimately that is not for the faculty to decide.

Folks in academe too often view the American public with contempt, as "a herd of lascivious sheep," as *Harper's* editor Lewis Lapham once put it, that "requires guidance and direction" from the really smart folk on campus. Actually, in a democracy, it's the sheep, "lascivious" or not, who will be providing the "guidance and direction" for public universities. And it's the Indiana sheep through their representatives on the board of trustees who will decide exactly what Indiana University will be and, ultimately, who will be coaching the basketball team.

For almost thirty years the flock chose Knight. Then the support began eroding. Maybe it was Knight's less than spectacular won-loss record in recent years that changed people's minds. Maybe they too were feeling embarrassed. Maybe it was a combination. Whatever the reason, the political climate changed and the voters drifted away. And while Myles Brand took advantage of the situation, in the end it wasn't Brand but the people of Indiana who fired Bob Knight.

"I haven't retired. I don't intend to retire," Bob Knight tells the Dunn Meadow crowd.

The coach is winding down and the students, sensing it, hoist their signs, bobbing them up and down.

"No one is better than the man in the sweater," reads a twenty-four-by-thirty-inch felt-tip-on-cardboard sign attached to a stick with silver duct tape.

"Re-hire the General. Fire the President," reads another.

"I had great kids and a great experience at West Point before I came here," continues Knight. "I had great kids and a great experience at Indiana while I've been here. I hope to have great kids and a great experience where I go from here to coach."

Then the man who eschewed pregame prayer following his first game as a head coach at West Point asks the students to pray for him. Only now does his voice get a little shaky.

"I'd like each of you to just take a minute, a full minute, to bow your heads, and in whatever way you do, wish myself and my family the very best, as I wish you the very best."

Knowing he's done, the crowd ignores the plea and begins to applaud and cheer as Bob Knight tosses off a final wave.

"Bob-*bee!* Bob-*bee!*" they chant as Knight turns and disappears into the crowd.

Ten minutes later, all of Dunn Meadow is in shadow, the treetops tinted a brilliant red-orange, catching the last of the sunlight. I see one black player being interviewed, a foot taller than the surrounding reporters. A white kid with a black Afro walks by pushing a bike with a boom box playing Dylan strapped to the handlebars. A streetlight comes on.

The crowd disperses quickly and soon the only significant cluster of students left is forming a backdrop for an ESPN reporter doing a live shot. When he signs off, they rush over to stand behind his CNN counterpart.

The last of the television cameras is off the risers by 7:10, the photographers packing up: collapsing tripods, coiling cables, stuffing canvas utility bags to the bursting point. A bevy of red-T-shirted IDS kids trailing trash bags pick up the fast-food debris scattered across the grassy field. By the time the CNN lights blink off, Dunn Meadow is all but deserted. I stand alone, not ready for it to be over. Can this really be it after thirty years of *Sturm und Drang?* No fireworks, no brass band, no nervous guys in ill-fitting suits swapping plaques for handshakes? Does it really end like this?

Yeah, afraid so. And with nothing left to report, I stuff my tape recorder in one pocket, my notepad in the other, and head out. On the way to the parking lot, I see fourteen cops come out of hiding and strut down Indiana Avenue, riot helmets dangling at the end of bare arms.

Part V

MEDIA WARS

Chapter 36

Midnight Madness

Lubbock, Texas, October 12, 2001. At Texas Tech's United Spirit Arena, the Midnight Madness festivities don't start at midnight, they start at 9:45. All eyes on court for the Wiener Nationals, a pseudo competition the corporate sponsors claim will lead to the crowning of the "fastest wiener dog in the nation." What it will really lead to is mondo exposure for a fast-food hot-dog vendor named Wienerschnitzel.

Organizers clad in Wienerschnitzel-yellow polo shirts with a Wienerschnitzel-red logo on the breast cover the middle of the basketball court with a twelve-foot-wide white runner that stretches from foul line to foul line. The crowd of ninety-four hundred begins to stir as the eight dachshunds (one long-haired) are carried out and placed in the Wienerschnitzel-yellow starting gates. The Texas Tech cheerleaders and "poms"—dancing girls—kneel shoulder to shoulder around the edges of the track to keep the dogs from going astray during the anticipated sprint to the finish line.

I leave my seat in the parents' section just behind the Texas Tech bench and move up by the starting gate, camera poised to record the action. I'm in town to do my second formal interview with Tech's new head coach, Bob Knight, the former "Emperor of Indiana." In the meantime, I'm taking in the local color.

And they're off! The dogs, stumpy legs a'blur, run in every direction, except toward the finish line some sixty feet away. They are distracted by the roaring crowd, the glaring lights, each other. One wanders toward the sidelines, something red, maybe a ball, in his mouth. Another turns and heads back toward the starting gates. A greyhound race this ain't. As the dogs meander around, folks in yellow polos toss foil-wrapped samples of Wienerschnitzel hot dogs into the stands.

Knight has sneaked out onto the court with two-and-a-half-year-old grandson Braden in tow. Both look like they're enjoying the spectacle. Could this be the same Bob Knight who only six months before fretted about the prospect of money changers taking over the temple at Indiana's Assembly Hall?

"You'll see a new Assembly Hall, I'm sure, when you go there this year," he cautioned students in his farewell speech at Dunn Meadow a year before. "There will probably be ads in it for everything from dog biscuits to Pepsi Cola, I would imagine. But we've always tried to keep it really free from commercialism. It's kind of a sacred place where students come to play and students come to cheer."

Apparently there's nothing sacred about Texas Tech's United Spirit Arena. While there are no ads for Pepsi and dog biscuits, there are plenty for hot dogs, Coca-Cola, Sprite, and Powerade. And looking around, at the sidelines, at the scoreboard, at the facing of the upper deck, I see billboards for sixteen national and local advertisers including United Supermarkets, the Lubbock-based regional grocery store chain that paid ten million dollars for arena naming rights. (Knight says he could've gotten twenty million.)

Who says Bob Knight can't change? Whatever objections he might have had to commercialism appear to have vanished somewhere between Bloomington and Lubbock. That can happen to a guy who is responsible for paying for a $62-million state-of-the-art, NBA-style basketball arena while working for an athletic department that lost $1.48 million on a total budget of $22 million the year before.

"Knight wasn't hired to win basketball games," wrote one cynic in *Texas Monthly*. "He was hired to make money for Texas Tech."

Tonight, Knight himself is wearing a charcoal gray pullover with a Minute Maid logo on the sleeve. Subtle to be sure, but advertising nevertheless. (Knight had starred in a commercial for the brand earlier in the year.) He wasn't so subtle back in March when, during a nationally televised news conference, he stopped in the middle of answering a totally unrelated question to say: "Now don't forget about drinking Minute Maid for breakfast now."

The Midnight Madness festivities continue. Around 11:30, Texas Tech's reigning superstar coach is introduced. That would be the Lady Raiders' Marsha Sharp, who has led her teams to fourteen NCAA appearances and one national championship during nineteen years at Tech. She talks for a bit and then brings on Knight, who delivers a variation on what one Texas reporter calls his "stump speech."

"We have a chance to make this arena the most special place for college basketball in America," Knight tells the cheering crowd, then tosses a bouquet to Lubbock and West Texas: "You folks underestimate, you underestimate what you've got here. This is a great community with exceptional people," says Knight and then lists some virtues of the region on the way to setting up his punch line: "Y'know, to hell with people who don't like West Texas."

That gets 'em going.

Lubbockians? Lubbockites? Lubbockers? Folks from these parts have good reason to be defensive. Visitors have said some really ugly things about their hometown. The place was once described as "a treeless, desolate waste of uninhabited solitude," if you believe "The Handbook of Texas Online," but that was before it became "a cosmopolitan, modern city."

More recently, outlanders have complained of the dust here in the "Hub City of the South Plains," which receives only fifteen inches of rain a year; of winds so brisk that local weathermen routinely issue "windcasts"; and of the isolation (Lubbock is a six- or seven-hour drive from any place you'd really want to be, like maybe Dallas or Austin). One smart-ass ESPN reporter even said Lubbock was "located somewhere between Mexico and 'Watch Out For That Snake, You Fool!'" It's safe to say nobody ever shows up here by accident. And anybody who's ever had to make their way to this remote part of West Texas will likely nod with recognition when they hear some smart aleck refer to it as "Lubfuckistan."

Time to update that vacation planner. Lubbock, population 190,000, hasn't been a place of solitude and desolation for a long, long time. Texas Tech University alone provides about as much company (around twenty-five thousand students) and civilization (courses in everything from fashion design to wind engineering) as most people need here in rock 'n' roll pioneer Buddy Holly's hometown.

Texas Tech claims to have the largest campus in the nation, and buildings are widely spaced on a sprawling physical plant that stretches from the "Meat Laboratory" on the west to the twin-towered Administration Building on the east. Most of the structures, even the United Spirit Arena (located, by the way, on Indiana Avenue), have a Spanish flair and are constructed of the same monotonous, buff brick. At the signature Administration Building, the Spanish influence looks to be genuine, while the design of the newer buildings has been toned down and homogenized, creating a crisp, pleasing style that would look about right for a taco factory in an industrial park on the outskirts of Albuquerque.

As for Knight, he had professed his love for Tech from the beginning.

"You've got a great, great university," Knight said on March 23, during the combination pep rally/news conference announcing his hiring.

Seventy-five hundred people flocked to United Spirit Arena for the gathering. That was about half again as many as showed up for a typical basketball game the year before. Donned in Texas Tech red, Knight gave the crowd a two-handed Tech "guns-up salute" and they returned a standing ovation.

The "Bob-*bee!* Bob-*bee!*" chant arose and six boys stood, letters crudely drawn on their chests spelling out "Bobby K." One of the boys (safe to say he wasn't an English major) held up a sign that proclaimed, "Bobby Knight rules and stuff." Another student waved a sign that read, "Put the women and children to bed. It's Knight time." But on that day an elated Knight was on his best behavior—mostly.

"We love you, Bobby!" wailed an adoring fan.

When the question-and-answer session began, reporters from CNN-SI and the *Dallas Morning News* mistakenly thought they were attending a real news conference and asked a couple of tough questions. One guy was all but shouted down by the partisan crowd when he asked if Knight was going to be grabbing Tech players like he grabbed Neil Reed. Knight kept his cool while brushing him off. A more typical media representative was Fawn Lindsey from Fox 34 Sports, who felt the need to suck up.

"For the record, you and I are good," she said, as if Knight cared. "No problem with you."

To Fawn's credit, her question prompted the best Knightism of the day.

"What is the biggest adjustment you face?" she asked.

"When you're kind of the man in charge, you don't have any adjustments to face," replied Knight.

The crowd liked that one.

After a half hour or so of this lovefest, Knight called it a day, and the cowed media went home. Knight had won the latest skirmish in his ongoing war with the press.

"No one has done more to demean the art of sportswriting than Knight," Mike DeCourcy once wrote in the *Sporting News.*

No one can pinpoint the exact moment when Knight's feud with the media turned into an all-out war. Perhaps it was in the sixties when the New York press branded him "Bobby T." Or maybe it was in 1973 when Knight fired this oft-quoted salvo in the direction of his pal, Bob Hammel, a Bloomington sportswriter: "All of us learn to write in second grade," quipped Knight, "but most of us go on to other things."

Or war might have been declared in the late seventies when Knight jokingly fired a starter's pistol at Russ Brown, the long-suffering IU beat reporter from the *Louisville Courier Journal,* or in 1980 when he refused to answer any questions at a postgame press conference until *Sports Illustrated*'s Curry Kirkpatrick left the room. Whatever. Years of skirmishing escalated into open war, and Bob Knight's contempt for the media has become as much a part of his public persona as the sideline tirades.

And even today, Knight is not ready for a truce. In his 2002 autobiography, Knight wonders whether "journalistic credibility" is an oxymoron, charges that sportswriters are jealous of athletes because "those were the guys getting girlfriends in high school," and opines that polls showing journalists garner less respect than used-car salesmen "are way too kind." Damn, Coach, tell us how you really feel.

Knight goes on to say that the only people he doesn't get along with "good to great" within a sports community that includes players, coaches, officials, fans, and media is the latter. He even blames the media for getting him fired. Specifically, he points to the cover of the May 22, 2000, edition of *Sports Illustrated* that followed Myles Brand's announcement of the zero-tolerance policy. The cover that week featured a near actual-size close-up of a scowling, red-faced Knight, brow knitted, mouth open in a full-throated roar, with "WHITEWASH!" plastered across his forehead in letters about an inch high. "Indiana caves, Bob Knight stays," read the subtitle.

"If I wasn't dead at Indiana before, I was the day that magazine cover hit Bloomington and was read by Brand and Simpson," wrote Knight in his autobiography.

On Knight's behalf, *SI*'s coverage was pretty brutal. In fact, the tone of the cover and the article inside were so angry that I sent a letter to the editor suggesting that perhaps the writer himself might want "to join Coach Knight in one of those anger management classes." (They didn't print that one.) But to suggest that the president of a major university would be shallow enough to pay any heed to a *Sports Illustrated* headline is a little farfetched. *Time* maybe. The *New York Times* sure. But *Sports Illustrated?* Nah.

As for Knight's other criticisms of the media, let's just say on behalf of all of my lyin', jealous, lightly regarded, hard-to-get-along-with colleagues out there, that guys who learned all they needed to know about writing in the second grade shouldn't be penning 375-page autobiographies.

So there.

Midnight Madness continues, and on this night the media will be the ones getting the last laugh. This year's first practice kick-off celebration has been promoted as "A Sharp-Knight in Texas" in honor of the two coaches. Special T-shirts have been designed for the occasion with the "Sharp-Knight" logo on the front and a red, white, and blue "Proud to Be an American" emblem on the back, the September 11 tragedy being barely a month old. And when the long-awaited practice finally begins, all the players, coaches, and managers don the shirts. Even Knight sheds his Minute Maid pullover in favor of the commemorative shirt, although there is not a T-shirt in the world that would look as good as "really bad" on the waistline-challenged coach. But the fearless Knight wears it anyway, and Associated Press photographer L. M. Otero is there to record the historic moment. And the next morning, the more than seven hundred thousand readers of the Sunday edition of the *Dallas Morning News* will get an up-close and personal look at a pot belly decades in the making. It's not a pretty sight.

Chalk one up for the media.

Chapter 37

Riding in Cars with Bob

Lubbock, Texas. Saturday, October 13. It had the makings for a great Bob Knight story, a surefire addition to that "lengthy pattern of troubling behavior" we've heard so much about.

I had come by the basketball office at one o'clock hoping to sneak in an interview with Knight between then and the start of practice at three. Instead I end up having lunch at Rosa's Cafe, the "tortilla factory," with Knight, Tech Athletic Director Gerald Meyers, and Mark Kram, a reporter from the *Philadelphia Daily News.*

When we've finished lunch, Kram and I hop in the car with Knight. I'm in front and Knight's driving his silver Lincoln Continental with black fabric top. Knight cranks the car without fastening his seat belt and the annoying chime starts going off: Ding! Ding! Ding!

Knight doesn't seem to notice. Ten minutes later we pull into the parking lot in front of United Spirit Arena and there's a car parked in Knight's private space.

Uh oh.

"Can't the son of a bitch read?" growls Knight, pulling past the car, still parallel to the sidewalk.

Knight has a point. The eye-level sign in front of his space says "RESERVED PARKING 24 HOURS DAILY" in green letters about two inches high. Couldn't be any clearer than that.

Now I don't know if this explains anything, but for lunch Knight had downed a couple of Rosa's hardy tortillas; a chicken fajita, "add queso, add chili"; chips, "add queso"; a side of sour cream; and a Coke. So his stomach may have been upset, or he might have been worried that he had strayed a bit from that low-cholesterol, low-cal diet the wife had been nagging him about.

"I'm gonna park it right here," says Knight. He then slips the car into reverse and backs up, blocking in the offending vehicle.

I glance to my right. There are a half-dozen open spaces a three-pointer away. I check out the tag on the errant car.

"They're from Kansas," I say, leaving it up in the air. Since the Texas Tech football team is playing Kansas State tonight, there are a lot of people in town from the Sunflower State. The car could belong to the governor, I'm thinking, the head football coach, a senator, whoever. But unless this is Osama bin Laden's vehicle, Bob Knight is coming out on the short end on this one.

I try to figure out what I'm going to do. Challenging Knight ain't an option. Maybe I can get my hands on his keys once we're back inside and move the car before there is another one of those "*SportsCenter* moments." Then Knight changes his mind. He slips the car into drive and in about three seconds we are parked in a slot two car lengths away.

Crisis averted. I breathe normally again, relieved I don't have another "Bob Knight story" to tell. Knight doesn't seem to understand that he's not just some guy schlepping around Lubbock. He's *Bob Knight,* a "big personality" with a reputation for creating confrontations out of thin air.

———◆———

Sunday, October 14. I'm sitting around the lobby of the basketball office at United Spirit Arena waiting for Knight. I've gotten up at 5:30 to prepare for a scheduled 8:30 interview. By nine my notes are smudged I've been through them so many times, and I start poking around, finger a videotape on the absent receptionist's desk: "Thank you. Not recruiting guards" reads the attached note.

A sleepy-looking Knight finally shows up at 9:15, just in time for a raspy-voiced coaches' meeting in the adjoining conference room. Practice starts at 10 A.M. and so that's that, I think. Blown off again.

This second interview was first scheduled for Midnight Madness in Bloomington a year ago, but then the Emperor got himself deposed. After Knight was coronated at Texas Tech in March, I rescheduled an audience for Lubbock in July, but he canceled again, and now I'm here for my third try. Actually "scheduled" is a misnomer with Knight. You never know when or if he'll actually talk to you, and over the years he's developed somewhat of a reputation for toying with, even standing up interviewers, and not just the small fry. *SportsCenter*'s Dan Patrick claims Knight once "blew [him] off in New York."

The way these things normally work is everybody agrees on a time and place for the interview *before* anybody actually books a hotel room or gets on an airplane. Not in Knightworld. In Knightworld you're told to show up and hang out until the mood strikes him.

Back in the late eighties writer Joan Mellen, author of *Bob Knight: His Own Man,* put her interview and her book at risk by actually calling him on it.

"I'm doing five things, you're only doing one," explained Knight.

Of course the "one thing" Mellen was doing was attempting to get an interview scheduled with a presumptuous basketball coach. Although you'll never see this type of thing mentioned in a story, it's a Knight habit that has to contribute to his often contentious relationship with the press.

"I think it's important to get 'em here twice a day," I overhear Knight telling the coaching staff. "Let 'em know this is major league."

After the meeting Knight motions me into the conference room. "When you leaving?" he asks. When I tell him I'm flying out the next day, he says he'll do the interview after that morning's practice.

Sure.

Practice over, Knight is on the way out the door with Jay Bilas from ESPN when he spots me in the lobby and invites me to tag along. That's how I will end up in a car with Bob Knight for the second time in two days. Knight is back in his charcoal gray Minute Maid pullover. Bilas is wearing a blue polo with white stripe, jeans, and running shoes, his black hair brushed straight back. On the way out, Bilas asks Knight what I was like as a player.

"Hardheaded, but a tough son of a bitch," says Knight.

"Hardheaded." "Tough." Makes you wonder why he ever let me in the door.

I walk out dwarfed by these two huge men, making note of Knight's signature gait. Shoulders rounded in a shallow crescent, eyes down, he walks like he's leaning into a stiff wind, his head eager to arrive ahead of his feet.

Ding! Ding! Ding!

Bilas and Knight are in the front seat. I'm in back. Makes sense. At about 6′9″ Bilas needs the leg room. We eat lunch at a deli inside some grocery store. The setup reminds me of the Marsh supermarket where Knight hung out in Bloomington. Knight recommends the barbecue sandwich but has lasagna himself.

When it comes to food, Knight revels in his lack of sophistication, his in-your-face, small-town tastes. Those looking for a little pecan-crusted sea bass with a tomato-basil cream sauce best not hang out with the Emperor. He likes Chinese, Mexican, Italian—all Americanized, of course—and a good steak. In his eating habits, at least, he's hung on to the Bob Knight from Orrville, like some Texan in a fru-fru Paris restaurant who insists on ordering a T-bone, rare.

The chat this day is for the most part casual, back and forth. Knight thinks this Texas Tech team is going to be "pretty good," will surprise some people. He turns out to be right. The team will actually make it into the NCAA tournament before losing in the first round.

Knight might be a "big personality," but today at least, he isn't throwing his psychic weight around. He doesn't try to charm, intimidate, pull rank, needle, dazzle, or steer the conversation. The gadzillionaire Knight doesn't even presume to lord over us by picking up the tab. He's merely a guy at lunch with a couple of other guys. It just so happens he has 763 wins more than we do.

Bilas raves about the barbecue and Knight seems pleased, saying he would've gotten it himself, but opted for a little variety despite the diminished fat grams. I keep it to myself, of course, but as I pick over my roast chicken with three veggies, I find it hard to believe that anybody still eats like Knight. It's a clear case of lasagna envy.

The talk turns to Knight's treatment by the press. Knight says he's going to change and "not try to entertain himself when he talks to the media." There's a pause and I jump in with something I'd been thinking about the night before.

"There's such a thing as a 'Bob Knight story,'" I say, then glance at Bilas. "If Coach starts raising kittens, that's not a story. If he starts raising rottweilers, that's got a chance of making *SportsCenter*."

In retrospect I wish I'd phrased it a little differently, but you get the idea.

Knight returns a blank stare. He doesn't get it. I shouldn't have been surprised. From past remarks it's obvious he doesn't understand why grabbing Kent Harvey is a "Bob Knight story" that's going to make every sports page and broadcast in the country while giving a hundred grand to StoneSong is not going to make it beyond the *Herald-Times* in Bloomington. He sees the Harvey and Neil Reed brouhahas as insignificant, isolated incidents. And he's right: taken alone they don't amount to much. But over the years a pattern has developed (see Brand, Myles Brand), leading to a stereotype that is familiar to every sportswriter in America. Anything Knight does that feeds that stereotype is news. A particular incident may be small, but the stereotype is big, really big, and dates back to his first, code-word-"volatile" days as a coach at West Point.

And it's not just the media feeding the stereotype. Friends and even Knight do it. Remember Tates Locke's story about the "fistfight" at American University and Knight's tale about threatening to kill the jump shot–challenged Danny Schrage?

Ding! Ding! Ding!

After lunch Bob Knight decides to show Bilas and his little friend in the backseat the house he and wife Karen are building on the outskirts of Lubbock.

Ding! Ding! Ding!

Lubbock is as flat as a Wal-Mart parking lot, and for visitors accustomed to a little relief in their terrain, subdivisions, universities, even cities seem to start and stop without rhyme or reason here at the "flattest place on earth." So housing developments aren't nestled in beautiful little valleys, on the sides of rolling hills, or just around the bend. There are no valleys, hills, or bends. There's just flat and plenty of it.

By now the seat belt chime has given up on Knight and we're cruising past a field of two-foot-high, green maize that stretches from the road to the horizon, planted to replace "a failed cotton crop," says Knight. Suddenly he turns left into a flat, treeless field. There's a cluster of new houses in this small, upscale-for-anywhere subdivision. The framers have just finished up on the work-in-progress Knight manse that is set on a thirteen-acre plot. Four lots, Knight says. He points out the gray, speckled brick on a nearby house, saying that's what he thinks the completed house will look like. He's not sure, he explains, because this is Karen's project. Only twelve minutes from the office, he says. We head back and Knight pulls up behind a pickup truck at a traffic light.

"A Lubbock Masserati," he quips.

The grand tour ends back at United Spirit Arena. So far it's been a slow day for the guy chaperoning the two out-of-towners around the greater Lubbock community. "College basketball's most combustible coach," as *Sports Illustrated* once called him, hasn't tried to wrestle any tape recorders away from inquiring *Playboy* interviewers, roughed-up anybody's kids, created any international incidents, or even blocked in a car belonging to some illiterate son of a bitch from Kansas.

Damn. No story here.

Chapter 38

Grandpa

Modesty aside, what have you contributed to the game of basketball?" I ask Knight as a tow-headed, two-and-a-half-year-old boy appears at the door.

"Come here," says Knight to grandson Braden. "Who's your buddy? Is Grandpa your buddy?"

A Winnie the Pooh fan, Braden has on his blue-on-gray Tigger T-shirt, matching blue shorts, and white running shoes. He's "as cute as a speckled pup in a red wagon," as they say back in Indiana.

"We got a ball or anything?" Grandpa asks, looking around the conference room. He digs a miniature basketball out of the rubble on the room-long table and gives it to the boy.

"I can't tell you how happy I am to see you," says Grandpa softly. "Are you gonna come down 'n' shoot today?"

"Um hmm," says the boy.

"Okay. Your dad wouldn't let you shoot the other night, would he? You should come ask Grandpa. Can I shoot, Grandpa? Can I shoot hoops?"

This is the same doting Grandpa who only the day before was bragging about his no-nonsense grandparenting skills to the *Philadelphia Daily News.*

"When I come into the room, he sits up and pays attention," Knight told reporter Mark Kram. "He knows better than to fool with me."

At the moment, the evidence suggests it's the other way around.

"He's captured his heart, Braden has," says Karen Knight.

Grandpa tosses off a quick answer to my question, the little one about what he's contributed to the game of basketball in the last thirty-five years—"Everything I can possibly contribute"—and takes another question as Braden climbs onto his lap.

So what *has* Bob Knight contributed to the game of basketball? Well, it's not the things you usually hear about: the pressure defense or the motion offense or even the discipline meant to reduce mistakes to a minimum. All those are derivative. What he's really added, I'm thinking, is intensity, the demand that his teams play the game as fiercely as it can be played every minute they are on the floor. It's an approach that proved to be contagious, spreading throughout the sport.

"You're gonna get dropped in the hatch, you know that?" says Grandpa, grasping the boy by both wrists.

The boy squeals.

"You ready?"

"Yeah!" says Braden and pauses. "Where is the hatch?"

"You're sittin on the hatch," says Grandpa, referring his clinched knees. "And the hatch is gonna"—he spreads his knees—"drop you! You like that, don't you?"

"Yeah!"

"Wanta go again?"

"Uh huh!"

They go again before Grandpa dispatches the boy on an important errand.

"Go see if Uncle Pat's down at his office. Tell me whether or not he's there or not."

There's a long pause and I can tell Grandpa is trying to remember the question I asked. Grandpa gives up. This man who can remember the exact score of games played when Braden's father was two and a half can't remember a question posed a minute before.

"What did you ask me?"

I had asked him to comment on a quote, the thesis of a book I was working on. The question had surfaced as I tried to figure out why Knight inspires such visceral reactions. I decided Knight had become a scapegoat for those who hate not him, but competition itself with its inherent violence, hostility, and aggression.

I read the quote back again.

"Over the last thirty-some years, Bob Knight has so shaped the game and the game so shaped him that the two are indistinguishable. Bob Knight is basketball incarnate. Hating Bob Knight is hating the game. Hating competitive sports. Hating major college basketball as it is now played."

"Who said that?" Grandpa Knight asks sternly.

"Oh shit!" I think. "I've pissed him off." The last reporter to do that, *Playboy's* Lawrence Grobel, had ended up in a wrestling match with Knight in the back of a car. "I want those goddamn tapes!" Knight had cried.

I suck in a quick breath. Eye my tape recorder. Not quick enough to make up a facile lie, I tell the truth.

"I said that. I wrote that," I said, and laughed, trying to defuse Grandpa.

"Well, I appreciate that, because I think I have really worked hard at the game of basketball and I think I've worked hard at passing things on in the game of basketball."

Knight is not pissed; he's pleased, his face suddenly aglow. Then without prompting he segues into what we were talking about at lunch, the kittens-rottweilers business, again demonstrating he doesn't get it.

"Writers cannot say, 'Y'know, I don't like the son of a bitch because he doesn't answer my phone calls.'"

That's because that's not news.

"The world saw the tape of that fucking Reed kid," says Knight out of the blue. "Well, on the spectrum of things that have mattered, where is that? It's inconsequential. Even more so is me telling some kid, 'Don't call people by their last names.' But in both cases monumental issues are made out of that."

Remember he's volunteering all this. I have no clue what this has to do with him being the walkin', talkin' personification of the game, the hating-him-means-hating-competitive-basketball quote I just read him. Maybe whenever he hears anything he regards as sympathetic, he feels free to vent.

"The whole thing with me has been I just didn't put up with the press's bullshit for all these years," Knight continues. "I didn't like 'em. I didn't make any bones about it. And then consequently instead of focusing on things that you could focus on that were genuine and positive, they chose to—as you said—get that negative thing."

That's because that "negative thing," the thing that feeds the stereotype, is the story. Other folks have had to labor under the heavy burden of stereotype. Take Dan Quayle. Remember any stories about him doing something smart? And when's the last time you heard a dumb redhead joke? Blondes are the dumb ones. Redheads are the ones with the bad tempers. Like Knight.

To paraphrase John Feinstein: Is that fair? No. Is that life? Oh yeah.

Braden pops his head in the door. "Grandpa, I'm thirsty."

"You're thirsty?"

"Yeah."

"I got somethin' that's really good, right here. Cold," says Grandpa, handing the drink to the boy. "If you don't like it, we'll get you something else. But that's pretty good. I drink that."

Braden takes a tentative sip. "I don't like that."

"You don't?"

"No."

"Okay, here's a little Dr. Pepper."

Another sip. "I like it!"

"You do?"

"Uh huh."

"Okay, you keep it. You hang onto it. Drink a little more."

What's the news coming out of this interview? It's certainly not a doting Grandpa who "sits up and pays attention" when his grandson comes into the room. It's whatever feeds the stereotype. Like this fusillade aimed at Mike Davis.

Davis was the source of a quote I used trying to get Knight to talk about the emotional intensity needed to play the game. But unlike most coaches and players, Knight doesn't believe emotion has anything to do with it. Rather "it's a total concentration on what the hell's happening," on what it takes to win the game. I keep plugging away, throw out Mike Davis's "harnessed rage" metaphor concerning the mind-set it takes to compete.

"Who's Mike Davis?" Knight asked.

I laugh. "Your former assistant coach."

"Oh shit! He wouldn't—that guy, he wouldn't have the first fuckin' clue!" exclaimed Knight. "'Harnessed rage.' That's such bullshit. I can't believe that. How do you harness rage? Rage is out of control. How the hell do you harness something that's out of control? That's bullshit."

Now that sounds like Bob Knight.

The stereotype dictates what "sounds like" Bob Knight and what doesn't. What's news and what isn't. Was allowing a two-and-a-half-year-old to continually interrupt an interview that took a year and a half to schedule "rude," or was it an example of a man who "has his priorities in order?" It could be written either way. In a "John Wooden story," it's an example of a kindly old gentleman having the right priorities. In a "Bob Knight story," it's bad manners. Throw in the yawning that began early on, the reading of the sports page in the midst of the interview, an almost grimace-for-grimace repeat of the famous 1992 "game face" mugging scene when I asked about the emotional element of the game, the attack on Davis, and the couple of times when he was visibly irritated by a question, and a reporter could easily make the case that Knight is a colossal jerk. That's the stereotype. That's news.

Knight's failure to recognize and accept that is a continuing source of grief. Despite the Minute Maid commercial that played off the stereotype, the one depicting Knight as a touchy-feely players' coach, he still doesn't seem to get it. He continues to get pissed off every time a reporter plucks the one thing out of the air that feeds the stereotype and ignores everything else. That's like raging at the tides and displays a total ignorance of what sports reporting, any reporting, is all about. Knight has often said that the media don't know anything about him or basketball. Maybe so. But the flip side is that Knight, after all these years, doesn't know a whole lot more about the media.

Here are just a few examples.

In his autobiography, Knight criticizes reporters for being "skeptical." That, of course, is their job. He seems surprised by the "nastiness of some of the criticism" when, following the announcement of the zero-tolerance policy, only a handpicked group of print reporters—"the sympathetic seven," as John Feinstein called them—were allowed to interview him. No journalist was surprised. In the business, allowing a subject to hand-pick interviewers is like allowing an ax murderer to pick his own judge and jury.

In another example, Knight criticizes the press for not being critical of each other. Hello. Anybody the least bit familiar with the business knows that analysts have turned media criticism into the General Motors of navel gazing. There are magazines like the *Columbia Journalism Review* and the *American Journalism Review* that do little else. Foundations. An endless procession of books. Television shows. Not a day goes by when there isn't a roundtable somewhere. Lest you think any of this is actually relevant, media critics are still carping about journalists' failure to report JFK's womanizing some forty years ago. This stuff seldom merits space in the local rag where Knight might see it because it's so stultifying it makes one of those typical C-SPAN snooze-a-thons look like a Wrestlemania main event featuring Hillary and Monica.

Enough.

I read Knight another self-authored quote. I've been holding off on this one, for obvious reasons.

"Coach Knight is a bully?" I read. "Of course, he's a bully. All coaches are bullies. All players too. That's what the game is all about. One guy trying to bully another. May the best bully win."

I throw in Coach Doug Collins's description of Michael Jordan. "He wants to cut your heart out and then show it to you," said Collins.

Knight dismisses all this as "melodramatic," then goes on to say that as a coach you "try to neutralize strengths of an opponent as much as you can." How? "You go right at their weaknesses."

Sounds like bullying to me.

"Kenyon Martin [of the New Jersey Nets] made a big mistake when he mentioned his back spasms to Michael Jordan," the Associated Press reported following a Nets-Wizards game in early 2002.

"I don't think he wants to tell me that," said Jordan. "I just started attacking from that point on."

Jordan scored forty-five in a 98–76 Washington win.

"Exploiting a man's weakness is the name of the game," wrote Jason Miller in his Pulitzer prize–winning play, *That Championship Season.* "You find his weak spot and go after it. Punish him with it."

Or as one former court bully put it: "Blessed are the meek, for they shall inherit the loser's bracket."

The defense rests.

"Did you really kick it?" chimes in Braden in a tiny voice as I'm asking Knight about the alleged chair incident at Madison Square Garden in 1966.

"I might have kicked a chair, yeah," says Grandpa sheepishly.

The interview is winding down. Knight's finished the sports page and it's almost time for the second practice of the day.

"I gotta put my other shoes on," Grandpa says to Braden. "You got your sneakers on, don't you?"

"Uh huh."

"Last question," I say. "Why do you think you really got fired at IU? Was it about money? Was it about public relations?"

Knight wanders around a little bit, blasts Indiana AD Clarence Doninger and the board of trustees, but finally gets to the nub of it.

"I think that everywhere they went, I was the one thing that was associated with Indiana University," Knight said quietly, "and I think they got tired of that."

Chapter 39

The Bob Knight Practice

S unday, October 14, 5 P.M. Call out the National Guard. Bobby Knight—"the Saddam Hussein of sport and a classic American bully," as sportswriter Brian Hewitt once described him—is about to start his fourth practice of the season. Expect lots of cussin', groveling players, and a smattering of handpicked toadies cowering in the stands.

It starts badly. A step behind Knight, I'm jabbering at his back, soliciting off-the-record comments about Myles Brand as he walks onto the court. Oh my God! The women's team is still on the floor. Knight doesn't even seem to notice, and moments later his players have split up into three groups for shooting drills.

"First shot's a three, second shot's a fake three, one dribble and a jump shot," Pat Knight tells the guards.

At another basket, the forwards sprint to the foul circle from on top, do a right-angle turn toward the sideline where they take the pass, and shoot a jumper. Meanwhile, at a third basket, the big men take a pass underneath with their back to the rim, shoot, then move outside for a sixteen-foot jump shot.

The players are in reversible red and black jerseys with white numerals and black shorts. Knight's got on the same old charcoal gray Minute Maid pullover (I hope he's got a closet full of these things), khakis, and white running shoes. It's constant motion, shoes screeching, both coaches and players yelling.

"Nice pass, Andre!" shouts Knight.

I'm leaving tomorrow morning and this will be my last chance to see some of that world-famous Bob Knight player abuse we hear so much about. I've been taking notes. At Midnight Madness, Knight grabbed his starting center, 6' 11" Andy Ellis, by the arm. When he was done talking, he patted him on the back of the head, a characteristic gesture that got Knight in big trouble when he loosed it on Joe B. Hall of Kentucky during a game years before. Inappropriate physical contact?

I hone in on another situation with potential for abuse. Players practicing free throws are supposed to do five fingertip push-ups for each miss. For a lousy foul shooter, that could easily mean a hundred push-ups in one practice. But the players I'm watching either only do a couple for each miss or don't do them on their fingertips or both. Nobody calls them on it.

Beginning with the early Sunday practice, Knight has been making threats. That morning when the players screwed up a chaotic passing drill that called for four interconnected sets of players, each with its own ball, to make three passes back and forth in a distance of twelve feet, Knight stopped play.

"I want you to step behind the guy that passed *period! Period!*" screamed Knight. "I don't wanta have to go through it again. If I have to go through it again, you're gonna have to run. And it'll be your fault that you made everybody run. You won't have to run, but everybody else will. Now, goddamnit, listen!"

That afternoon, after players don't listen when told to pass the ball four times before shooting, Knight will make good on the threat. The "abusive" penalty run will last less than two minutes before the players are back executing the five-on-five block-out/fast-break drill.

There is discipline on display at the practices. It shows not in what the players do, but in what they don't do. There is no idle chatter, no grab-assing, and nobody bounces the ball when the coaches are talking. Everything is strictly business. There are no breaks. The team is either running drills or shooting free throws, which is the only time the players are allowed to catch their breath. Not that there is much breath to be caught. Nobody's huffing and puffing. Owing to those preseason "voluntary workouts," the players are in pretty good shape. No need to run these guys 'til they drop.

All in all it's a pitiful showing by Knight. So far he hasn't even kicked a water cooler. (All the players have individual water bottles these days.) Maybe I need to come back after he's lost a couple of big games. What I'm looking for is the kind of abuse dished out by Clair Bee after his Long Island University team gave up a steal, foul, lay-up, technical—a rare four-point play—to San Francisco in Madison Square Garden back in December of 1950.

"[Bee] was practically out on the court to meet the players as they came back to the bench," then San Francisco coach Pete Newell told his biographer Bruce Jenkins. "And they all stood there in a row as he slapped each one of them on the face. Bang! Bang! I mean, really hard."

Now that's the kind of thing a reporter can work with. But the only physical "abuse" I'll see in the four Knight practices I attend is dished out by the players. The day before, a 6'4" guard named Jesus Arenas had been poked in the eye by one of his teammates and ended up writhing around on the floor. As I watched, I was struck by the comparative violence involved in this routine mishap on the court and what happened with Neil Reed. Of the two, Jesus clearly got the worst of it, and he was back on the floor in ten minutes. Still the threat of being seriously injured is always there.

"We're not teaching kids to play canasta," Knight once said. "This is a game where kids get bloody noses, they get broken legs, they get hurt."

Of course, the difference between the Reed and Arenas encounters is that the Neil Reed "choking" is considered "outside the game."

"Think! Think! Think! You can't play with your ass!" Knight screams during a fast-break drill.

Today Knight is in hands-off mode. No physical abuse here. Maybe I'll have better luck with verbal abuse.

"When we go over something, goddamnit, don't forget it three minutes later!" Knight screamed at the 3 P.M. Saturday practice.

Then on Sunday morning Knight had singled out starting guard Andre Emmett during a block-out drill. Knight tells the team they should "protect" Andre because "as long as he's around, you won't be the worst" block-out artist on the team.

During the four practices I attend, Knight will raise his voice, but he's never really angry, just tough. I will hear the word "fuck!" every now and again, but it's not coming from Knight. It's coming from the players.

Knight says he's trying to tone down his language and at one practice, he will suggest Pawel Storozynski, a 6' 8" forward born in Poland and raised in France, take one of his big-at-Dodge-City-Junior-College moves the coach doesn't want to ever see again and "make a rectal deposit." This is wasted on the befuddled Storozynski, whose command of English doesn't include the nuances of American slang. So Knight will end up telling him to "stick it up his ass" anyway. But Knight would balance this "abuse" with praise.

"Good move!" screams Knight, as practice continues.

"If you keep track of the negative things and the positive things [in practice]," Knight once told William Gildea of the *Washington Post,* "the positives are overwhelming."

Meanwhile the hand-picked visitors are milling around in the stands refusing to act like toadies. Some are even talking, quietly of course, respecting the decorum of what Knight calls his classroom. But, let's face it: seen one practice, seen them all, and after a while the whole process is kind of boring. And while "being an S-O-B is a coach's J-O-B," as one wag put it, today at least, spectators will not be entertained by a coach pushing his players to the limit. Maybe the intensity will pick up when the team starts preparing for conference play against Big 12 teams like Kansas and Oklahoma.

During his last stand in Bloomington, Knight kept saying he was first a teacher. And while you'll never hear him brag about where he ranks as a basketball coach—"Let somebody else judge that," he says—when it comes to teaching he'll be the first to tell you he's up there with Socrates.

Here's his take on the "little nickel-and-dime" Methods of Coaching class he taught at Indiana.

"I taught it for twenty-nine years," said Knight. "I can't even begin to tell you the number of notes I got from kids or ran into people that had been in that class over the years that said it was far and away the best class they ever took in college."

"I'd be willing to bet that 99 percent of the faculty members at Indiana," continued Knight, "never got a letter from any kid saying this was the most important class or the best class for the future that I ever had to take. And I heard that constantly."

The practice is winding down. For a big chunk of it, Big Bad Bob Knight has been carrying grandson Braden around on his shoulders.

"You don't have to be big, quick, fast, or strong. Just smarter," Knight tells the players, losing his voice.

The taskmaster will end practice forty minutes early on this day. After the players clear the floor, one of the assistant coaches wrestles the south basket down until it's only a couple of feet off the floor. Soon Braden is working on his monster slam, "shooting hoops" just like Grandpa promised.

After practice, Knight invites a bunch of us to join him for supper out at the Hong Kong Restaurant on Fiftieth Street. I go through the buffet line loading up on moo goo gai pan, sweet and sour pork, egg rolls, steamed rice. Jay Bilas and Knight sit on one side of the table while I join Mark Kram and a retired high school coach from Pennsylvania on the other.

Knight has brought Braden along without backup. There's no mom, dad, or Karen hovering at Knight's elbow, ready to step in and rescue Grandpa should the boy start acting like a typical two-and-a-half-year-old. The boy's with him. He'll take care of it. It's the final bit of proof that all this doting grandpa business over the last three days was not for the benefit of me and Kram and Bilas, the media. As Knight himself might put it: "This sumbitch is a real grandfather."

Like I said. No story here.

Conclusion

An American Institution

It's been almost four decades since the "brat from Orrville," the skinny kid with the black crewcut, made his college coaching debut at West Point. Now the hair is silver and the paunch ample, but the question for Knight-watchers remains the same. As one plebe put it during that first surreal Bob Knight practice at the Academy: "Who *is* this son of a bitch?"

Well, back in 1984, here's what Knight said he would like chiseled on his tombstone: "He was honest and he didn't kiss anybody's ass." He got it half right. It has been a long, long, long time since Bob Knight, the best coach of his generation, has even felt the need to kiss anybody's ass. For more than thirty years, he's been the one getting his ass kissed. As for honesty, that's given way to something else that should be carved on that tombstone: "He was a great competitor." Like at West Point, winning matters, it matters a lot, even when the truth is at stake.

Who *is* this son of a bitch?

Here's wife Karen's take for those who imagine family and friends cowering in the wake of the legendary bad boy: "People have often referred to him having a temper," she said. "And I just see everyday what I call a *huge* passion for living. He has a passion for every *thing* he does. Everything."

Especially basketball.

"The game means more to me than anything else," Knight said.

Who *is* this son of a bitch?

Many accuse Knight of being an egomaniac. It's just the opposite. He still conducts himself like some *enfant terrible,* a scratching, clawing underdog with something to prove on the floor and off.

"All the world must be in the game," Frank Deford wrote of Knight's approach to life. "All the people are players for or against, to be scouted, tested, broken down, built back up if they matter. Life isn't lived, it's played."

And it's "us against them" behind the barricades of fortress Knight. Knight's paranoia is given voice by a collection of quotes of the to-thine-own-self-be-true variety that have been plastered on his office walls over the years. There are quotes from heroes such as President Harry Truman, who decided to "do what I think is right and let them all go to hell"; from General George S. Patton, who warned that as you near success "some you thought were loyal friends, will suddenly show up doing their hypocritical goddamndest to trip you, blacken you, and break your spirit"; and this one from Abraham Lincoln:

> I desire so to conduct the affairs of this administration so that if at the end, when I come to lay down the reins of power, I have lost every other friend on earth, I shall at least have one friend left, and that friend shall be down inside me.

"There are a lot of times," said Knight, "when I feel like I'm a lone ship on a stormy sea and I don't have any sail."

Who *is* this son of a bitch?

Bob Knight is one part West Point to two parts basketball. He's a teacher straight out of the fifties. He's a classic hothead. Throw all that together and you get a surrogate parent who, in the face of an often disapproving public and press, is willing to yell, curse, embarrass, tease, insult, humiliate, manhandle, and, yes, even praise players if that's what it takes to make them play as hard as the rules allow, if that's what it takes to make them better. When it comes to Bob Knight, the coach's reach exceeds the player's grasp.

"Find someone who will kick you in the ass once in a while," Knight once said, "because that's the person that cares about you."

It's an approach that worked for the most part at there-is-no-substitute-for-victory West Point.

"I had to be just as tough as the very toughest tactical officer [scary guy] there," said Knight.

Meanwhile at Indiana University, and in American society at large, there's an ongoing debate about how hard mentors should push students in the name of sports or anything else. To many, civility is an end in itself. And Myles Brand can talk all he wants about a "commitment to excellence" being "at the heart of all we do," but in the Knight case, Brand demonstrated that being nice matters more. And when like-minded critics see Knight discipline a player, they are left thinking, "Nothing is worth this." So the Bob Knights and Myles Brands of the world are left tossing brickbats across an unbreachable kick-ass, don't-kick-ass, philosophical divide.

So Knight was right after all. There are philosophical differences. Those differences take Knight far beyond the game of basketball and place him dead center of America's ongoing culture wars. An icon for conservatives, Knight has come to symbolize all that used to be right with America before the tofu-eating pantywaists took over in the sixties. The rugged individualism. The toughness. The determination in the face of overwhelming odds. A man's man in a girly world, Bob Knight is the John Wayne of his generation. An American institution.

Bob Knight is also an icon for those on the other side of the divide. This "ultimate alpha male" has come to symbolize all that was wrong with a necktied, fifties America overrun by tyrannical white men in wing tip shoes and black nylon socks. He's become a target for all those who hate the military and West Point, sports and competition in general; for feminists who see Knight as a misogynistic, "typical white male"; for aging peace activists still fighting the Vietnam War; for those who label as "fascist" anyone who demands "instant unquestioning obedience"; and even for some sportswriters who think big-time sports should be "fun."

"[Knight] believes in pushing people to their limit, an approach that, inexplicably, seems to bother so many sportswriters," wrote Joan Mellen, a professor at Temple. "But they are not teachers; they do not understand how difficult it is to change the behavior of students, and how great and unrelenting a physical and mental effort it demands of the teacher."

This from an English professor.

While the rest of us may not know what it takes to get boys moving in the right direction, Bob Knight is convinced he does. His teaching methods are based on more than thirty years of extraordinarily successful coaching, and all he asks is that we "get out of the goddamned way."

But even if Knight were to adopt a "no touch, no yell" style tomorrow, that wouldn't make a dent in the level of perceived abuse. For whatever the technique, he is still left with Red Blaik's goal of pushing players past their limit today so he can push them past it again tomorrow. That's how players get better. And that requires some ass-kicking, at least metaphorically.

There are convincing, three-NCAA-championship arguments in favor of Knight's ass-kicking style. Still there's a world of difference between being tough and lashing out in anger. While the first may be justifiable, the other is unacceptable. And that's a judgment shared by those on both sides of the kick-ass, don't-kick-ass divide. Too many times over the years, Knight has shocked both friends and detractors alike with his angry outbursts. "Sometimes the devil grabs your soul," he once said.

"I've understood for a long time, maybe way back when I was even playing in high school, that temper is a problem for me," Knight has said.

What Knight doesn't seem to understand is that temper is not a problem: it is *the* problem. Protest as he might, the source of most of Knight's troubles over the years is not the media or disgruntled players or spin doctors or even back-stabbing university presidents and athletic directors. The source is his own self-destructive behavior when he's determined he's right and everybody else is wrong. And his is not a get-mad, then-get-over-it kind of temper. He dwells on things for days, months, years, even decades and will still heat up at the mere mention of Lou Eisenstein, the official who "cost" Army the BYU game in 1966.

And while there are a few rare exceptions, such as the Kent Harvey run-in, Knight's bad temper is behind most of the incidents that have made it onto the *SportsCenter* lowlight reel and the list of unseemly episodes the Associated Press calls "a chronology of events involving Indiana basketball coach Bob Knight." In short, without the temper, there is no Bob Knight stereotype. At least not the one we know today.

Given all that, should we expect to see some major changes in the Bob Knight "method of operation"? Nah. For despite his crucifixion at Indiana and subsequent resurrection at Texas Tech, Knight claims he is not a changed man.

"I haven't changed a bit. I'm exactly like I was. Only you're just payin' attention now," Knight said, speaking of the media in general. "You're tryin' to find somethin' now instead of makin' up somethin' and there isn't anything."

Well, there has been somethin'. But not often. There are fewer than two dozen incidents spread over his long career. Not that there won't be somethin' again. Especially on court. Here's a hot-tempered man with a high-pressure job that would have a "nonviolence-my-ass!" Mohandas Gandhi kicking British butt on a trying day. And unacceptable or not, you can bet the house, car, and bass boat that some time in the future, the harness will slip and Bob Knight will again provide the world with a glimpse of the rage that fuels high-level athletic competition. And when that happens, when the true nature of competition shows, everybody from Myles Brand to Bryant Gumbel will again be appalled. They want good-natured camaraderie, "fields of friendly strife" as General Douglas MacArthur once put it. Ask around. There's nothing friendly about big-time basketball, on the floor or on the bench. That's the nature of the game. And as long as Coach Knight keeps the proverbial chair on the floor, chances are he will continue to get away with an occasional outburst.

As for off court, Knight says he has it all figured out.

"I have to be able to do all the time basically what I've done most of the time now," said Knight.

So Knight must consistently curb his anger and swallow that surrogate parent's "impulse always to teach someone a lesson." Meanwhile all those who love and respect Coach Knight will be left to stand by helplessly, hoping that when one of those angry impulses does arise, Coach Knight will think twice, slip the car back into drive, and slide into the parking spot ten feet away.

—————

In mid-November, Texas Tech will host and win the Ford Red Raider Classic, a four-team mini-tournament that kicks off Tech's 2001–02 season. In the opening round, Tech will beat William and Mary 75–55 in a game that's never close. But just before halftime Tech gives up five points in nineteen seconds including a "virtually uncontested lay-up before the buzzer." An angry Knight "stomped off the court," and ESPN cameras were there to capture the moment. That night on *SportsCenter*, the featured video from the Texas Tech debut of the winningest active coach in America is a shot of Knight huffin' and puffin' his way toward the locker room.

Predictable.

Even Lubbock's Knight-friendly *Avalanche Journal* follows suit, with a front-page picture of a scowling Knight screaming at players during a time-out "midway through the first half."

The stereotype is alive and well.

After the game, I join a large contingent of Knight friends who have gathered to celebrate the coach's debut at Texas Tech. The soiree is held in the City Bank conference room located on an upper level of United Spirit Arena. There must be a hundred people in attendance, including Celtic great John "Hondo" Havlicek; golfer Fuzzy Zoeller; John Ryan, the Indiana University president who first hired Knight; ex-Globetrotter Marques Haynes; and the usual contingent of well-wishers from West Point and Indiana.

All are men who wish Knight the best. Yet they are men who will, as often as not, preface even the most extravagant praise of the coach with an "I-don't-always-agree-with-what-he-does" disclaimer. And they are also men who, when watching a Knight-coached game, can't help but share a sentiment first expressed by Knight's mother, Hazel, a generation before: "I just hope he behaves."

Somebody needs to tell him all that. And as I watch the group milling around, I think there's got to be at least one guy in this bunch Knight would actually listen to. Somebody he deeply respects. Somebody who could grab him by the crook of the arm a la Kent Harvey, pull him aside, and provide a bit of guidance and direction.

I spot John Havlicek towering above the crowd. He looks like he can still take a punch. Maybe he's the one to corner Knight—we'll back you all the way, Hondo—and pass along a little brotherly advice. You can start out with the "friends are worried" thing, Hondo, and go on to the "hope he behaves" quote before wrapping it up with that minimalist, time-honored guideline that floated to the surface during the zero-tolerance debacle. Just tell him, "Hey Coach, on court or off, now and forever, no matter how much somebody deserves it, don't be an asshole."

Just tell him that, Hondo. *Sotto voce* for sure. No use stirring things up unnecessarily. Then, uh, what with the past being prologue, you might want to, y'know, keep an eye on his hands. Never can tell when old "Dragon" might unleash one of those signature thrusts to the jugular.

Index

Abdul-Jabbar, Kareem, 43
Agent Orange, 9
Agnew, Spiro, 83
Alcindor, Lew, 43
Alford, Steve, 231, 233
Ali, Muhammad, 5
Allen, Edgar, 146
Allen, Forest "Phog," 101
Allen, Woody, 194
Ambrose, Stephen E., 60–61, 77–78
Andreas, Harold, 71, 90
Arenas, Jesus, 309
Ashbaugh, Brian, 105, 162
Assembly Hall, 234
Atkinson, Rick, 65, 93
Auer, Bruce, 125–27
Austin, John, 157

Backer, Stephen, 266–67
Barkley, Charles, 240
Barry, Rick, 103
Bee, Clair, 101, 175–76, 201–2, 309
Benner, Bill, 255
Bergen, Candice, 282
Bergen, Edgar, 282
Berger, Phil, 45, 90, 162, 229
Berkow, Ira, 91
The Best American Sports Writing
    1999 (Stout, ed.), 273
Bilas, Jay, 296–99, 311
Bird, Larry, 39
Bjarkman, Peter C., 101, 133
Blaik, Earl "Red," 44, 116, 128,
    139, 316
Bliss, Dave, 7
Bloody Sunday, 114, 276
Blum, Larry, 199
Bob Knight: His Own Man (Mellen),
    139, 229, 269, 296
Bobby Ball, 130, 132, 159, 181–82,
    196, 200, 216

Boehlert, Eric, 143
Bomba, Brad, 258
Bonnecaze, Louis "Buddy," Jr.,
    269–70
Booz, Oscar L., 66
Boroff, David, 80, 83–84
Boston College scrimmage, 4,
    156–57
Bowen, William G., 274
Bradley, Bill, 103, 141, 179
Brand, Joshua (son), 254
Brand, Myles, 250, 252–53, 282;
    biography of, 253–55; and Knight
    firing, 221, 228, 235–36, 262,
    292; and zero tolerance, 13,
    255–62. See also zero-tolerance
    policy
On Brave Old Army Team, 117
Breckenridge, Cora, 267
A Brief History of Time (Hawking),
    83
Broudy, Feets, 162
Brown, Russ, 291
Bryan House, 233–36
Bryan, William Lowe, 234
Bubas, Vic, 119
Buckner, Quinn, 23

Caldwell, Dana, 243
Camp Buckner, 91–95
Cardillo, Rich, 119, 162, 209–12
Carlesimo, P. J., 26
Carnesecca, Lou, 139, 185, 187–88
Carnevale, Ben, 191
Carpenter, Bill, 44
Caught in the Net (Locke and Ibach),
    73
Chamberlain, Wilt, 198
That Championship Season (Miller),
    306
charging violation, 28

Civil Rights Act, 150. *See also* racial discrimination
Clarke, Towney, 168, 170
Class of 1966: AOT (Army Orientation Training) 108–10; in Beast Barracks, 54–59, 61–69, 74; and branch selection, 189–91; at Camp Buckner, 91–95; at June Encampment, 108; motto of, 64; plebe basketball team of, 87–88
Clemens, Roger, 163–65
Clinton, Carver, 179–81
Cohen v. California, 14–15
Cohen, Paul Robert, 14
Collegiate Basketball Officials Association, 208
Collins, Doug, 305
competition, 164–65
Congdon, Jeff, 205-6
Continental Basketball Association, 244–45
Corps of Cadets: cadet life, 56–57, 75–78, 110, 112, 137–38, 151; cadet profile, 83–84; dating and, 94, 203–5; organization of, 75
Cousy On the Celtic Mystique (Cousy and Ryan), 157, 162
Cousy, Bob, 156–57, 162, 269
Cry Me a River, 76–77
Cuban Missile Crisis, 87
Cullum, Bill, 102

Daley, Chuck, 119
Davis, Antoine (son), 244, 275
Davis, Bill (brother), 240
Davis, Janice (sister), 240
Davis, Jefferson, 61
Davis, Lateesha (daughter), 244
Davis, Mary Ann, 6, 27, 232
Davis, Mike, 33; biography, 239–44; and Kent Harvey incident, 223–24, 226–27; hiring of, 233, 237–47, 275–76; Knight on, 304; loyalty of, 245–47
Davis, Mike, Jr., 241, 244, 246
Davis, Nicole (daughter), 244
Davis, Tamilya (wife), 241, 244, 275

Davis, Van (brother), 240
Davis, Vandella (mother), 239–41
Dawkins, Pete, 44
DeCourcy, Mike, 291
defense, pressure, 99–101, 113, 301
Deford, Frank, 70, 113, 216, 314
Deluca, Bob, 87, 144
Devoe, Don, 89
Dietzel, Paul, 44, 81, 85, 99
discipline, 11–12, 52, 142, 136
Doninger, Clarence, 238–39, 242–43, 258
Dooley, Vince, 147
draft (military), 44, 50, 89
Drisell, Lefty, 81
Duderstadt, James J., 275
Dunn Meadow, 279–80

Eakins, Jim, 205
École Polytechnique, 78
Edwards, Jerry, 87
Egli, John, 181
Eisenhower, Dwight D., 56
Eisenstein, Lou, 206–9, 211–12, 316
Eliot, Charles, 133
Elliot, Ramblin' Jack, 251
Ellis, Andy, 308
Ellis, Joe, 199
Emmett, Andre, 310
Engberg, Eric, 250–51
ESPN interview (Digger Phelps, Roy Firestone), 25, 27, 30, 251
ESPN interview (Jeremy Schaap), 252–53, 255, 257–60, 263–67

Far West Classic, 28
Feinstein, John, 6, 70–71, 186, 224–25, 303, 305
Fidgeon, Bud, 206–8
field house (West Point), 128–29
Fife, Dane, 32, 237–38, 242–43, 247
finesse players, 133–34, 159
Firestone, Roy, 25, 27
Fisher, Orville, 205
Fitzpatrick, Frank, 149
Flirtation Walk, 94
Foley, Bob, 82

Foley, Red, 187–88
Ford Red Raider Classic, 318
Ford, Richard, 273
Foster, Chris, 270
Foster, Kathy, 235
Fourth Class System, 58, 60. *See also* hazing
Fratwell, Dorothy, 258–59
Freeman, Don, 160–61, 178
Fretwell, Norm, 190

The Game of Life (Shulman and Bowen), 274
Gamina, Russ, 199
Gelling, Peter, 228–29, 280
General Electric, 171
Gildea, William, 310
Goldwater, Barry, 110
Grant, Ulysses S., 61
Graves, Ray, 148
Green, Dudley, 147
Grobel, Lawrence, 265, 302
Gulf of Tonkin Resolution, 110
Gumbel, Bryant, 317
Gyovai, Mike, 23–24, 30, 37–39

Hammel, Bob, 291
Harlan, John, 14
Harper's, 80, 83, 283–84
Harvey, Kent, 223–28, 236, 259–62, 298
Harvey, Kevin (brother), 223–24, 230
Harvey, Kyle (brother), 223
Haskins, Clem, 147
Haskins, Don, 213
Haston, Kirk, 37, 247
Havlicek, John, 48, 69, 71, 318–19
Hawking, Stephen, 83
Hayes, Woody, 40, 116
hazing, 58–62, 66–69, 76
Heiner, Paul, 116, 129–30, 153, 157, 168–69; and academics, 168, 170–71; and Knight marriage (first), 106–7; and Princeton incident, 142; recruiting of,

106–7; as a starter, 153–55, 157, 168
Helkie, Bill, 81–82, 85; 1965–66, 145, 152–55, 157, 161, 168, 173, 175, 189; in high school, 82; at Indiana Classic, 8–9; as an intellectual, 82–85; and Knight hiring, 122; in the military, 8–9; and Mike Silliman, 82–85; at NIT (1966), 195, 198–201, 206–7; recruiting of, 82–83
Helms Foundation, 115, 175
Hewitt, Brian, 307
Holiday Festival at Madison Square Garden, 151, 154–55, 157–58
Holman, Nat, 101
Hoopla: A Century of College Basketball (Bjarkman), 101
Hoosier Hundred, 10
Howitzer, 149
Hughes, Neal, 85, 122, 130, 135, 173, 176–77, 181
Hunt, Richard L., 72
Hunter, George, 43–45, 88–89, 99

Indiana University: Board of Trustees, 252, 256, 267–68, 283–84; and code of conduct (athletic), 13, 256; image of, 13, 15, 282–84, 306; values of, 217
Intending and Acting: Toward a Naturalized Action Theory (Brand), 254
Irish, Edward "Ned," 192–93
Isenhour, Jack, 4–5, 9, 11–12, 155, 157, 168, 170, 297

Jannarone, Ann, 118, 127, 169–70
Jannarone, John, 36, 118, 126–27, 169–71, 216
Jeffries, Jared, 243, 275
Jenkins, Bruce, 309
Jimas, Jim, 207
Johnson, Lyndon B., 5, 110, 114
Johnson, T. Loftin, 62
Jones, Rich, 160–61

Jordan, Ed, 24, 96, 132, 178–83, 198–99
Jordan, John, 46, 48
Jordan, Michael, 240, 306–07
Jordan, Ralph, 148

Katz, Andy, 221
Kaurin, Pauline, 246
Keady, Gene, 19
Kennedy, John F., 96–97
Kennedy, Josephine, 241–42
King, Larry, 268–69
Kinney, Bob, 50, 119, 128–29, 173, 180–81, 193; and Knight incidents, 161–62, 207, 209–11
Kirkpatrick, Curry, 291
Klingelhofer, Kit, 269
Knight, Bob: and anger management, 26–28, 30; biography of, 69–72, 90–91, 106–7, 226–27, 254–55; bosses, relationships with, 265–66; at Cuyahoga Falls, 71–72, 90–91; as a grandfather, 300–1, 303–4, 306, 311; as an icon, 315; and loose ball drill, 131–34; memory of, 37; and Mike Davis, 33, 242–47, 304; at Ohio State, 69–71, 90, 130; and school for basketball, 31–33; on sports, 273, 288–89; and StoneSong, 251; as a teacher, 138–39, 229, 265, 310–11, 314–16; at Texas Tech, 288–91, 293, 307–11, 318–19; on Vietnam War, 38
Knight, Bob and basketball, 22, 313; as "basketball incarnate," 229, 302; contributions to game, 34, 101, 133–34, 196–97, 301–2; discipline and, 11–12, 32–33, 119, 142, 308; on intensity of game, 304, 309; philosophy of, 32, 130–31, 134, 138–39, 155, 159, 314–16; on winning, 215–16, 218, 268, 270, 274
Knight, Bob, character traits: as a "bully," 305-6; as a competitor, 119, 165, 268, 302, 313; elders,

respect for, 90, 223–27; generosity of, 134, 302; honesty of, 30, 252, 261, 268–70, 313; intensity of, 224, 227–28, 313; loyalty and, 243, 245–47; modesty of, 34–36, 202, 301, 310; paranoia of, 314; profanity of, 143, 227, 309–10; temper of, 13, 25–27, 186–88, 313, 316–19. See also Knight, Bob, incidents
Knight, Bob, and firing: and Christopher Simpson, 225, 250–51, 256–58, 266–68, 277–78, 281–82; ESPN interview, 252–53, 255, 257–60; farewell speech, 281–82, 284; and Kent Harvey incident, 221, 223–30; and Indiana University Board of Trustees, 252, 267–68; in local media accounts, 271–72, 275–78; Knight reaction to, 252–53, 255, 302–3; loyalty and, 243, 245–47; on Miles Brand and, 252, 272–74, 315; player reaction to, 30, 242–43, 252; public opinion and, 251–52, 267–68, 283–84; reasons for, 253–55, 262, 265, 272–73, 282–84, 292, 306, 315; and student riot, 222, 233–36; and zero tolerance, Knight reaction to, 6–7, 12–13, 259–60. See also zero-tolerance policy
Knight, Bob, incidents: and behavior "outside the game," 163–65, 309; "chokings," 13, 160, 268–70 (see also Neil Reed); at Cuyahoga Falls, 90–91; at Indiana University, 13, 25, 143, 223–30, 258–60, 268–70, 304, 308–9 (see also Kent Harvey, Neil Reed); involving Jeremy Schaap, 263–65; involving Lou Eisenstein, 206–11; involving Playboy, 265; involving Ray Murphy, 209–12; temper and, 188, 316–19; at West Point, 28–29, 102–3, 119, 142–43, 160–63, 186–89, 206–12

Knight, Bob, and the media, 7, 291–93; ignorance of, 304–5; on perspective, lack of, 302–3; scheduling difficulties, 296; stereotype and, 7, 25, 153, 294–95, 298, 302–5, 317–18; at West Point, 146, 157–58, 207–10, 215

Knight, Bob, at West Point, 96, 105, 129–135, 141, 173; on academics, 79; career recap of, 20–21, 191; on coaching challenges, 120; and Ed Jordan, 24, 96, 178–83; and Florida job offer, 214–15; hiring as assistant coach, 43–45, 88–89; hiring as head coach, 117–122; influences of, 136–39, 215–18, 258; and Mike Silliman, 36, 99, 126, 175–76; and the military draft, 44–45, 89; and recruiting, 20, 36, 50, 159; as a scary guy, 137–38, 315; and Tates Locke, 35–36, 104, 113, 115–16; and values of, 215–18, 268, 313

Knight, Braden (grandson), 288, 300–1, 303–4, 306, 311

Knight, Hazel (mother), 226–27, 318

Knight, Karen (second wife), 281, 298-99, 301, 311, 313

Knight, Nancy (first wife), 106–7, 281

Knight, Pat (father), 89, 226–27

Knight, Pat (son), 245–46, 252, 263–65, 301, 307

Knight, Tim (son), 119

Knightmares (Wolfe), 269

Korean War, 190–91

Kornheiser, Tony, 273

Kraft, Jack, 155

Kram, Mark, 294, 301, 311

Kramer, Steve, 205–6

Krzyzewski, Mike, 21, 168

Ky, Nguyen Cao (Marshal), 118

Lambert, Ward "Piggy," 101

Lancaster, Harry, 47

Lapchick, Joe, 37, 101, 113, 115, 175, 185–86, 208

Lapham, Lewis, 283–84

Lee Clyde, 37, 144–47

Lee, Robert E., 61

LeMay, Curtis, 110

Lennon, Jim, 158

Lindsey, Fawn, 291

Liston, Sonny, 5

Lloyd, Bobby, 174

Lo Balbo, Al, 18–19, 36–39, 99–100, 131

Locke, Nancy (first wife), 45, 73, 95, 116

Locke, Tates, 35–36, 59, 84, 115, 134; 1963–64, 98–99, 101–6; 1964–65, 28–29, 111–13; biography, 73; and Knight, 45, 88, 102–3, 117–18; and Lou Eisenstein incident, 207–9, 211; and Mike Silliman, 46, 49–51, 53, 73, 109–11, 126; and recruiting, 45–46, 49–51, 53, 73–74, 86–88; and resignation, 115–17; temper of, 103–5

Lombardi, Vince, 114

London, Julie, 76

The Long Gray Line (Atkinson), 65, 93

Long, Russell, 85–86

loose ball drill, 131–34, 138

Lubbock, Texas, 289–90, 299

Lucas, Jerry, 47–48, 69, 167

Lupica, Mike, 176

MacArthur, Douglas, 21–22, 62, 90, 215, 217, 317

Maertens, George K., 127

McCarthy, Babe, 148

McCarthy, Charlie, 282

McDaniel, Susan Silliman (sister), 46–47, 83

McGee, Jack, 156

McGuire, Al, 177

McGuire, Frank, 197

McIntyre, Bob, 187

Malone, Karl, 194

Marsh, Irving T., 161, 196, 200

Martin, Kenyon, 306

Martin, Tommy, 149

Massinino, Rollie, 122

Melchionni, Bill, 154, 212
Mellen, Joan, 139, 160, 227,
    229–30, 269, 296, 315–16
Methods of Coaching (Knight class),
    255, 260, 311
Meyers, Gerald, 294
Mikula, John "Jocko," 173; 1965–66,
    144–45, 154; and academics, 168,
    170–71; in Beast Barracks, 95–96;
    and Christmas in Dayton, 111; at
    Indiana Classic, 8–9, 18; on
    Knight, 96, 138; in the military,
    8–9
Miller, Jason, 306
Miller, Norm, 155, 158, 197, 200
Minh, Ho Chi, 38
Minute Maid, 288–89, 304
Montgomery, Sarah, 43, 227
Mueller, Edwin, 198–99, 201
Mullan, Thomas L., 125–26
Mullan, Elizabeth (wife), 125–26
Murphy Brown, 282
Murphy, Ray, 36, 86, 129, 149, 185,
    199, 214–16; and Knight hiring,
    118–21; and Lou Eisenstein inci-
    dent, 209–12
Murray, Dick, 103–4, 113; 1965–66,
    126, 134–35, 154, 156–57, 175,
    186–89, 193; on Knight, 105,
    139, 186–89; and Knight hiring,
    118, 121–22

Naismith, James, 101
Napoleon, 114
National Invitation Tournament. See
    NIT
National Press Club, 282
Nemelka, Dick, 205–7
Newell, Pete, 37, 175, 194, 201, 309
Newton, Jeffrey, 32, 243
Nicholas, Charles P., 137
NIT, 35, 105–6, 112, 191–202,
    205–13
Noonan, Mike, 121–22, 132, 149,
    175; in high school, 12; at
    Indiana Classic, 11–12, 22–23;
    kicked off team, 191, 193–94;

and Knight hiring, 121; recruiting
    of, 12, 121–22
Northington, Nat, 147
Nowell, Mel, 165
Novak, Leo, 20

offense, controlled, 101, 113
O'Neal, Shaquille, 163–64
Otero, L.M., 293

Palone, Joe, 130
Parsels, Bill, 89
Parseghian, Ara, 116, 120
Patrick, Dan, 296
Peletta, Pete, 198, 200
Phelps, Digger, 25, 27, 251
Piazza, Mike, 163–64
Pillings, Ed, 141, 173–74, 209–11
Piskun, Walt, 104
Platt, Billy, 139, 152, 156; and
    Knight hiring, 117, 121–22; quits
    team, 169; recruiting of, 87
Playboy, 265

Quayle, Dan, 303

racial discrimination, 147–50, 213
Raymond, Craig, 205
Recondo, 92-93. See also Class of
    1966, at Camp Buckner
Reed, Neil, 13, 268–70, 291, 298,
    302, 309
Reibel, Joe, 47, 49
Reorganization Week, 75–77, 95
Ritch, John, 82
Robbins, Marty, 34–35
Robinson, David, 36
Rollins, Tree, 35
Romo, Joe, 200
Roosevelt, Franklin Delano, 44
Rupp, Adolph, 46–48, 176
Ryan, John, 318

Salon.com, 143
scary guys, 65–66, 79, 94, 110,
    125–26, 137–38, 171
Schaap, Dick, 252

Schaap, Jeremy, 242, 252–53, 255, 257–260, 263–66
Schrage, Danny, 145, 178–80, 198–99, 206; and choking incident, 160, 269
Schuler, Mike, 131, 153, 179
Schutsky, Billy, 115, 122, 131, 152–53, 161, 181, 184, 201
Scott, Winfield, 60
A Season on the Brink: A Year with Bob Knight and the Indiana Hoosiers (Feinstein), 6, 177, 186, 224
Seigle, Bobby, 85, 98, 154, 158; in high school, 86; at Indiana Classic, 19–25, 30; on Knight, 21–22, 139; in the military, 22, 24–25; recruiting of, 86–87; on Silliman, 126–27
Selma, Alabama, 114, 182, 275–76
Sex and the City, 143
Sharp, Marsha, 289
Shaw, Mark, 225–26, 228
Shulman, James L., 274
Silliman, Betty (mother), 48–49, 72
Silliman, Greg (brother), 47–48
Silliman, Gus (father), 48, 50, 72, 101, 125
Silliman, Jerry (uncle), 72
Silliman, Mike, 49, 110; 1962-63, 82, 85, 88; 1963-64, 99, 103, 105–6; 1964-65, 110–13; 1965-66, 134–35, 139, 152–53, 157, 159–61, 166–68, 172–76, 200; attitude toward West Point, 77, 92, 95; in Beast Barracks, 59, 65, 67, 72–74; at Camp Buckner, 91–93; drinking and, 110–11, 125–27; in high school, 36, 46–50, 72, 152; as an intellectual, 83–84; knee injuries of, 72–74, 173–76; recruiting of, 46–51, 53
Simpson, Christopher, 225, 236, 250–51, 256–58, 266–68, 277–78, 282
Skinner, Roy, 147
Slover, Pat, 49

Slum and Gravy, 195–96
Smart, Keith, 254
Smith, Dean, 176
Smith, Don, 184
Smith, Harvey, 15
Smitherman, Joe, 276
Sorge, Robert E., 79
Southwood, Jerry, 145–47, 199
Sperber, Murray, 15
sports: commercialism in, 288–89; importance of, 273–75; and universities, 273–75
Sports Illustrated, 292
Sprewell, Latrell, 26
Stewart, Potter, 257
Stilwell, Richard G., 59-60, 65–67, 137, 211
Stockton, John, 194
StoneSong, 251, 298
Storozynski, Pawel, 310
St. Xavier High School (Louisville), 46–47

tactical officers. *See* scary guys
Tarbox, Robert M., 66, 137
Taylor, Fred, 43, 45–46, 48, 70, 167, 207, 214–15, 226
Texas Tech University, 290
Texas Western, 213
Thayer Hall, 51
Thayer, Sylvanius, 78–79, 151
Thomas, Isiah, 3, 36, 182, 252
three-point play, 155
Treloar, John, 31, 231, 238, 242–45, 247
Truman, Harry, 149, 217

United Spirit Arena, 288
United States Corps of Cadets. *See* Corps of Cadets
Unseld, Wes, 37, 152–53

Valvano, Jim, 175
van Breda Kolff, Butch, 141
Vanderbilt Invitational Tournament, 144–147
Vesser, Dale, 84

Voting Rights Act, 150. *See also*
　　racial discrimination
Vietnam War, 110, 114, 129,
　　143–44, 190–91; and 1965–66
　　team, 8–9, 22, 38–39, 190; and
　　recruiting 20

Walda, John, 13, 256, 283
Walker, Jimmy, 171
Wallace, Jim, 98, 102, 154, 172–74
And the Walls Came Tumbling Down:
　　Kentucky, Texas Western, and the
　　Game That Changed American
　　Sports (Fitzpatrick), 149
Washington Hall, 61–62
Westmoreland, William C., 83, 87,
　　92
West Point: academics of, 77–80,
　　83–84, 137, 168; attrition rate,
　　59; racial discrimination and,
　　149; values of, and Knight, 45,
　　215–18, 268, 313–15
West Point basketball: 1963–64,
　　98–99, 101–06; 1964–65,
　　110–13; media stereotype of,
　　158–59, 200–1; player profile
　　83–85, 113–14; and recruiting,
　　49–53; and West Point Football
　　Bill, 85–86
West Point basketball, 1965–66:
　　academic losses of, 167–71;

Boston College scrimmage, 4,
　　156–57; games, regular season,
　　141–47, 150, 152–55, 157–58,
　　160–61, 166–68, 172–77,
　　179–82, 184, 186–89, 191;
　　games, NIT, 194–201, 205–7, 212
　　(*see also* NIT); at Holiday Festival,
　　151, 154–160; prospects for, 115;
　　season recap, 205; at Vanderbilt
　　Invitational Tournament, 144–47
West Point Football Bill, 85–86
Wetzel, Dan, 213
White, Gordon S., Jr., 158, 189
White, Tom, 251
Wienerschnitzel, 287–88
WISH-TV, 276–78
Wittman, Randy, 33
Wolfe, Rich, 269
Wooden, John, 43, 176, 304
World War II generation, 216–17

Yogi's (restaurant), 23, 30

Zeglin, Peg, 235, 254
zero-tolerance policy: and
　　Christopher Simpson, 256–57;
　　definition of, 13, 255–56; freedom
　　of speech and, 13–15; and Knight
　　"violations," 257–62; Miles Brand
　　and, 13, 255–62; as "unclear and
　　ill-formed," 256–62

About the Author

A West Point graduate and decorated Vietnam veteran, Jack Isenhour averaged a whopping 1.6 points per game as a backup guard on Bob Knight's first team in 1965–66. After going mysteriously undrafted by his beloved Celtics, Isenhour settled into a career as a television journalist where most recently he was the co-creator and executive producer of a nationally syndicated PBS talk show. Over the years, he has received numerous national honors for his television journalism including Headliner and Robert F. Kennedy Awards. Currently working as a writer and artist, Isenhour lives in Nashville with wife, Dana Moore. He has one son, Will.